American Indian

Uncovering the Past: Documentary Readers in American History
Series Editors: Steven F. Lawson and Nancy A. Hewitt

The books in this series introduce students in American history courses to two important dimensions of historical analysis. They enable students to engage actively in historical interpretation, and they further students' understanding of the interplay between social and political forces in historical developments.

Consisting of primary sources and an introductory essay, these readers are aimed at the major courses in the American history curriculum, as outlined further below. Each book in the series will be approximately 225–50 pages, including a 25–30 page introduction addressing key issues and questions about the subject under consideration, a discussion of sources and methodology, and a bibliography of suggested secondary readings.

Published

Paul G. E. Clemens
The Colonial Era: A Documentary Reader

Sean Patrick Adams
The Early American Republic: A Documentary Reader

Stanley Harrold
The Civil War and Reconstruction: A Documentary Reader

Steven Mintz
African American Voices: A Documentary Reader, 1619–1877

Robert P. Ingalls and David K. Johnson
The United States Since 1945: A Documentary Reader

Camilla Townsend
American Indian History: A Documentary Reader

In preparation

Brian Ward
The 1960s: A Documentary Reader

Jeremi Suri
American Foreign Relations Since 1898: A Documentary Reader

Steven Mintz
Mexican American Voices: A Documentary Reader

Nancy Rosenbloom
Women in Modern America, 1880–Present: A Documentary Reader

American Indian History

A Documentary Reader

Edited by

Camilla Townsend

A John Wiley & Sons, Ltd., Publication

This edition first published 2009

Blackwell Publishing was acquired by John Wiley & Sons in February 2007. Blackwell's publishing program has been merged with Wiley's global Scientific, Technical, and Medical business to form Wiley-Blackwell.

Registered Office
John Wiley & Sons Ltd, The Atrium, Southern Gate, Chichester, West Sussex, PO19 8SQ, United Kingdom

Editorial Offices
350 Main Street, Malden, MA 02148-5020, USA
9600 Garsington Road, Oxford, OX4 2DQ, UK
The Atrium, Southern Gate, Chichester, West Sussex, PO19 8SQ, UK

For details of our global editorial offices, for customer services, and for information about how to apply for permission to reuse the copyright material in this book please see our website at www.wiley.com/wiley-blackwell.

Library of Congress Cataloging-in-Publication Data

American Indian history : a documentary reader / edited by Camilla Townsend.
p. cm. – (Uncovering the past–documentary readers in American history)
Includes bibliographical references and index.
ISBN 978-1-4051-5907-4 (hardcover : alk. paper) – ISBN 978-1-4051-5908-1 (pbk. : alk. paper)
1. Indians of North America–History–Sources. 2. Indians of Mexico–History–Sources. I. Townsend, Camilla, 1965–
E77.A4963 2009
970.004'97–dc22

2008048195

A catalogue record for this book is available from the British Library.

Set in 10/12pt Sabon by SPi Publisher Services, Pondicherry, India
Printed in Singapore by Ho Printing Singapore Pte Ltd

01 2009

Contents

Series Editors' Preface viii
Acknowledgments x

Introduction 1

Chapter 1 Indian Ways 9
1 Maya Glyphs at Piedras Negras 9
2 Ancient Nahuatl Prayers from the Florentine Codex 12
3 Pueblo Bonito of Chaco Canyon 14
4 Images of Secotan 17
5 Two Versions of the Haudenosaunee (Iroquois) Creation Story 21

Chapter 2 First Contact 27
1 Arrival of the Spaniards in the Annals of Tlatelolco 27
2 Response to the Spanish by Native Priests 29
3 Don Luis Travels the World 31
4 The Arrival of the Dutch at Manhattan in Native Memory 33

Chapter 3 The Expectations of the Strangers 39
1 Christopher Columbus's Journal 39
2 Cabeza de Vaca's Experiences in North America 41
3 Thomas Harriot's Observations at Roanoke 43
4 John Smith's Visit to Werowocomoco 44
5 Edward Waterhouse's Report on the Events of 1622 46

Chapter 4 The Long Struggle for American Lands 50
1 A Jesuit's Story of the 1639 Smallpox Epidemic 50
2 Gandeaktena's Decision to Become a Christian 52
3 Metacom's Grievances 55
4 Mary Rowlandson's Narrative 57
5 The Declaration of a Rebellious Christian Indian in the Pueblo Revolt 61

Chapter 5 Eighteenth-Century Power Shifts 64
1 The Refusal of Some English Prisoners to Return to English Life 64
2 The Abenakis' Forceful Statement to the English 68
3 The Chickasaws' Political Vision in 1723 72
4 Sir Jeffery Amherst Suggests the Smallpox 76
5 The Chickasaws after the Revolution 81
6 George Washington's Indian Policy 84

Chapter 6 What the New Nation Portended for Indians 89
1 Lewis and Clark in the Pacific Northwest 89
2 Russian Settlements in Alaska 91
3 Tecumseh's Demands 94
4 The Cherokee Syllabary and Newspaper 99
5 The Cherokee Debate in Washington 102
6 Black Hawk's Autobiography 112
7 William Apess's Condemnation of White America 118

Chapter 7 The Losing of the West 122
1 Charles Ohiyesa Eastman's Childhood Memories 122
2 Lone Dog's Winter Count, 1800–1870 125
3 Sarah Winnemucca's Choices 135
4 The Views of George Armstrong Custer 136
5 Black Elk's Memories of the Battle of the Little Big Horn 138
6 Elaine Goodale's Observations of the Ghost Dance 142
7 Charles Ohiyesa Eastman's Visit to Wounded Knee 144
8 Geronimo's Story of His Life 146

Chapter 8 Surviving Assimilation and the National Imagination 154
1 The 1887 Statement of the Commissioner of Indian Affairs 154
2 Francis La Flesche's Memories of Boarding School 157
3 A Navajo Girl's Letters Home from Boarding School 161
4 William Stoddard's *The Talking Leaves* 164
5 The Arguments of *The Quarterly Journal* 166

Chapter 9 Mid-Twentieth-Century Changes 171
1 The Arts and Crafts Act of 1935 171
2 The Navajo Contribution to the War Effort 175
3 The Musings of an Iroquois High Steel Man 177
4 The Menominee Struggle against Termination 181

Chapter 10 The Upheavals of the 1960s and 1970s 184
1 The 1961 Declaration of Indian Purpose 184
2 The Alcatraz Proclamation 186
3 Vine Deloria's *Custer Died for Your Sins* 189
4 The Thoughts of Mary Crow Dog 192
5 A Reporter's Comments on the Deaths at Pine Ridge 195

Chapter 11 The End of the Twentieth Century: A New Era? 198
1 The Origins of the Native American Graves Protection and Repatriation Act (NAGPRA) 198
2 Growing Pan-Indian Activism and the Native Press 201
3 Louise Erdrich's "Dear John Wayne" 205
4 President Clinton's 1994 Conference with Native Leaders 207
5 Struggles over the Indian Gaming Regulatory Act 211
6 An Elder's Stories for Future Generations 216
7 List of Federally Recognized Tribes Today 219

Selected Bibliography 233
Index 240

Series Editors' Preface

Primary sources have become an essential component in the teaching of history to undergraduates. They engage students in the process of historical interpretation and analysis, helping them understand that facts do not speak for themselves. Rather, students see how historians construct narratives that recreate the past. Most students assume that the pursuit of knowledge is a solitary endeavor; yet historians constantly interact with their peers, building upon previous research and arguing among themselves over the interpretation of documents and their larger meaning. The documentary readers in this series highlight the value of this collaborative creative process.

Documentary readers can be used in a variety of ways. The introduction for each reader discusses the kinds of sources available for the study of the subject under investigation and suggests how the documents can be adapted to various classroom situations. The books in the series introduce students in American history courses to two important dimensions of historical analysis. They enable students to engage actively in historical interpretation, and they further students' understanding of the interplay between social and political forces in historical developments.

Consisting of primary sources and an introductory essay, the readers are aimed at the major courses in the American history curriculum. The documents include such items as illustrations of material artifacts, letters and diaries, sermons, maps, photographs, song lyrics, selections from fiction and memoirs, legal statutes, court decisions, presidential orders, speeches, and political cartoons.

Each volume in the series is edited by a specialist in the field who is concerned with undergraduate teaching. The goal of each volume is not to provide a comprehensive selection of material but to choose items that reflect major themes and debates and that illustrate significant social, cultural, political, and economic dimensions of an era or subject. The editor of each volume has written an introduction which discusses the central questions that have occupied historians in the field and the ways historians have used primary sources to answer them. In addition, the introductory essay contains an explanation of the kinds of materials available to investigate a particular subject, the methods by which historians analyze them, and the considerations that go into interpreting them. Each source selection is then introduced by a short head note that gives students the necessary information and a context for understanding the document. In addition, each section of the volume contains questions to guide student reading and stimulate classroom discussion.

Camilla Townsend's *American Indian History: A Documentary Reader* provides an array of documents dealing with the history of Native Americans from before they encountered Europeans until the twenty-first century. This is a formidable task to achieve in a single, small volume, but Townsend accomplishes it with great success. Divided into eleven chapters, the book starts out with pre-European Indian settlements in Central and North America and covers the period of Spanish, English, Dutch, and French explorations that led to challenging and tragic encounters. It discusses the efforts of a wide variety of Native Americans to come to grips with attempts of foreigners to subdue and conquer them from the sixteenth to the nineteenth centuries. It focuses attention not only on policies pursued by the colonial and United States governments, but on the responses and strategies of Native American tribes to resist as well as accommodate to change. *American Indian History* also relates the twists and turns of native history in the twentieth century, as Indian tribes once again asserted their independence within the context of other human rights struggles in the nation. The voices of Native Americans are mingled with Euro-Americans to present a full picture of the interrelated history of these peoples. The sources Townsend presents range from Mayan pictorial glyphs, portraits of Indian leaders such as Black Hawk, and native autobiographies to journals of white explorers, statements of US political and military leaders from George Washington to George Armstrong Custer and Bill Clinton, and pronouncements from the Bureau of Indian Affairs. In providing an assortment of documents covering over six centuries of history, Townsend has selected and organized the material from the perspective of a historian and with the sensitivity of an anthropologist to underscore the complicated dialogue that existed between Native Americans and those who followed them to the New World. Indeed, it is a story that continues to unfold.

Steven F. Lawson and Nancy A. Hewitt

Acknowledgments

All academic projects are to some extent collaborative, and this one has been no different. The book has benefited from both the chance comments and concerted efforts of a number of scholars from a range of fields. I would especially like to thank James Axtell, Alejandro Delgado, Dan Goldstein, Michel Launey, James Lockhart, Frederick Luciani, Susana Matallana, Jane Merritt, Lloyd Moote, Amy Schutt, Chris Vecsey, Wendy Wall, and Nicolas Wey-Gómez. People who patiently answered specific questions include José Barreiro (National Museum of the American Indian), Deanna Beacham (Virginia Council on Indians), Paul DeMain (*News from Indian Country*), and Dan Littlefield (American Native Press Archives).

At Rutgers University, my many colleagues in the history department have made my professional life a delight in the past few years. Graduate students Sandra Mendiola, Robin Chapdelaine, and Jahaira Arias helped me with the images and charts and generally attempted to bring me into the modern age. In the library, Tom Glynn offered high-speed help when I needed it most. Two sections of my Modern Native American History class happily served as guinea pigs as I developed some of these units; I am eternally grateful for their thoughtful responses.

Blackwell Publishing has been a joy to work with. Peter Coveney, Deirdre Ilkson, and the entire editorial team, could not have been more helpful. Series editors Nancy Hewitt and Steven Lawson provided excellent guidance. And the critiques of the anonymous reviewers rendered each iteration better than the last.

Perhaps I have trespassed most on the patience of my family – my beloved partner, John; my sons, Loren and Cian; and my parents, Carolynn and Ken, who need me now as I once needed them. I thank you all for giving me the time I asked for, and for sharing your love with me.

Text and image credits

The editor and publisher gratefully acknowledge the permission granted to reproduce the copyright material in this book:

1.1 Courtesy of Linda Schele, from 'Breaking the Maya Code' by Michael D. Coe. © Michael D. Coe. Reprinted by kind permission of Thames & Hudson Ltd., London.

1.2 Charles Dibble and Arthur J. O. Anderson, eds., *General History of the Things of New Spain*. Book 6. *Rhetoric and Moral Philosophy*. (University of Utah Press, 1969), pp.35–36 and 167–68. N.B. Editor has slightly altered their translation. Reprinted with permission of the University of Utah Press.

1.5 Carl Klinck and James J. Talman, *The Journal of Major John Norton, 1816* (The Champlain Society, 1970), pp.88–89. Reprinted with permission The Champlain Society, Canada.

2.1 Excerpt from: James Lockhart, ed., *We People Here: Nahuatl Accounts of the Conquest of Mexico* (University of California Press, 1993), pp.257–59. Reprinted by permission of Wipf and Stock Publishers www.wipfandstock.com.

3.1 *Diario of Christopher Columbus's First Voyage to America 1492–1493*, edited by Oliver C. Dunn and James E. Kelley Jr., Excerpts "Friday 12 October, 1942" and "Saturday 13, October, 1942", pp.67–71 English text only. Published by University of Oklahoma Press, 1989. Reprinted with permission of the publisher.

3.2 Reprinted from *The Narrative of Cabeza de Vaca,* edited, translated, and with an introduction by Rolena Adorno and Patric Charles Pautz by permission of the University of Nebraska Press © 1999/2003 by the University of Nebraska Press. Reprinted with permission.

3.3 Thomas Harriot, "A Briefe and True Report of the New Found Land of Virginia" (1590) in Peter Mancall, ed., *Envisioning America: English Plans for the Colonization of North America, 1580–1640* (Bedford Books, 1995). Reprinted with permission of Palgrave Macmillan.

3.4 Extract from *The Complete Works of Captain John Smith, 1580–1631* edited by Philip L. Barbour, with a foreword by Thad W. Tate. Published for the Omohundro Institute of Early American History and Culture. Copyright © 1986 by the University of North Carolina Press. Used by permission of the publisher.

4.5 "Declaration of one of the rebellious Christian Indians who was captured on the road. El Alamillo, September 6, 1680." In Charles Wilson Hackett, ed., *Revolt of the Pueblo Indians of New Mexico and Otermín's Attempted Reconquest, 1680–1682* (University of New Mexico Press, 1942), pp.60–2. Reprinted with permission of University of New Mexico Press.

5.4 British Museum, MS. 21634, Amherst to Bouquet, July 7, 1763, folio 313 and 243 [envelope], and July 16, 1763, folio 323 and 241 [envelope]. Bouquet to Amherst, July 13, 1763, folio 321. British Library

6.1 Reprinted from *The Journals of the Lewis and Clark Expedition*, Vol. 6, edited by Gary E. Moulton by permission of the University of Nebraska Press. Copyright © 1990 by the University of Nebraska Press.

6.2 Excerpts from Georg Heinrich von Langsdorff, *Remarks and Observations on a Voyage Around the World from 1803 to 1807*, Vol. 2, edited by Victoria Joan Moessner and Richard A. Pierce (Fairbanks, Alaska: Limestone Press, [1811] 1993), pp.1–2, 35–8, 45–6. Reprinted with permission of the University of Alaska Press.

6.5.1 Gary E. Moulton, ed., *The Papers of Chief John Ross*, Volume I (University of Oklahoma Press, 1985), pp.154–57. Reprinted with permission.

6.6 Roger Nichols, ed., *Black Hawk's Autobiography* (Iowa State University Press), pp.56–61. Reprinted with permission of Wiley-Blackwell USA.

7.5 John Neihardt, *Black Elk Speaks, being the Life Story of a Holy Man of the Oglala Sioux,* SUNY Press. pp.82–86 and 98–99. Reprinted with permission of SUNY Press.

7.6 Reprinted from *Sister to the Sioux: The Memoirs of Elaine Goodale Eastman, 1885–1891*, edited by Kay Graber, by permission of the University of Nebraska Press. © 1978 by the University of Nebraska Press.

8.2 Francis La Flesche, *The Middle Five: Indian Schoolboys of the Omaha Tribe*. Copyright © 1963 by the Board of Regents of the University of Wisconsin System [1900]), pp.xv–xix, 96–100. Reprinted by permission of the University of Wisconsin Press.

8.3 Alice Becenti's letters found in National Archives, Laguna Niguel, printed in Peter Iverson, ed., *"For Our Navajo People": Diné Letters Speeches & Petitions, 1900–1960* (University of New Mexico Press, 2002), 82–85 Reprinted with permission of University of New Mexico Press.

9.2 Sally McClain, *Navajo Weapon* (Tucson, AZ: Rio Nuevo Publishers, 1994.) Reprinted with permission of the author and the publishers.

9.3 Joseph Mitchell, "The Mohawks in High Steel," appearing as a foreword to Edmund Wilson, Apologies to the Iroquois (New York: Farrar, Straus and Cudahy, 1959), 27–36. Copyright © 1949 Joseph Mitchell. Reprinted with permission of the Estate of Joseph Mitchell c/o Dunow, Carlson & Lerner Literary Agency.

10.3 Reprinted with permission of Scribner, a Division of Simon & Schuster Adult Publishing Group, from *Custer Died for Your Sins: An Indian Manifesto* by Vine Deloria, Jr.. Copyright © 1969 by Vine Deloria, Jr. Copyright renewed © 1997 by Vine Deloria, Jr. All rights reserved.

10.4 Mary Crow Dog with Richard Erdoes, *Lakota Woman*, pp.3–11. Copyright © 1990 by Mary Crow Dog and Richard Erdoes. Used by permission of Grove Atlantic Inc.

11.1 Joseph L. Benthall, *Archaeological Investigation of the Shannon Site, Montgomery County, Virginia* (The Virginia State Library, 1969), pp.44–52. Reproduction of these materials granted courtesy of the Library of Virginia, Richmond, Virginia and is granted solely for the present work.

11.3 "Dear John Wayne" by Louise Erdrich, Copyright © 1984, Louise Erdrich, appears in *Jacklight*, published by Holt, Rinehart, and Winston. Reprinted with permission of The Wylie Agency (UK) Limited.

11.6 Ann Fienup-Riordan, ed., *Stories for Future Generations: The Oratory of Yup'ik Elder Paul John* (University of Washington Press, 2003), pp.18–25. Reprinted by permission of the University of Washington Press Seattle.

Figures

1.1.1 Maya Glyphs at Piedras Negras. Image © John Montgomery, reproduced with kind permission of The E. S. Agency, Citrus Heights, CA.

1.3.1 Artist's reconstruction of Pueblo Bonito looking north, by Lloyd K. Townsend, *Mysteries of the Ancient Americas*. © 1986 by the Reader's Digest Association.

1.3.2–1.3.5 John R. Stein, Dabney Ford, and Richard Friedman, "Reconstructing Pueblo Bonito," in Jill Neitzel, ed., *Pueblo Bonito*: *Center of the Chacoan World* (Smithsonian Books, 2003), pp.44–50.

1.4.1 John White, *Indian Village of Secotan* (watercolor), © British Museum.

1.4.2 Theodor de Bry, *Indian Village of Secotan* (engraving), British Library.
1.4.3 John White, *Indians Fishing* (watercolor), © British Museum.
1.4.4 Theodor de Bry, *Indians Fishing* (engraving), © British Museum.
5.3.1 Conch shell (*c.*1400) found at Spiro, Oklahoma. Timothy R. Pauketat, *Ancient Cahokia and the Mississippians* (Cambridge University Press, 2004), p.142.
5.3.2 Chickasaw map (1723) Map CO 700/North Colonies General 6 (2). Reprinted with permission of the National Archives Image Library.
5.3.3 Line drawing of the 1723 Chickasaw map. Gregory Waselkov, "Indian Maps of the Colonial Southeast," in Peter H. Wood, Gregory A. Waselkov and M. Thomas Hatley, *Powhatan's Mantle: Indians in the Colonial Southeast* (University of Nebraska Press, 1989), pp.324–9.
6.6.1 George Catlin, *Múk-a-tah-mish-o-káh-kaik, Black Hawk, Prominent Sac Chief* (1832), oil, 29 × 24 in., Smithsonian Institute. Reprinted with permission.

Every effort has been made to trace copyright holders and to obtain their permission for the use of copyright material. The publisher apologizes for any errors or omissions in the above list and would be grateful if notified of any corrections that should be incorporated in future reprints or editions of this book.

Introduction

For thousands of years, American Indian history was taught by American Indians to American Indians. Elders taught it to young people sitting around fires within their lodgings or out in the open air, trying to catch the breeze. Priests taught it to laypeople in ceremonial settings. They put the history into songs, poems, stories, and jokes. To aid their memories or vividly illustrate their points, they used pictures and symbols painted on bark or maguey paper or deer hides or buffalo robes. If they had been in one place long enough to begin to build, they carved references to their past into their wooden houses or totem poles or stone lintels. Their histories offered layers of meanings – simple messages for children, so that they might learn where they came from; political statements designed to convince general audiences that their chief was indeed the rightful chief or their band's course of action the best one; and more complicated discourses intended to make adults think carefully about right and wrong and their own role in the ongoing lives of their people.

Today most of that history-telling is lost to us. The passage of the stories from generation to generation was interrupted by conquest and the erosion of people's traditional way of life. To the extent that it is known, American Indian history is now generally taught as a subsection of the history of the United States. And yet it runs against the grain of "American history." It makes a poor fit, for it does not offer a story of increasing prosperity or a tale of a struggle for justice that is eventually attained. Sometimes it is reduced to a mere reminder – a reminder in an otherwise optimistic story that all has not always been well. But the people who kept their own stories alive for millennia would not have wanted to be reduced to a reminder. They would have wanted to shape the telling of a much greater, more significant narrative about the importance of their traditions, and the heroism and pain that come of unequal struggle.

People attempting to understand Native American history on its own terms, in a way that truly makes room for indigenous perspectives, face a serious challenge. Most of the surviving sources were produced by Europeans and European Americans, not by Indians, or if by Indians not until many years after the events. Scholars argue among themselves about whether or not it is imperative to move away from a chronology derived from European history. (That chronology runs something like this: "The Indians lived in such-and-such a way in the years just before 1492. Then the Europeans came. Then certain European wars occurred in which Indians participated. Then the colonies broke free from Europe." And so on.) Of course it would be best if we could move away from a narrative that was not of the Indians' own choosing and which does not reflect many of their immediate realities. (For example, what about those who were living beyond the Mississippi when the Europeans came?) The problem with attempting to free the narrative entirely, however, is that we are left taking sources out of context. For example, if we want to begin the story of the Haudenosaunee (or Iroquois) with a discussion of their ancient political life, we must take at face value the account we have, which was actually written down in particular circumstances in the year 1900. We are not really looking through a window onto Iroquoian thought and actions in the 1300s. We cannot do so; we can only wish that we could. We would never accept a document from 1900 as a source on fourteenth-century France or England. In my opinion, although it is lamentable, it is more honest to follow the European trajectory: in that unfolding drama, written records were produced by and about Native Americans that we can fully understand or "decode" because we are looking at them in their own historical context. In this way, I believe, we may ultimately be more faithful, not less, to indigenous people's realities as they once were.

It is crucial, though, that even as we follow the chronology produced by the colonizers, we always seek the perspective of the colonized. We should ask ourselves with heightened energy and especially open-minded interest the questions historians always ask themselves: Who produced this document, and when? What was going on around the person who wrote it that would explain the choice of words? What did the writer hope to accomplish? It is particularly important that we do a thorough job in this regard because Europeans, not Native Americans, were most often the ones holding the pens, and they wrote about what interested them. In earlier eras, even when a speech or statement of an Indian is recorded in a document, we must remember that the recorder was probably a white man. He might have misrepresented what was happening on purpose, or he might not have fully understood it. Or an Indian translator might have been present who did indeed understand all that was in the speaker's mind, but whose English or Spanish or French was not good enough to present the leader's views in all their complexity. Even if a statement was recorded verbatim in an indigenous language, we have the problem of scholars' continuing need to refine their knowledge of native languages, which are not nearly as well known to them as, for example, French is to scholars of French history. Even after years of study this remains true, as scholars are working without the accumulated wisdom of generations of people who have been paying attention to a particular document or genre.

It is not only the difficulties related to learning all that was once said that have been the causes of significant misperceptions, but also *our willingness to assume that there is little more we need to know.* Americans are familiar, through movies, novels, and even some history books, with Indians who speak only truncated or child-like English and nothing else. Thus we have tended to assume their perspectives are rather simple. We often do not challenge the veracity of sources that present them either as more naive or more one-dimensional than Europeans. Francis LaFlesche, an Omaha Indian, bemoaned this fact as long ago as 1900, when the records that we now assume reveal all that happened in the nineteenth century were still very much in the making:

> The misconception of Indian life and character so common among the white people has been largely due to an ignorance of the Indian's language, of his mode of thought, his beliefs, his ideals, and his native institutions. ... No native American can ever cease to regret that the utterances of his fathers have been constantly belittled when put into English, that their thoughts have been frequently travestied and their native dignity obscured. The average interpreter has generally picked up his knowledge of English in a random fashion, for very few have ever had the advantage of a thorough education, and all have had to deal with the difficulties that attend the translator. The beauty and picturesqueness, and euphonious playfulness, or the gravity of diction which I have heard among my own people, and other tribes as well, are all but impossible to give literally in English.[1]

In this book I have tried to remind readers that they are accustomed to seeing only muted translations – and that much may therefore be lost to us – by including a few sentences in the original language whenever it is possible to do so. I have written explicitly about who translated the material, and whether or not I have felt it necessary to change the translation in cases where I was qualified to do so. When we do not have a transcription of the original language, I have commented on who it was who was doing the writing in English (or French or Spanish) and whether or not he or she had a deep familiarity with the relevant native language.

[1] Francis La Flesche, *The Middle Five: Indian Schoolboys of the Omaha Tribe* (University of Nebraska Press, 1963 [1900]), pp. xviii–xix. See Ch. 8 for a longer excerpt from this work.

I believe it is necessary to ask a painful but important set of questions at the outset: Why were the Europeans the ones holding the pens? Why did the Europeans have so much more power than the Native Americans? Why were they able to defeat the Indians – not in every battle, but in every war? Not so long ago, many people believed that the explanation was that the white race was superior to the red. In the latter part of the twentieth century, a majority of people finally rejected that notion and argued that there was no question of inferiority or superiority: that the two peoples were simply profoundly different in a cultural sense, with different inner wellsprings, and that whites were either more ambitious or ruthless, depending on one's point of view. Most recently of all, biologists and archaeologists have offered an important breakthrough, which is particularly meaningful to those of us who believe that all races of people are profoundly similar rather than dissimilar. (Individuals and small groups of individuals, of course, vary. But within each race, similar variations can be seen.)

What was that breakthrough? It has long been known that when hunter-gatherers began to rely more on agriculture and to settle down in one place, increasingly complex political hierarchies and technological innovations appeared. Populations grew, and there was a need to organize irrigation, labor contributions, the storage of food surplus, etc. In all parts of the world, we see the development of each region's most ancient complex societies whenever and wherever agriculture was adopted in a serious way. In the Old World, specifically the Fertile Crescent, agriculture became a way of life thousands of years before it did anywhere else, thus giving the Old World a significant time advantage in the development of technology. The question that follows is – why did the Eurasians choose to become farmers so much earlier than anyone else? In the 1980s and 1990s, thanks to improved radiocarbon-dating techniques, biologists and archaeologists found a scientific explanation: simply put, the Fertile Crescent had a constellation of protein-rich plants, upon which people could easily live. They had wheat, barley, and peas. Other areas did not have such a useful set of plants. The New World did have corn, but the ears of wild corn were tiny, even paltry, things. For millennia the indigenous people of Mexico occasionally planted the kernels, almost as a hobby, until they gradually bred larger ears, and then discovered that when corn was eaten together with beans, it made a completely filling meal. At that point, the central Mexicans did indeed become full-time agriculturalists, but they could not have done so any sooner. By that time, the people of the Old World had been full-time farmers for at least 5,000 years, and had already developed all the accoutrements of sedentary life: steel weapons, navigation equipment, writing, etc. The Europeans, having borrowed all that their neighbors in the Fertile Crescent had to offer rather early on, had an obvious advantage when 1492 came round.

The mistake that is all too easy to make is to take from this that there is an associated difference in intelligence. My forebears may have developed the electric blender over the course of many generations, but if one blender is placed before me and another blender before an indigenous person in the Amazon basin, the Amazonian person may well figure out before I do how the gadget works. One group of people may have conquered an empire, and another may live in small bands, answering to no higher authority than their own separate chiefs, but the poems both recite in the evenings will be equally beautiful, the jokes they tell equally witty, and the reflections of their wise men and women on the nature of divinity equally profound. Intelligence never had anything to do with the long-term differences that arose between the peoples of the various continents. It was, rather, due to the plants that were present thousands of years ago.

Another question that we should ask is why we study American Indian history in the context of the boundaries of the United States. Clearly the borders of that nation have nothing to do with native borders or native traditions. Still, we must live within the real world, and in the real world of the American academy, courses are offered in geographic categories in keeping with modern times. A course that attempted to cover the history of the Inuit of Canada and the Mapuche of Chile as well as that of all groups in between would be confusing to everyone, professors and students alike. So I leave other excellent books to cover those fields.[2] However, the borders of the modern United States will have to be seen as somewhat porous within the confines of this book, or else it would be impossible to be intellectually honest. In the centuries before the conquest, the central valley of Mexico was the throbbing pulse of North America. There lay the Aztec city of Tenochtitlan, one of the largest urban areas in the world, and from it radiated a huge long-distance trade network that affected much of the future United States as well. Corn gradually spread outward from Mexico and began to change the lives of many of the people to the north. In addition, because the cultures of Mexico had been sedentary longer than any others in the hemisphere, they had the most advanced writing systems, and so, through them, we can catch the clearest glimpses of pre-contact modes of thought that we are ever going to get. Thus it is that this book opens in Mexico. Later, when the book treats the Iroquoian and Algonkian

[2] In many ways this decision is problematic. The Spanish were eager to teach the Indians the roman alphabet, and the Aztecs and others were eager to learn it. Thus in the sixteenth century, the Mesoamerican Indians recorded thousands of pages of their own traditions in their own languages, using the foreigners' alphabet phonetically. This material makes a crucial contribution to modern knowledge of Native American life. Students who are interested should begin by consulting Matthew Restall, Lisa Sousa, and Kevin Terraciano, eds., *Mesoamerican Voices: Native-Language Writings from Colonial Mexico, Oaxaca, Yucatan, and Guatemala* (Cambridge University Press, 2005).

peoples of the northeast, it would be impossible to proceed without including material produced in what today we call Canada. The indigenous world of that time was not divided along today's borders between nations.

*

So much for my explanation of why the book is organized as it is, and how I believe we should try to approach the documents it contains. What remains to be done, so as to maximize the book's transparency and thus its usefulness, is to think about alternative ways in which it might have been organized and other documents it might have included. It might, for example, have been organized according to themes that seem relevant to Native American life in more than one era. Those that come to mind include the nature of warfare and captivity, women's lives as compared to men's, native reactions to "Western culture," and the use of humor as a strategy for survival. Students interested in these topics might take the time to look through each section, to find at least one document from each time period that casts some light on the subject. They will find that they can easily do so.

Choosing which documents to include and which to exclude has not been an easy task, as may well be imagined. Historical documents offer us snatched glimpses of times and places now gone; we do not always see the most representative moments, not even in one person's life. For example, at one point I had in my hand the comments made by L. Frank Baum, author of *The Wonderful Wizard of Oz* (1900), after the massacre of hundreds of Lakota Sioux at Wounded Knee Creek in 1890. Baum was an educated easterner, interested in socialism and women's rights. He had not long before published a humorous story mocking people who were afraid of Indians, who after all were the victims, in his view, not the villains. But in January 1891 he was living with his four young sons in nearby Aberdeen, South Dakota, and he panicked. He feared the Indians would seek retribution, and his children might pay the price. Against character, he suddenly wrote that, having wronged the natives for so many generations, the army had better just finish the job and kill them all before anything happened. In vain I looked for evidence that he was using his famous sarcasm. He was not. There were people in the nineteenth century who were quite serious about killing the remaining Indians as a final solution (if I may borrow a term anachronistically from a later era). Baum was not normally one of them. George Armstrong Custer, on the other hand, was. And so in the end it was Custer's statement that I chose to illustrate the point. But other editors might have looked for moments that were least typical in various individuals' lives, or most discordant in the context of the overall tone of the era, to show the depths or the heights people could reach.

Beyond the question of selecting the documents that appeared to me to be fairest or most illuminating, there was the simple question of numbers. For pragmatic reasons I was to reduce five centuries and a continent full of varied peoples to a collection of no more than 60 documents. In the fields that I know most deeply, leaving certain elements out was positively painful. No doubt experts in other fields will be chagrinned by all that I have not included from the times and places they know best. If students use this book to launch research projects, it is my hope that they come to understand a segment of history so thoroughly that they put themselves in a position to write to me and recommend inclusion – at some future point – of other documents they have come across in their work. Certainly their professors are welcome to do so. Still, I believe students and their teachers will find that in its present form, the book does, broadly speaking, represent the major types of documents that are available to us from each era, as well as the most important historical themes. It is not intended to be comprehensive, but rather illustrative.

*

There are two final points to be addressed. First is the question of terminology. In different parts of the country and in different tribes, preferences vary for "Native American" or "American Indian." Out of respect for both groups, I use the two interchangeably. In Mexico, people prefer the word "indigenous" and in Canada, "First Nations," so these terms also sometimes appear. Second, many tribes call themselves by names different from those that have traditionally been attached to them by outsiders, raising the complicated question of what we should call them here. The Iroquois, for example, were given that name by the French; they are really the Haudenosaunee. The Aztecs never called themselves by that name; they were the Mexica. After long internal debate, I have elected to use the names most familiar to an American audience, though generally coupled with the more accurate name preferred by the tribe. Francis La Flesche, whom I quoted earlier, made a similar decision in his own published work, and for similar reasons. Just as he was, I am concerned that if I only use the labels particular peoples prefer for themselves – while it may be truer to their desire on one level – I will actually be perpetuating a deeper problem: most people, when faced with numerous "foreign" terms they have never heard before, find that they blend together in their mind and they cannot remember them, or if they struggle successfully to remember them, they then do not focus on the more important elements of the drama. In essence, names that are "exotic" or strange to us are distracting and make the bearers of those names seem less real, less immediately human. As it is, the book is full enough of material brand new to most college students. I decided to do my best to make my introductory comments as easily accessible as possible and will thus use the generally familiar names invented by the colonists side by side with the less familiar names preferred by the peoples themselves.

Last but not least, I would like to answer a question occasionally posed to me by my own students. They have sometimes wanted to know if any part of me is genetically Indian. They are especially curious about this when I read aloud to them in Nahuatl. The answer is no. On my father's side, my people were among the wave of European migrants who displaced the Algonkians of the eastern seaboard in the seventeenth century. On my mother's side, they were among the Swedes and Norwegians who poured into Minnesota in the 1860s, displacing the Dakota Sioux. My great grandmother remembered seeing the Indians who came to the house frequently when she was a little girl, not to wreak vengeance – the time for that had passed – but to beg for food: the white people's farms had destroyed their hunting grounds, and so their own children, girls and boys my great-grandmother's age, were gradually dying of starvation. I believe that attaining true wisdom involves studying not only who we are but who we are not, that it involves pushing ourselves to adopt perspectives that do not come easily, that it requires listening to many voices – not only those of our own ancestors – and that we are all capable of this.

Chapter 1 Indian Ways

1. Maya Glyphs at Piedras Negras

The first Native Americans to become full-time farmers were the Mesoamericans. As sedentary people, they soon produced monumental architecture, a complex calendar system, and written histories. Because of this, we can still catch glimpses of their lives. In the year 711, for example, a Maya sculptor carved into a great flat stone (or stela, *as archaeologists call it) a story that had come to be important to his people. On July 7, 674, a noble girl-child was born in a place called* Man *(pronounced "Mahn"), in the vicinity of her people's highest-ranking line of chiefs, known as the Turtle lineage, whose seat was at today's Piedras Negras, in Guatemala. She would later be called Lady Katun Ahau. When she was 12 years old, she was "adorned," married to the heir apparent of Piedras Negras, Yo' Acnal, who later became high chief. When she was 33, she gave birth to a daughter, Lady Kin Ahau. When Lady Katun Ahau had been queen for 24 years, she participated in a ceremony called "grasping the staff," celebrating rulership. The current* katun, *or set of twenty 365-day years, ended 99 days later, in December of 711 in the Western calendar. As the scribe told the story of Lady Katun Ahau, he emphasized how worthy of homage was the young princess, Lady Kin Ahau, who was clearly poised to have an important role in the future.*

We can read this history today because Maya scholars in the second half of the twentieth century dramatically succeeded in breaking the code embedded in the glyphs that cover the ancient ruins scattered throughout Mexico and Guatemala. It had long been thought that the glyphs made mystical references to the spiritual world, that is, that a particular sculptor represented the divinities he worshipped with pictures he and others in his world felt were fitting. Finally one scholar realized that certain glyphs commonly appeared as appendages (prefixes or affixes) and apparently had meanings like "in this place of —" or "it happened on —" or "became king of —." The texts, then, were actual histories – tales of the real world, of kings and queens and wars. Later, other scholars who had a grasp of at least one Mayan language began to take seriously the idea that many of the main glyphs were phonetic, that certain images represented certain syllables. A colonial friar named Diego de Landa had asserted this in the sixteenth century and, using his examples to begin with, scholars began to make rapid progress. There now exists a nearly complete Maya syllabary.

As you look at this example of a translated text, try to participate in the scholarly sleuthing. After you see how numbers are represented, can you easily pick out other glyphs that contain numbers? See if you can identify symbols that are found in different glyphs – "lady," "she was born," "kin" (sun), "katun," etc.

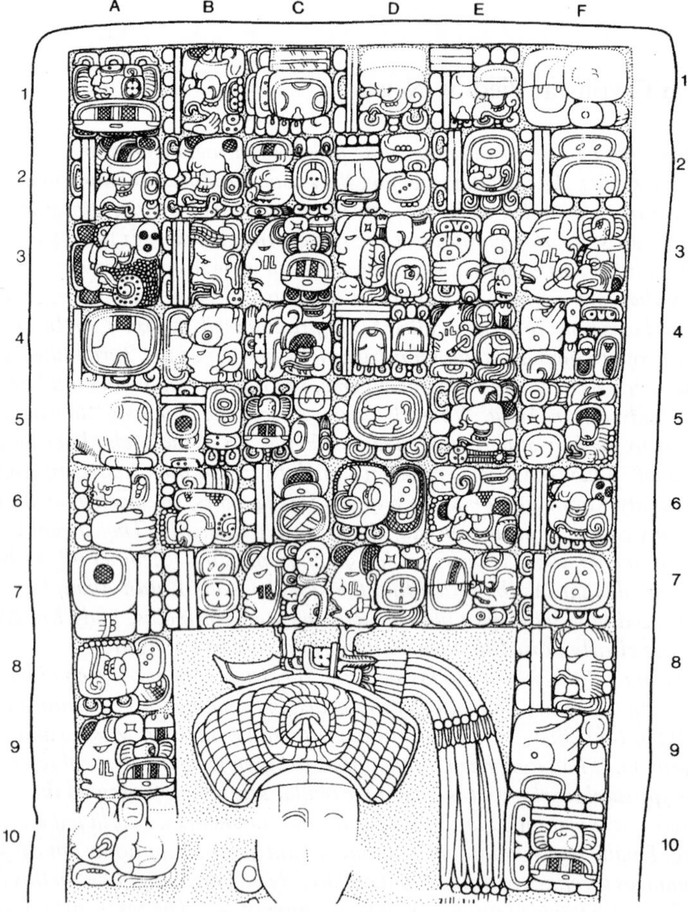

Figure 1.1.1 Maya Glyphs at Piedras Negras

A1 *tzic yaxkin*
the count [date] is in yaxkin
B1 *bolon pih*
9 baktuns
A2 *lahcham katun*
12 katuns
B2 *cha tun*
2 tuns
A3 *mi uinic*
0 uinals
B3 *buluch kin*
11 kins
A4 *ho chibin*
5 cib
B4 *nah*
Seventh Lord of the Night
A5 *ch'a hun*
tied on the headband
B5 *uac kal huliy*
27 days after [the moon] arrived
A6 *cha tzuc u*
two moons are worn out
B6 *ux sac uitz ku*
Three White Mountain God[1]
A7 *uinic bolon*
29 days
B7 *chanluhum yaxkin*
14 yaxkin
A8 *sihi*
she was born
A9 *na katun ahau*
Lady Katun Ahau
A10 *nana man ahau*
matron (noblewoman) from *Man*

C1 *mi, luhum uinicihi*
0 kins, 10 uinals
D1 *lahcham tuni*
12 tuns
C2 *iual ut hun chibin*
it came to pass on 1 cib
D2 *chanlahum uniu nauah*
14 kankin, she was adorned
C3 *na kutun ahau*
Lady Kutun Ahau
D3 *nana man ahau yichnal*
matron of *Man* with
C4 *makina yo' acnal*
Great Sun Yo' Acnal
D4 *luhum, buluch uinicihi hun tuni*
10 kins, 11 uinals, 1 tun
C5 *hun katun, iual ut*
1 katun, it came to pass
D5 *chan chamal*
on 4 cimi
C6 *chanlahum icat*
14 uo
D6 *sihi*
she was born
C7 *na hun tan ac*
she, cherished one of the Turtle lineage
D7 *na kin ahau*
Lady Kin Ahau

E1 *holuhum, uaxac uinicihi, ux tuni*
14 kins, 8 uinals, 3 tuns
F1 *iual ut*
it came to pass
E2 *buluch imix*
on 11 imix
F2 *chanluhum yaxkin*
14 yaxkin
E3 *u ch'amua lom*
she grasped the staff
F3 *na katun ahau*
Lady Katun Ahau
E4 *nana man ahau*
matron from *Man*
F4 *homi u ho tun*
it ended, the fifth tun
E5 *hun katun lati*
1 katun after
F5 *ti ahuale yo'*
his kingship, Yo'
E6 *acnal*
acnal
F6 *bolonluhum, chan uinicihi*
19 kins, 4 uinals
E7 *iual ut*
it came to pass
F7 *uac ahau*
on 7 ahau
F8 *uxluhum muan*
13 muan
F9 *homi*
it ended
F10 *u chanluhum katun*
its fourteenth katun

Source: Linda Schele's translation of Stela 3, Piedras Negras, Guatemala, in Michael D. Coe, *Breaking the Maya Code* (Thames & Hudson, 1992), pp. 266–7, courtesy of Thames & Hudson.

Study: Linda Schele and David Freidel, *A Forest of Kings: The Untold Story of the Ancient Maya* (William Morrow, 1990).

Further exploration: Students who wish to launch themselves into the study of the Maya glyphs should begin with Michael D. Coe and Mark Van Stone, *Reading the Maya Glyphs* (Thames & Hudson, 2001). A classic article that became a touchstone in the development of the field and demonstrates how scholars developed the syllabary is David Stuart, "Ten Phonetic Syllables," *Research Reports on Ancient Maya Writing* 14 (1987).

[1] This is probably the name of the lunation.

2. Ancient Nahuatl Prayers from the Florentine Codex

The Nahuas inhabited central Mexico from the tenth century onward. They came down in waves from today's Arizona and New Mexico and made lives for themselves among people who had been farmers for at least two millennia. One of the last groups to arrive, the Mexica (pronounced "Me-SHEE-ka"), had risen to great power by the time the Spanish came, ruling over at least a quarter of a million people. We know them now as the Aztecs. Their priests and healers led the people in memorized prayers that were recited on the appropriate occasions. Here we have an excerpt of a prayer offered to the rain god, Tlaloc, in a time of drought, followed by a prayer of thanksgiving traditionally offered by a midwife after a woman had successfully given birth. Most likely these words were sung or chanted.

Surprisingly, perhaps, we have the texts of the prayers today thanks to the efforts of Christian missionaries. In the 1560s, 40 years after the Spanish conquest, a Franciscan friar named Bernardino de Sahagún orchestrated a huge project in which Nahuatl-speaking assistants interviewed Indian elders on many aspects of their former lives. He called the resulting multivolume work The General History of the Things of New Spain. *Because the work was eventually taken to Florence, Italy, it is known today as the Florentine Codex.*

Uncan mitoa in tlatolli: in uel iniollocopa quitoaia in iquac quitlatlauhtiaia in tlaloc ...

Auh iz nelle axcan ca ie tlaihiiouitoc in tonacaiutl, ca ie ma uilantoc in teteu inueltiuh: in tonacaiutl ca ie teuhpachiuhtoc, ca ie tocatzaoalquimiliuhtoc ca ie tlaihiiouia, ca ie tlaciaui ...

Here are told the words which they uttered from their hearts when they prayed to Tlaloc: "Behold now, earthly fruit[2] lies suffering, the elder sister of the gods lies outstretched. The earthly fruit lies covered with dust, wrapped in cobwebs. There is fatigue, exhaustion."

Behold the common folk, who are the tail and the wings.[3] They are disappearing. Their eyelids are swelling, their mouths drying out. They become bony, twisted, stretched. Thin are the commoners' lips and blanched are their throats. With pallid eyes live the babies, the children, those who totter, those who crawl, those who spend their time turning dirt and potsherds in their hands, those who live with their eyes bent to the ground, those who lie on the boards, who fill the cradles. All the people face torment, affliction. They witness that which makes humans suffer.

[2] The word *tonacaiutl* is difficult to translate. It literally means "that which is intrinsically tied to the shining of the sun."

[3] This metaphor is used to express the crucial importance of the commoners to all of society.

Already there are none who are passed over; all the little creatures are suffering. The troupial bird, the roseate spoonbill drag their wings. They are upended, tumbled headfirst. They open and close their beaks [from thirst]. And the animals, the four-footed ones of the lord of the near, of the nigh, just wander here and there. They can scarcely rise; to no purpose do they lick the ground. They are crazed for water. Already there is death, all are perishing. The common folk and the animals are dying.

*

Uncan mitoa: in quenin ticitl quitlatlauhtiaia, in piltzintli in ooallacat ...

Auh in otlalticpac quiz piltzintli: niman tzatzi in ticitl, tlacaoatza, quitoznequi: ca ouel iaot in cioatzintli, ca onoquichtic, ca otlama, ca ocacic in piltzintli ...

Here is told how the midwife exhorted the baby who had been born:

When the baby had arrived on earth, then the midwife shouted; she gave war cries, which meant that the woman had fought a good battle, had become a brave warrior, had taken a captive, had captured a baby.

Then the midwife spoke to it ... You have suffered exhaustion, you have suffered fatigue, my youngest one, my precious noble child, precious necklace, precious feather, precious one. You have arrived. Rest, find repose. Here are gathered your beloved grandfathers, your beloved grandmothers, who await you. Here into their hands you have arrived. Do not sigh! Do not be sad! Why have you come, why have you been brought here? Truly you will endure the sufferings of torment and fatigue, for our lord has ordered, has disposed that there will be pain, affliction, misery [in our lives on earth]. There will be work, labor for morning and evening sustenance. [But] there is sweat, weariness and labor so that there will be eating, drinking, and the wearing of raiment. Truly you will endure ...

Source: Charles Dibble and Arthur J. O. Anderson, eds., *General History of the Things of New Spain*, Book 6: *Rhetoric and Moral Philosophy* (University of Utah Press, 1969), pp. 35–6, 167–8. (I have amended their translations slightly.)

Study: Inga Clendinnen, *Aztecs: An Interpretation* (Cambridge University Press, 1991); James Lockhart, *The Nahuas after the Conquest: A Social and Cultural History of the Indians of Central Mexico, Sixteenth through Eighteenth Centuries* (Stanford University Press, 1992).

Further exploration: Students wishing to delve into the study of the Nahuatl language, in which we have more surviving indigenous texts than in any other Native American tongue, should begin with James Lockhart, *Nahuatl as Written* (Stanford University Press, 2001).

3. Pueblo Bonito of Chaco Canyon

The complex of corn, beans, and squash that sustained Mesoamerican civilization eventually spread outward through long-distance trade. Along with it traveled hallmarks of their culture: for example, towering pyramids or large mounds and nearby ceremonial ball courts. Archaeologists have found such sites as far south as San Salvador, in Central America, and as far north as Cahokia, near St. Louis. Other peoples, however, although they gradually adopted corn and thus became sedentary, did not adopt other elements of Mesoamerican civilization. They proceeded along their own unique paths.

In the San Juan River basin, for example, and especially at Chaco Canyon, in the northwestern corner of today's New Mexico, people experimented with agriculture in the ninth, tenth, and eleventh centuries, adopting it for a few generations and then, when times grew tougher, breaking into smaller nomadic groups once again and abandoning the settled communities. They built impressive stone and wood villages organized around kivas, *large communal ceremonial chambers. The largest of these sites is now called Pueblo Bonito. Archaeologists have pieced together which parts were built when, and have proven that the people were well aware of their history. A small original construction became the ceremonial heart of the large village built around it several generations later; there the people concentrated their rich burials, reliquaries, and precious goods, which included some products brought from faraway Mexico. As many as 1,000 people may have lived there at the town's height.*

Figure 1.3.1 Artist's reconstruction of Pueblo Bonito looking north, by Lloyd K. Townsend

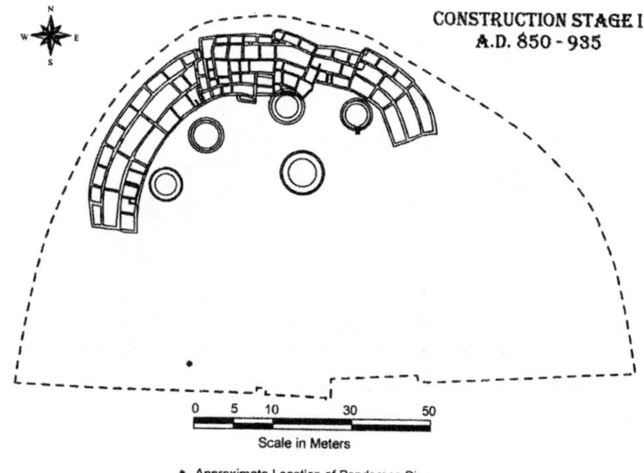

Figure 1.3.2 Pueblo Bonito floor plan: construction stage 1 (850–935)

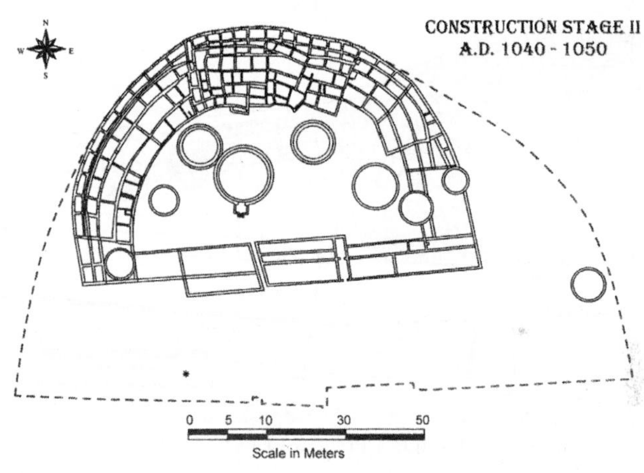

Figure 1.3.3 Construction stage 2 (1040–1050)

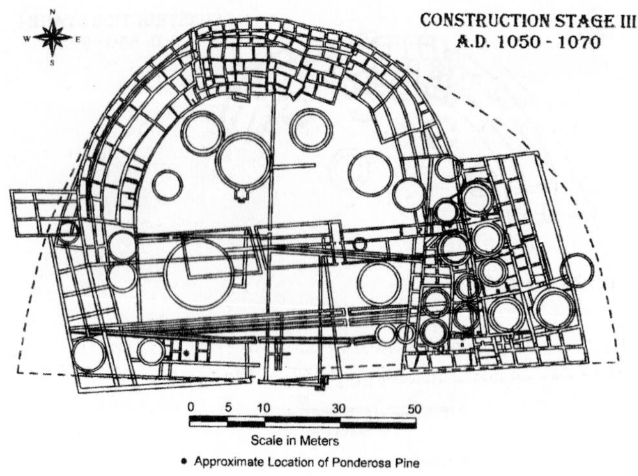

Figure 1.3.4 Construction stage 3 (1050–1070)

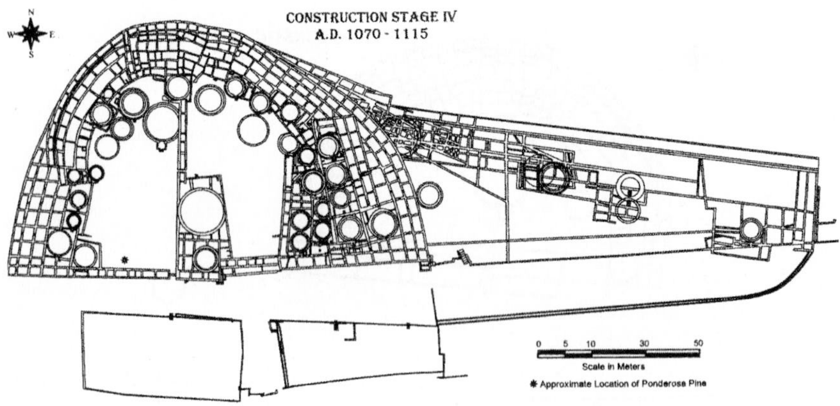

Figure 1.3.5 Construction stage 4 (1070–1115)

Source: John R. Stein, Dabney Ford, and Richard Friedman, "Reconstructing Pueblo Bonito," in Jill E. Neitzel, ed., *Pueblo Bonito: Center of the Chacoan World* (Smithsonian Books, 2003), pp. 44–54.

Study: David E. Stuart, *Anasazi America* (University of New Mexico Press, 2000).

Further exploration: If students want to pursue archaeological remains as texts, one of the most compelling examples would be Cahokia. Unfortunately, there is a great deal of misinformation available from enthusiastic but uninformed writers. A highly scholarly but readable synthesis is Timothy R. Pauketat, *Ancient Cahokia and the Mississippians* (Cambridge University Press, 2004).

4. Images of Secotan

Eventually, corn, beans, and squash made their way through the eastern woodlands of the future United States. When the Europeans first landed, they met people who had been part-time farmers for a few hundred years. The population relied to some extent on agriculture, but also continued to hunt, fish, and gather wild plants. In the 1580s, artist John White traveled to the English colony of Roanoke, in today's North Carolina, and painted the people of the village of Secotan. Fortunately for us, he brought his paintings back to London before the colony and all its inhabitants disappeared. In 1590 his watercolors were made into engravings by Theodor de Bry. (The engravings were used to illustrate a book written by Thomas Harriot, a selection from which appears in Chapter 3, as an example of the kind of preconceptions European visitors brought with them.) These images provide some of the most detailed information we have about pre-colonial Native American life in the region. Think about what we can and cannot learn from them. How did the engraver in Europe change the images that were given to him by the watercolor artist who had actually known the people?

Sources: All of John White's paintings and Theodor de Bry's engravings are available on the Jamestown website: www.virtualjamestown.org/images/white_debry

Study: There are many studies of the ways the eastern woodlands Indians lived in today's southeastern United States, among them Helen Rountree, *The Powhatan Indians of Virginia: Their Traditional Culture* (University of Oklahoma Press, 1989).

Further exploration: Students can see all of the images on the Jamestown website (see above). To put these images in the context of their era, see Peter C. Mancall, ed., *Envisioning America: English Plans for the Colonization of North America, 1580–1640* (Bedford/St. Martin's, 1995). For a full-color facsimile of a sixteenth-century edition, see Thomas Hariot, *"A briefe and true report of the new found land of Virginia": The 1590 Theodor de Bry Latin Edition* (University of Virginia Press, 2007).

Figure 1.4.1 John White, *Indian Village of Secotan* (watercolor), © British Museum

Figure 1.4.2 Theodor de Bry, *Indian Village of Secotan* (engraving), British Library

Figure 1.4.3 John White, *Indians Fishing* (watercolor), © British Museum

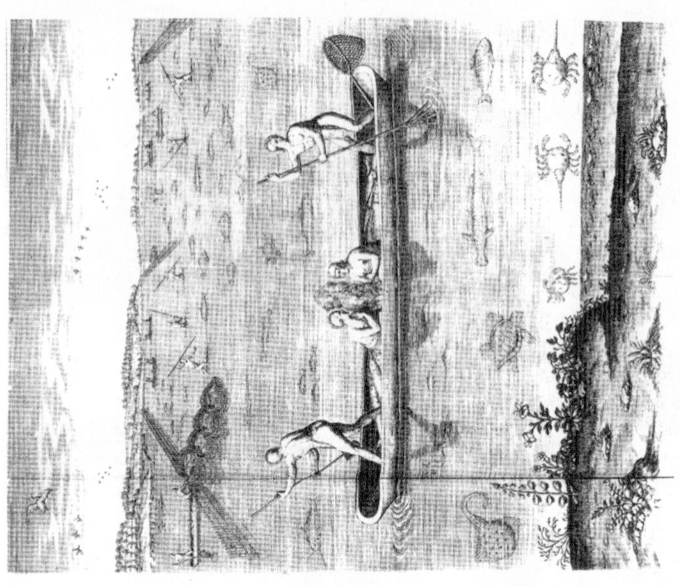

Figure 1.4.4 Theodor de Bry, *Indians Fishing* (engraving), © British Museum

5. Two Versions of the Haudenosaunee (Iroquois) Creation Story

Because the indigenous peoples north of Mexico did not have an alphabetic tradition, scholars have long sought to record oral religious traditions and other stories in hopes of capturing ancient modes of thought. Documents of this nature, however, were produced by people who had lived all their lives with some degree of exposure to a colonial power.

In 1816, a man named John Norton wrote down one version of the Iroquois creation myth for an English audience. Norton's father was Cherokee and his mother a Scottish servant, but he himself had been adopted by the Mohawk nation of the Iroquois and spoke their language. He worked closely with such renowned Iroquois leaders as Joseph Brant and was passionately committed to being a spokesman for Indian peoples in their relationships with the white world.

In the 1890s, a white man named John Hewitt interviewed a number of elders living on the Iroquois reservations in New York state and Canada, writing down their versions of the same story in their own languages. Seth Newhouse, a respected man in the Mohawk community, told the story given here in 1896.

The Journal of John Norton

The tradition of the Nottowegui or Five nations says that "in the beginning before the formation of the earth; the country above the sky was inhabited by Superior Beings, over whom the Great Spirit presided. His daughter having become pregnant by an illicit connection, he pulled up a great tree by the roots, and threw her through the Cavity thereby formed; but to prevent her utter destruction, he previously ordered the Great Turtle, to get from the bottom of the waters, some slime on its back, and to wait on the surface of the water to receive her on it. When she had fallen on the back of the Turtle, with the mud she found there, she began to form the earth, and by the time of her delivery had increased it to the extent of a little island. Her child was a daughter, and as she grew up the earth extended under their hands. When the young woman had arrived at the age of discretion, the Spirits who roved about, in human forms, made proposals of marriage for the young woman: the mother always rejected their offers, until a middle-aged man, of a dignified appearance, his bow in his hand, and his quiver on his back, paid his addresses. On being accepted, he entered the house, and seated himself on the birth [bunk] of his intended spouse; the mother was in a birth on the other side of the fire. She observed that her son-in-law did not lie down all night; but taking two arrows out of his quiver, he put them by the side of his bride: at the dawn of the day he took them up, and having replaced them in his quiver, he went out.

"After some time, the old woman perceived her daughter to be pregnant, but could not discover where the father had gone, or who he was. At the time of delivery, the twins disputed which way they should go out of the womb; the wicked one said, let us go out of the side; but the other said, not so, lest we kill our mother; then the wicked one pretending to acquiesce, desired his brother to go out first: but as soon as he was delivered, the wicked one, in attempting to go out at her side, caused the death of his mother.

"The twin brothers were nurtured and raised by their Grandmother; the eldest was named Teharonghyawago, or the Holder of Heaven; the youngest was called Tawiskaron, or Flinty rock, from his body being entirely covered with such a substance. They grew up, and with their bows and arrows, amused themselves throughout the island, which increased in extent, and they were favoured with various animals of Chase [hunting]. Tawiskaron was the most fortunate hunter, and enjoyed the favour of his Grandmother. Teharonghyawago was not so successful in the Chase, and suffered from their unkindness ...

*

Seth Newhouse's Relation

Ratinakere` ne ēnekě$^{n}$ nene iă de`hatiiěñtēri nene āio^{n}shěñtho` nok onĭ` ne āiāĭ`heie. Ne onĭ` ne dji rotino^{n}soto^{n}` ne skahwădjiratsho$^{n}$`, kano^{n} sowaně^{n}, něñ tähno^{n}` ě$^{n}$s kano$^{n}$ses ne dji ratitero$^{n}$`...

In the regions above there dwelt man-beings who knew not what it is to see one weep, nor what is it for one to die; sorrow and death were unknown to them. And the lodges belonging to them, to each of the ohwachiras [families] were large, and very long, because each ohwachira usually abode in a single lodge.

Within the circumference of the village there was one lodge which claimed two persons, a male man-being and a female-man-being. Moreover, these two man-beings were related to each other as brother and sister, and the two lived in holy seclusion ...

Then, after a time, it came to pass that the female's parent perceived that, indeed, it seemed she was in delicate health; one would indeed think that she was about to give birth to a child. So then they questioned her, saying, "To whom of the man-beings living within the borders of the village art thou about to bear a child?" But she, the girl child, did not answer a single word.

At last the day of her confinement came, and she gave birth to a child, and the child was a girl; but [the mother] persisted in refusing to tell who the father was.

In the time preceding the birth of the girl child the man-being at times heard his kinfolk in conversation say that his sister was about to give birth to a child. Now the man-being spent his time in meditating on this event, and after awhile he began to be ill. And moreover, when the moment of his death had arrived, his mother sat beside his bed, gazing at him in his illness. She knew not what it was; never before had she seen anyone ill.

[*The family experienced grief for the first time when the man-being died. They placed his preserved body in an alcove that they reached by climbing a ladder. His daughter – for it turned out that the baby was his – grew up. At first her weeping knew no bounds when she realized her father was dead, but she became reconciled to losing him when she found she could always climb the ladder, sit by his remains, and communicate with him, sometimes even laughing at the stories he told her. Eventually he told her it was time for her to marry. She embarked on a difficult journey, and finally married, at his direction, a man who was cruel to her, though he provided her family with venison. She endured her experiences with fortitude because her father's spirit regularly gave her advice and even told her ahead of time how her life would probably be. At last her husband grew ill and no one could cure him.*]

When they failed to cure his illness, his people questioned him, saying: "What should we do so that thou mayest recover from thy illness?" Then he answered them, saying: "I am thinking that, perhaps, I would recover from my illness if you would uproot the tree standing in my dooryard." . . . When they had uprooted the tree, he said to his spouse: "Do thou spread for me something there beside the place where stood the tree." Thereupon she did spread something for him there, and he then lay down on it. And so, when he lay there, he said to his spouse: "Here, sit thou beside me." She did sit beside his body as he lay there. He then said to her: "Do thou hang thy legs down into the abyss." For where they had uprooted the tree there came to be a deep hole, which extended through to the nether world, with earth all around it.

Truly it came to pass, that while he lay there his suffering was mitigated. . . . When he had, seemingly, recovered from his illness, he turned himself over . . . and looked into the hole. After a while he said to his spouse: "Do thou look thither into the hole to see what things are occurring there in yonder place." She bent forward her body and looked in. Whereupon he placed his fingers against the nape of her neck and pushed her, and she fell into the hole.

... She kept falling in the darkness. After a while she passed through it. She looked about her in all directions and saw on all sides of her that everything was blue in color ... She knew nothing of the thing she saw, but in truth she now was looking on a great expanse of water, though she did not know it.

This is what she saw: on the surface of the water, floating about hither and thither, like veritable canoes, were all the kinds of ducks. Loon noticed her, and he suddenly shouted, "A female man-being is coming up from the depths." Then Bittern spoke, saying, "Indeed she is not coming up out of the depths. She is falling from above." Whereupon they held a council to decide what they should do to provide for her welfare. They finally decided to invite the Great Turtle to come.

[*The birds flew close together and caught the protagonist on their backs, setting her down gently on the Turtle. Then the water animals – the beaver, the otter and the muskrat – each in turn volunteered to dive down deep and bring up some mud, turning her new home into the earth. The female man-being fell asleep, and each time she woke she saw that more plants and grasses had grown.*]

Now, when the time had come for her to be delivered, she gave birth to a female man-being, a girl child. Then, of course, they two, mother and daughter, remained there together. It was quite astonishing how rapidly the girl child grew. ... When she had grown up, her mother had the habit of admonishing her child, saying "Thou wilt tell me what manner of person it is who will visit thee, who will say, 'I desire that thou and I should marry.' Do not give ear to this, but say, 'Not until I first ask my mother.'"

First one suitor, then another, came along, and she customarily replied, "Not until I first ask my mother," ... But after a while the maiden said, "One who has a deep fringe along his legs and arms paid a visit." The elder woman said, "That is the one, I think, that it will be proper for you to marry." ... Then it was that he paid court to her. But, I think, they did not lie together. When she lay down to sleep, he laid one of his arrows beside her body. Thereupon he departed. Then, at his return, he again took his arrow and departed, carrying it away with him. He never came back.

After a while the elder woman became aware that the maiden was growing in size, caused by the fact that she was pregnant.

When the day of her delivery had come, she brought forth twins, two male infants. During the time that she was in labor, the maiden heard the two talking within her body. One of them said: "This is the place through which we two shall emerge from here. It is a much shorter way." But the other said, "Not at all. Surely we would kill her by doing this thing. Let us go out that other way, the way that, having become human beings, we will use as an exit. We will turn around and in a downward direction we two will go." ... At that time, then, he turned about, and at once he was born. So at that time his grandmother took him up and cared for him. Then she laid him aside. She gave her attention to her daughter, for another travail she did suffer. But that other one emerged in another place. He came out of her armpit. So that one, he killed his mother. His grandmother took him up and attended to his needs also. She completed this task and laid him alongside of the one who had first come. Then she devoted her attention to her child who was dead. Turning to the place where she had laid the two infants, she said, "Which of you two destroyed my child?" One of them answered, saying, "Truly, he it is, I believe." This one was a marvelously strange person. His flesh was nothing but flint. Over the top of his head there was a sharp comb of flint. ... He who was guilty did not swerve from his denial, so he finally won his point. Their grandmother seized the body of him whose flesh was truly that of a man-being and with all her might cast him far into the bushes. But the other, whose flesh was flint, was taken up and cared for by her. And it was amazing how much she loved him ...

Sources: Carl Klinck and James J. Talman, eds., *The Journal of Major John Norton, 1816* (Champlain Society, 1970), pp. 88–9; J. N. B. Hewitt, "Iroquoian Cosmology," *Twenty-First Annual Report of the Bureau of American Ethnology, 1899–1900* (US Government Printing Office, 1903), pp. 255–95. Hewitt provided a painstaking transcription and word-by-word translation parallel to his colloquial translation. I have changed his colloquial translation only where his nineteenth-century English might obstruct a modern understanding and never in any way that might violate the word-by-word translation. I have also omitted his marks indicating which syllables to stress, as I have not included them in other language samples in this book.

Study: Daniel K. Richter, *The Ordeal of the Long-House: The Peoples of the Iroquois League in the Era of European Colonization* (Institute of Early American History and Culture, 1992).

Questions for consideration

1. What do these documents reveal about the types of changes that may begin to take place in people's lives when they adopt agriculture and thus become sedentary?
2. Judging from the remnants of ancient indigenous lives recorded here, what issues would you say were of paramount importance to the people? Were they spiritual or political? Did they feel that their lives were richly rewarding or frighteningly precarious or both?
3. Were any ancient Native Americans interested in memorializing themselves as individuals? Were they interested in memorializing their lineage or their entire people? Could all of these desires be compatible?
4. Which elements of the images of the Algonkian coastal village reveal the hands of European artists? Which elements are most helpful to you in envisioning Native American life?
5. How do the two versions of the Mohawk creation story differ? Which version seems to reveal the influence of European values? What do we gain by reading a version prepared for readers of English and what do we lose? Why is it dangerous to draw conclusions about any native people based on brief statements made by visitors?

Chapter 2 First Contact

1. Arrival of the Spaniards in the Annals of Tlatelolco

A persistent story about First Contact has been that the Native Americans perceived the arriving Europeans to be gods. Nowhere has this story become better known than in the case of the Aztecs, who are supposed to have thought that Hernando Cortés was the god Quetzalcoatl returning from the east. In fact, there is no evidence dating from the years of contact to indicate that the indigenous believed any such thing; they apparently saw the newcomers as visiting priests representing a foreign land. At the same time, there is significant evidence that the story was developed years later in the 1560s by Spanish priests and their Indian aides, who were eager to offer an explanation for the spectacular losses experienced by the hitherto powerful Aztecs.

Before the Spanish conquest, the Aztecs kept track of their history in pictographic records that were designed to elicit complicated recitations on the part of trained historians. After the conquest, when they learned the Roman alphabet, they continued their writing tradition using the new phonetic symbols. This set of annals was written down in Tlatelolco, which was part of Tenochtitlan, the city of Mexico. It almost certainly dates from the 1540s, recording an oral tradition that had developed in the 1520s and 1530s; it is the oldest indigenous account of the conquest in existence.

In the year of Thirteen Rabbit the Spaniards were seen on the water. It was also when some Mexica went to the ocean and died. In the year of One Reed the Spanish appeared at Tecpantlayacac. Thereupon the Captain [Hernando Cortés] came.

When he appeared at Tecpantlayacac, Cuetlaxtecatl met him; there he gave him suns of precious metal, one yellow [gold] and one white [silver], and a mirror for the back, and a golden helmet, and a golden shell head cover, and a head fan of plumes, and a shell shield. Sacrifices were made before the Captain, at which he was angered. They gave the Captain blood in an eagle vessel, and because of it he killed the person who was giving him blood, striking him with a sword. At that, the meeting party dispersed.

Moteucçoma [the king] himself gave [the gifts] to the Captain [as tribute] so that the Captain would go back. [Presenting the gift] was the task of Cuetlaxtecatl.

He [Cortés] reached Tenochtitlan very quickly. He arrived [in the month of] Quecholli, on a day Eight Wind. When he reached Tenochtitlan, we gave him turkey hens, turkey eggs, shelled white maize, and white tortillas, as well as providing water and delivering deer fodder [for the horses] and wood. The Tenochca people and the Tlatelolca people each made their contribution separately.

Then the Captain left for the seashore; he left behind don Pedro de Alvarado, Tonatiuh [the Sun, named for his golden hair]. Then Alvarado asked Moteucçoma how they celebrated the festivity of their god. He said to him, "How is it? Set up all the equipment for it and do it."

When Tonatiuh gave the order, Moteucçoma was already being detained, along with Itzquauhtzin, the Tlacochcalcatl [political leader] in Tlatelolco. At this time [the Spanish] hanged the nobleman of Acolhuacan, Neçahaulquentzin, at the wall near the water. The second one who died was the ruler of Nauhtla, named Cohualpopocatzin. They shot him with arrows [from a crossbow]; when they had shot him, he was burned while he was still alive.

... They told them that [the figure of] Huitzilopochtli [the god of war] should be adorned. Then they set up Huitzilopochtli, outfitted with all his paper garments and accoutrements; they prepared it all. Then the Mexica danced and sang ...

The second day that they danced and sang was when the Tenochca and the Tlatelolca died. While dancing they went bare [of weapons], with only their net cloaks, their turquoise ornaments, their lip plugs, their necklaces, their forked heron-feather ornaments, their deer's hooves. The old men who beat the cylindrical drums had their tobacco pots and their rattles. It was them they first attacked; they struck off their hands and lips. Then all who were dancing, and all who were looking on, died.

They were killing us for three hours. When they had finished killing people in the temple precinct, they went into the buildings and killed those who carried water, provided deer fodder, ground maize, swept, and kept watch.

And the ruler Moteucçoma of Tenochtitlan, accompanied by Itzquauhtzin, said to them, "O our lords, let it be enough. What are you doing? The people are suffering. Do they have shields and war clubs? They go unarmed."

Source and study: Annals of Tlatelolco in James Lockhart, ed., *We People Here: Nahuatl Accounts of the Conquest of Mexico* (University of California Press, 1993), pp. 257–9. The best study of this text appears in the introductory materials of the same volume.

Further exploration: Students can compare this account of events to the much more stylized one that appeared as Book 12 of the Florentine Codex more than a generation later in a work created under Spanish supervision. That account also appears in *We People Here* (see above). A different translation of Book 12 is Miguel León Portilla, *The Broken Spears: The Aztec Account of the Conquest of Mexico* (Beacon Press, 1962). Advanced students will be able to see what a tremendous difference the translator makes. He or she can adjust phrases to make the speaker sound more naive or more sophisticated, and minor errors can create major differences in meaning. The field of Nahuatl translation made major strides forward between 1962 and 1992.

2. Response to the Spanish by Native Priests

Everywhere the Europeans went, they presented the tenets of Christianity and asked native peoples to accept their religion as the one true faith. Usually we can gauge very little of what the indigenous were thinking in the early period: some converted and some resisted. In the case of the Aztecs, we know more, because of the plethora of sources in their own language. (See section 1 above.)

A group of 12 Franciscan friars, representing the 12 apostles, arrived in Mexico in 1524, three years after the conquest. They orchestrated a series of official meetings with high-ranking Aztec political leaders and priests. On several of these occasions, the Europeans took notes. Years later, in the 1560s, another Franciscan wrote up a collection of these notes as though the exchange he was recording had occurred on a single occasion, though he was really creating a composite picture. Here is a direct translation from the Nahuatl of what he claimed the Aztec priests said after having listened for several hours to the messages of the Christians. Notice that what has them truly incensed is not so much the idea of adding a new god as the demand that they abandon the old.

You say that we do not recognize the being who is everywhere, lord of heaven and earth. You say our gods are not true gods. The new words that you utter are what confuse us; due to them we feel foreboding. Our makers [our ancestors] who came to live on earth never uttered such words. They gave us *their* laws, their ways of doing things. They believed in the gods, served them and honored them. They are the ones who taught us everything, the gods' being served and respected. Before them we eat earth [kiss the ground]; we bleed; we pay our debts to the gods, offer incense, make sacrifice. ... indeed, we live by the grace of those gods. They rightly made us out of the time, the place where it was still dark. . . . They give us what we go to sleep with, what we get up with [our daily sustenance], all that is drunk, all that is eaten, the produce, corn, beans, green maize, chia. We beg from them the water, the rain, so that things grow upon the earth.

The gods are happy in their prosperity, in what they have, always and forever. Everything sprouts and turns green in their home. What kind of place is the land of Tlaloc [the god of rain]? Never is there any famine there, nor any illness, nor suffering. And they [the gods] give people virility, bravery, success in the hunt, [bejeweled] lip rings, blankets, breeches, cloaks, flowers, tobacco, jade, feathers and gold.

Since time immemorial they have been addressed, prayed to, taken as gods. It has been a very long time that they have been revered, since once upon a time in Tula, in Huapalcalco, Xochitlapan, Tlamohuanchan, in Teotihuacan, the home of the night. These gods are the ones who established the mats and thrones [that is, the inherited chieftainships], who gave people nobility, and kingship, renown and respect.

Will we be the ones to destroy the ancient traditions of the Chichimeca, the Tolteca, the Colhuaca, the Tepaneca? [No!][1] It is our opinion that there is life, that people are born, people are nurtured, people grow up, [only] by the gods' being called upon, prayed to. Alas, o our lords, beware lest you make the common people do something bad. How will the poor old men, the poor old women, forget or erase their upbringing, their education? May the gods not be angry with us. Let us not move towards their anger. And let us not agitate the commoners, raise a riot, lest they rebel for this reason, because of our saying to them: address the gods no longer, pray to them no longer. Look quietly, calmly, o our lords, at what is needed. Our hearts cannot be at ease as long as we cannot understand each other. We do not admit as true [what you say]. We will cause you pain. Here are the towns, the rulers and kings who carry the world. It is enough that we have lost political power, that it was taken from us, that we were made to abandon the mats and thrones. We will not budge; we will just end [this conversation]. Do to us whatever you want. This is all with which we return, we answer, your breath, your words, o our lords.

Source: Miguel León Portilla, ed., *Coloquios y doctrina cristiana* (Universidad Autónoma de México, 1986). This text has generally appeared in English as a translation from the Spanish, but I preferred to translate directly from the Nahuatl words as the overall effect is somewhat different.

[1] Nahuatl texts are full of rhetorical questions, the answer to which is clearly meant to be a resounding "No!"

Study: James Lockhart, *The Nahuas after the Conquest: A Social and Cultural History of the Indians of Central Mexico, Sixteenth through Eighteenth Centuries* (Stanford University Press, 1992).

3. Don Luis Travels the World

In the period of first contact, Europeans of all nationalities were in the habit of kidnapping Native Americans to act as intermediaries and translators. They preferred their captives to be taken young, so that they would more easily be able to adapt and learn the language. Today we can catch glimpses of these people only in the comments made by the Europeans who knew them – or thought they knew them – during their years abroad.

One of the better known examples was an Algonkian named Paquiquineo who was kidnapped by the Spanish from the shores of the Chesapeake in 1561. He and a companion were taken to Spain, where they met the king. Paquiquineo refused to convert to Christianity and begged the monarch to send him home. His wish was granted, but he was sent first to Mexico; thence he was to be taken to the northern territories. He wasn't. Instead, he became a Christian and was baptized "don Luis de Velasco," in honor of the viceroy. He is well known to historians because years later, in 1570, after traveling to Havana and to Spain for a second time, he joined a Jesuit expedition to his homeland – and once home, led his people in killing all the missionaries. Why would he do this, people have wondered, after becoming a Christian and living for so many years among Europeans?

In a Spanish archive there is a letter that offers many clues to his painful and frustrating experiences among his captors. It was written by the head of the Dominican order in Mexico City soon after Paquiquineo had been placed in his keeping. The friar was alight with zeal: he had in his hands a young man whom he believed would be a perfect intermediary in a major Dominican effort to proselytize in the northern territories. Try to read between the lines to figure out how Paquiquineo might have told the same story.

Sacred Catholic Royal Majesty:

In the last fleet there came to New Spain two Indians whom Captain Antonio Velazquez brought before Your Majesty, and whom Your Majesty ordered Captain Pedro Menendez to return to their homeland as they were not baptized at the time they left the kingdom [of Spain]. As soon as they arrived in this city they got so sick and arrived at such a point that it was not thought they would escape death. For that reason, having learned of their desire to be baptized, as they had asked for it more than once, they were given the sacrament of baptism. Our lord was moved to give them back their health. The religious [brothers] of this your Convent of Santo Domingo begged your Viceroy to keep them here among us so we might instruct them in the things of our holy Catholic Faith and also so that they would become tied by affection to the friars. It was done, and thus they have been and still are among us, and have been treated like sons and taught the things of our faith. Seeing that they are now Christians and members of the church, and that if they were returned to their land alone without ministers who could keep them from straying from the faith and from Christian law, and if they were to return to their rites and idolatries and thus lose their souls, their baptism would have caused them to be damned. Permitting all of that to happen would seem to be a great inhumanity, even a grave offense against our Lord, and a disservice to Your Majesty. It is believed that your desire to return them to their land depended on their being pagans, as they were when they left you. Considering as well the fine presence and capacity of this Indian, and what he tells us of his land, that it is well populated with peaceful people, and believing as we do that Our Lord has arranged all of this business and sent this Indian so that he may be the means of saving all of that land, your Viceroy, with the zeal of a true Christian and a Catholic and a vassal of Your Majesty … communicated with the Provincial and other leading men of our Dominican Order what we might do assuming we received the permission of Your majesty so that the excellent opportunity we had been offered by means of the conversion of this Indian would not be lost. Thus the Order offered to send religious brothers on this project … And to be more effective your Viceroy, desirous of being of service to Our Lord and to Your Majesty, offered to pay expenses himself … There then arrived the moment to deal with the captain [of the royal convoy] Pedro Menendez about the necessary measures for the execution of this business … Because he did not have the necessary orders, or because Our Lord ordered it otherwise, wanting the expedition to be better guided by Your Majesty's hands, he denied the departure of the religious …

The Archbishop[2] then ordered Pedro Menendez not to return the Indians to their homelands since no ministers would go with them. If he wanted to bring them back to Spain to go before Your Majesty, of course he could do that. The Indians were at full liberty to go to Spain and even encouraged to do so, but they said that if they were not going to return to their land, they preferred to stay here than to go all the way to Spain. Thus they remained here and are still among us, who take care to teach them the doctrine and all that is appropriate. Your Viceroy takes a special interest in them and oversees their good treatment …

[2] The Archbishop at the time was a Dominican. He was a friend of the Provincial of the Order and strongly in favor of any plan that would help the Dominicans gain influence in the New World.

Understanding the desire that exists on the part of the Order to serve Our Lord and Your Majesty and the opportunity that exists just now to save those people [of the northern territory] and the misfortune it would be if this opportunity were lost, it seems Your Majesty was well served. Those people are peaceful, and it is believed that they would be even more so if this Indian were to go there and give an account of what he has seen and the benefits he has received. No more than forty or fifty men would have to go with the religious, in one ship, which would be able to pacify the people there ... May Our Lord keep the holy person of Your Majesty and augment your territories for his service ... Mexico City, February 13, 1563.

Fray Pedro de Feria

Source: Archivo General de Indios, Seville, Spain. Record Group Mexico, vol. 280, Feb. 1563.

4. The Arrival of the Dutch at Manhattan in Native Memory

The Delawares and Mahicans lived on the coast of today's New Jersey and in the Hudson River region when the Dutch first arrived at Manhattan in 1609. Gradually, as more Europeans arrived, they were pushed westward, carrying their memories and stories with them. By the middle of the eighteenth century, they were living in the Ohio valley.

A man named John Heckewelder came to live among them. He had been born in England to parents who were Moravians. When he was 11, the whole family traveled to the New World to undertake missionary work. At first he lived in Bethlehem, Pennsylvania, the center of the Moravian community, but in the 1760s, when he was in his early twenties, he went to serve in the Ohio valley and began to learn indigenous languages and record many of the people's customs and histories. In later years, he would act on behalf of George Washington as a spy among the Indians.

After you have read the story about the arrival of the Dutch over 150 years earlier, read Heckewelder's commentary on how to interpret native accounts, and consider whether this narrative was more likely given to him as a serious historical account or as a humorous tall tale.

A great many years ago, when men with a white skin had never yet been seen in the land, some Indians who were out a fishing, at a place where the sea widens, espied at a great distance something remarkably large floating on the water, and such as they had never seen before. These Indians immediately returning to the shore, apprised their countryman of what they had observed, and pressed them to go out with them and discover what it might be. They hurried out together, and saw with astonishment the phenomenon which now appeared to their sight, but could not agree upon what it was;

some believed it to be an uncommonly large fish or animal, while others were of opinion it must be a very big house floating on the sea. At length the spectators concluded that this wonderful object was moving towards the land, and that it must be an animal or something else that had life in it; it would therefore be proper to inform all the Indians on the inhabited island of what they had seen, and put them on their guard. Accordingly they sent off a number of runners and watermen to carry the news to their scattered chiefs, that they might send off in every direction for the warriors, with a message that they should come on immediately. These arriving in numbers, and having themselves viewed the strange appearance, and observing that it was actually moving towards the entrance of the river or bay; concluded it to be a remarkably large house in which the Mannitto (the Great or Supreme Being) himself was present, and that he probably was coming to visit them. By this time the chiefs were assembled at York island, and deliberating in what manner they should receive their Mannitto on his arrival. Every measure was taken to be well provided with plenty of meat for a sacrifice. The women were desired to prepare the best victuals. All the idols or images were examined and put in order, and a grand dance was supposed not only to be an agreeable entertainment for the Great Being, but it was believed that it might, with the addition of a sacrifice, contribute to appease him if he was angry with them. The conjurers were also set to work, to determine what this phenomenon portended, and what the possible result of it might be. To these and to the chiefs and wise men of the nations, men, women and children were looking up for advice and protection. Distracted between hope and fear, they were at a loss what to do; a dance, however, commenced in great confusion. While in this situation, fresh runners arrived declaring it to be a large house of various colors, and crowded with living creatures. It appears now to be certain, that it is the great Mannitto, bringing them some kind of game, such as he had not given them before, but other runners soon after arriving declare that it is positively full of human beings, of quite a different color from that of the Indians, and dressed differently from them; that in particular one of them was dressed entirely in red who must be the Mannitto himself. They are hailed from the vessel in a language they do not understand yet they shout or yell in return by way of answer, according to the custom of their country; many are for running off to the woods, but are pressed by others to stay, in order not to give offence to their visitor, who might find them out and destroy them. The house, some say large canoe, at last stops, and a canoe of a smaller size comes on shore with the red man, and some others in it; some stay with his canoe to guard it. The chiefs and wise men, assembled in council, form themselves into a large circle, towards which the man in red clothes approaches with two others. He salutes after their manner. They are lost in admiration [stunned surprise]; the dress, the manners, the whole appearance of the unknown strangers is to them a subject of wonder; but they are particularly struck with him who wore the red coat all glittering with gold lace,[3] which they could in no manner account for. He, surely, must be the great Mannitto, but why should he have a white skin? Meanwhile, a large *Hackhack* [gourd] is brought by one of his servants, from which an unknown substance is poured out into a small cup or glass, and handed to the supposed Mannitto. He drinks – has the glass filled again, and hands it to the chief standing next to him. The chief receives it, but only smells the contents and passes it on to the next chief, who does the same. The glass or cup thus passes through the circle, without the liquor being tasted by any one, and is upon the point of being returned to the red clothed Mannitto, when one of the Indians, a brave man and a great warrior, suddenly jumps up and harangues the assembly on the impropriety of returning the cup with its contents. It was handed to them, says he, by the Mannitto, that they should drink out of it, as he himself had done. To follow his example would be pleasing to him; but to return what he had given them might provoke his wrath, and bring destruction on them. And since the orator believed it for the good of that nation that the contents offered them should be drunk, and as no one else would do it, he would drink it himself, let the consequence be what it might; it was better for one man to die, than that a whole nation should be destroyed. He then took the glass, and bidding the assembly a solemn farewell, at once drank up its whole contents. Every eye was fixed on the resolute chief, to see what the effect the unknown liquor would produce. He soon began to stagger, and at last fell prostrate on the ground. His companions now bemoan his fate, he falls into a sound sleep, and they think he has expired. He wakes again, jumps up and declares, that he has enjoyed the most delicious sensations, and that he never before felt himself so happy as after he had drunk the cup. He asks for more, his wish is granted; the whole assembly then imitate him, and all become intoxicated.

After this general intoxication had ceased, for they say that while it lasted the whites had confined themselves to their vessel, the man with the red clothes returned again, and distributed presents among them, consisting of beads, axes, hoes, and stockings such as the white people wear. They soon became familiar with each other, and began to converse by signs. The Dutch made them understand that they would not stay here, that they would return home again, but would pay them another visit the next year, when they would bring them more presents and stay with them awhile; but as they could not live without eating, they should want a little land of them to sow seeds, in order to raise herbs and vegetables to put into their broth. They went away as they had said, and returned in the following season, when

[3] Note that this is not really how Dutch officers dressed in 1609. It is, however, how British officers dressed in the eighteenth century, when the story was recorded.

both parties were much rejoiced to see each other; but the whites laughed at the Indians, seeing that they knew not the use of the axes and hoes they had given them the year before; for they had these hanging to their waists as ornaments, and the stockings were made use of as tobacco pouches. The whites now put the handles to the former for them, and cut trees down before their eyes, hoed up the ground, and put the stockings on their legs. Here, they say, a general laughter ensued among the Indians, that they had remained ignorant of the use of such valuable implement, and had borne the weight of such heavy metal hanging to their necks, for such a length of time. They took every white man they saw for an inferior mannitto attendant upon the Supreme Deity who shone superior in the red and laced clothes. As the whites became daily more familiar with the Indians, they at last proposed to stay with them, and asked only for so much ground for a garden lot, as, they said the hide of a bullock would cover or encompass, which hide was spread before them. The Indians readily granted this apparently reasonably request; but the whites then took a knife, and beginning at one end of the hide, cut it up to a long rope, not thicker than a child's finger, so that by the time the whole was cut up, it made a great heap; they then took the rope at one end, and drew it gently along, carefully avoiding its breaking. It was drawn out into a circular form, and being closed at its ends encompassed a large piece of ground. The Indians were surprised at the superior wit of the whites, but did not wish to contend with them about a little land, as they had still enough themselves. The white and red men lived contentedly together for long time, though the former from time to time asked for more land, which was readily obtained, and thus they gradually proceeded higher up the mahicannittuck [Hudson River], until the Indians began to believe that they would soon want all their country, which in the end proved true.

*

The language, then is the first thing that a traveler ought to endeavour to acquire, at least, so as to be able to make himself understood and to understand others. Without this indispensable requisite he may write about the soil, earth and stones, describe trees and plants that grow on the surface of the land, the birds that fly in the air and the fishes that swim in the waters, but he should by no means attempt to speak of the disposition and characters of the human beings who inhabit the country, and even of their customs and manners, which it is impossible for him to be sufficiently acquainted with. And indeed, even with the advantage of the language, this knowledge is not to be acquired in a short time, so different is the impression which new objects make upon us at first sight, and that which they produce on a nearer view . . .

There are men who will relate incredible stories of the Indians, and think themselves sufficiently warranted because they have Indian authority for it. But these men ought to know that all an Indian says is not to be relied upon as truth. I do not mean to say that they are addicted to telling falsehoods, for nothing is farther from their character; but they are fond of the marvelous, and when they find a white man inclined to listen to their tales of wonder, or credulous enough to believe their superstitious notions, there are always some among them ready to entertain him with tales of that description, as it gives them an opportunity of diverting themselves in their leisure hours, by relating such fabulous stories, while they laugh at the same time at their being able to deceive a people who think themselves so superior to them in wisdom and knowledge. They are fond of trying white men who come among them, in order to see whether they can act upon them in this way with success.

Source: John Heckewelder, *An Account of the History, Manners, and Customs of the Indian Nations, who once inhabited Pennsylvania and neighboring states* (Historical Society of Pennsylvania, 1876 [1819]), pp. 71–5, 321–2.

Study: Paul Wallace, *Thirty Thousand Miles with John Heckewelder* (University of Pittsburgh Press, 1958). For a more modern perspective on Heckewelder, see Barbara Alice Mann, "'I Hope You Will Not Destroy What I Have Saved': Hopocan before the British Tribunal in Detroit, 1781," in Barbara Alice Mann, ed., *Native American Speakers of the Eastern Woodlands: Selected Speeches and Critical Analyses* (Greenwood, 2001).

Further exploration: Put Heckewelder's work in the context of all that has been pieced together about the Indians he once knew. Read Amy Schutt, *Peoples of the River Valley: The Odyssey of the Delaware Indians* (University of Pennsylvania Press, 2007).

Questions for consideration

1. Is there any evidence in the documents included in this chapter that the Nahuas in general, or the Aztecs in particular, believed the arriving Europeans to be gods? Is there any evidence against the assertion?
2. We generally assume that Indian travelers in the European world experienced a form of awe. What else does the story of don Luis (or Paquiquineo) suggest that they might have felt?
3. How might we weigh the seriousness or humor of the account of the arrival of the Dutch? After reading the original words of the Aztecs, does it seem more or less likely that other Indians believed the Europeans to be gods? What do the details in the account tell us? Does it seem likely, for example, that the creators of the tomahawk would be unable to determine an ax's use? Would the makers of leggings not recognize knitted stockings?
4. We know that centuries of sedentary living are required for people to develop widespread writing systems, calendars, monumental architecture, metalwork, etc. Often these developments are conflated with a people's mental aptitude. Judging from the documents in this section and the last, does it seem that people whose cultures are relatively new to agriculture are any less intelligent than others?

Chapter 3 The Expectations of the Strangers

1. Christopher Columbus's Journal

In the late fifteenth century, all educated Europeans knew the world was round. Cristoforo Colombo, whom we call Christopher Columbus in English, was a Genoese sailor who believed the globe was much smaller than it actually is. He thought that the ships of his era would be able to carry enough food and water to make it to Asia by sailing across the Atlantic, thus circumventing the Muslim merchants of the Middle East who had dominated the trade routes for centuries. Eventually, he convinced the Spanish monarchs Isabel of Castile and Ferdinand of Aragon to fund an experimental voyage. Columbus was lucky: while trying to make it to Asia, he stumbled upon the Americas. He thought he was near the coast of India, and so named the people he met in the Caribbean "Indians."

Columbus kept a log during the course of the expedition. The original journal was later lost, but not until after a copy had been made by a Spanish friar named Bartolomé de las Casas. Las Casas paraphrased some sections, but seemed to copy faithfully word by word in other places. He was particularly interested in what Columbus had to say about the indigenous people whom he met for the first time on Friday, October 12, 1492.

They are very well formed, with handsome bodies and good faces. Their hair [is] coarse – almost like the tail of a horse—and short. They wear their hair down over their eyebrows except for a little in the back which they wear long and never cut. Some of them paint themselves with black, and they are of the color of the Canarians,[1] neither black nor white; and some of them paint themselves with white, and some of them with red, and some of

[1] Columbus is referring to the people of the Canary Islands, off the coast of Africa.

them with whatever they find. And some of them paint their faces, and some of them the whole body, and some of them only the eyes, and some of them only the nose. They do not carry arms nor are they acquainted with them, because I showed them swords and they took them by the edge and through ignorance cut themselves. They have no iron. Their javelins are shafts without iron and some of them have at the end a fish tooth and others of other things. All of them alike are of good-sized stature and carry themselves well. I saw some who had marks of wounds on their bodies and I made signs to them asking what they were; and they showed me how people from other islands nearby came there and tried to take them, and how they defended themselves; and I believed and believe that they come here from *tierra firme* [the mainland] to take them captive. They should be good and intelligent servants, for I see that they say very quickly everything that is said to them; and I believe that they would become Christians very easily, for it seemed to me that they had no religion. Our Lord pleasing, at the time of my departure I will take six of them from here to Your Highnesses in order that they may learn to speak. No animal of any kind did I see on this island except parrots.

Saturday, 13 October

As soon as it dawned, many of these people came to the beach. . . . They came to the ship with dugouts that are made from the trunk of one tree, like a long boat, and all of one piece, and worked marvelously in the fashion of the land, and so big that in some of them 40 and 45 men came. And others smaller, down to some in which came one man alone. They row with a paddle like that of a baker and go marvelously. And if it capsizes on them they then throw themselves in the water, and they right and empty it with calabashes that they carry. They brought balls of spun cotton and parrots and javelins and other little things that it would be tiresome to write down, and they gave everything for anything that was given to them. I was attentive and labored to find out if there was any gold; and I saw that some of them wore a little piece hung in a hole that they have in their noses. And by signs I was able to understand that, going to the south or rounding the island to the south, there was there a king who had large vessels of it and had very much gold. I strove to get them to go there and [only] later saw that they had no intention of going.

Source: Oliver Dunn and James Kelley, Jr., eds., *The Diario of Christopher Columbus's First Voyage to America, 1492–1493* (University of Oklahoma Press, 1989), pp. 67–71.

Study: Margarita Zamora, *Reading Columbus* (University of California Press, 1993); Nicolás Wey-Gómez, *The Tropics of Empire: Why Columbus Sailed South to the Indies* (Duke University Press, 2006).

Further exploration: Geoffrey Symcox and Blair Sullivan, eds., *Christopher Columbus and the Enterprise of the Indies: A Brief History with Documents* (Bedford/St. Martin's, 2005), puts the Columbus voyage in context. Students can consult for themselves a wide-ranging collection of Columbus's writings as well as other relevant accounts from the era.

2. Cabeza de Vaca's Experiences in North America

For several decades after the European public realized that Columbus had discovered a previously unknown landmass ambitious young people were engaged in a veritable frenzy of exploration and attempts at conquest. There were some spectacular victories, such as that of Hernando Cortés over the Aztecs, but there were also many failures. The more mobile an Indian population was, the more difficult it was for the Europeans to render any victory permanent. In 1528, a Spanish expedition was wrecked off the coast of Florida. The survivors eventually fled from the hostile Indian population in rafts that they built. Ultimately only four men survived – three Spaniards and one North African who had been a slave. They lived for years along the coast of today's Texas, where they gained a reputation as healers among the local people. In 1535, they wandered into Spanish settlements in northern Mexico and reentered European society. One of them, Alvar Núñez Cabeza de Vaca, wrote a long narrative about his experiences among people who had never seen a white man – or a black man – before.

The Indians from the Island of Malhado ... are warlike people, and they have as much cunning to protect themselves from their enemies as they would have if they had been raised in Italy and in continuous war. When they are in a place where their enemies can attack them, they set up their houses at the edge of the most rugged woods and of the greatest density they find there. And next to it they make a trench and sleep in it. All the warriors are covered with light brush, and they make their arrows. And they are so well covered and hidden that even if their heads are uncovered, they are not seen. And they make a very narrow path and enter into the middle of the woods. And there they make a place for their women and children to sleep. And when night comes, they light fires in their houses, so that if there should be spies, they would believe that they are in them. And before dawn, they again light the same fires, and if by chance their enemies come to attack the houses themselves, those who are in the trench surprise them and from the trenches do them much harm without those outside seeing them or being able to find them. ... While I was with the ones of Aguenes, they not being warned, their enemies came at midnight and attacked them and killed three of them and wounded many others, with the result that they fled from their houses forward through the woods. And as soon as they perceived that the others had gone, they returned to them. And they gathered up all the arrows that the others had shot at them, and as secretly as they could, they followed them and were near their houses that night without being perceived And in the early morning they attacked them and they killed five of them and injured many others, and made them flee and leave their houses and their bows with all their possessions ...

The manner in which they fight is low to the ground. And while they are shooting their arrows, they go talking and leaping about from place to place, avoiding the arrows of their enemies, so much so that in such places they manage to suffer very little harm. The Indians are more likely to make fun of crossbows and harquebuses [than to fear them] because these weapons are ineffective against them in the flat, open areas where they roam free. They are good for enclosed areas and wetlands, but in all other areas, horses are what must be used to defeat them, and are what the Indians universally fear. Whoever might have to fight against them should be advised to prevent them from perceiving weakness or greed for what the [Indians] have. And as long as war lasts, they must treat them very badly, because if they know that their enemy has fear or some sort of greed [that may affect their decisions] they are people who know how to recognize the times in which to ... take advantage of the fear [or greed] of their enemies.

Source and study: Rolena Adorno and Patrick Charles Pautz, eds., *The Narrative of Cabeza de Vaca* (University of Nebraska Press, 2003), pp. 127–9.

Further exploration: The journey of Cabeza de Vaca has received an immense amount of attention in recent years. Two writers who have retold the story are Andrés Reséndez, *A Land So Strange: The Epic Journey of Cabeza de Vaca: The Extraordinary Tale of a Shipwrecked Spaniard who Walked across America in the Sixteenth Century* (Basic Books, 2007) and Paul Schneider, *Brutal Journey: The Epic Story of the First Crossing of North America* (Henry Holt, 2006). Mexican film-maker Nicolás Echevarría beautifully captured the tensions intrinsic to the situation in *Cabeza de Vaca* (1991), available with English subtitles. Of the scholarly writing on the events, David Howard most directly addresses the party's interactions with the indigenous: *Conquistador in Chains: Cabeza de Vaca and the Indians of the Americas* (University of Alabama Press, 1997).

3. Thomas Harriot's Observations at Roanoke

By the 1580s, Spain had many successful colonies in the Americas; other European nations dreamed of catching up with them. Spain had managed to impose a kind of labor tax over the Indians, requiring individuals to work for part of each year for the European to whom their village had been assigned. As the English began to explore North America, they hoped they would soon be able to do the same. In 1585, an experimental colony was planted at Roanoke, an island off the coast of today's North Carolina. Later, all traces of the colonists would disappear, but not until after men in the first boatload had made careful observations of what they found and brought their records back to London. John White painted the land and people (see Chapter 1, section 4), and Thomas Harriot, a talented linguist and mathematician, did his best to learn an Algonkian language and talk to the people. He later published A Briefe and True Report of the New Found Land of Virginia, *which was published along with engravings made from White's paintings and became a bestseller by sixteenth-century standards.*

In respect of us they are a people poore, and for want of skill and judgement in the knowledge and use of our things, doe esteeme our trifles before things of greater value: notwithstanding, in their proper maner (considering the want of such meanes as we have), they seem ever ingenious. For although they have no such tooles, nor any such crafts, Sciences and Artes as wee, yet in those things, they doe, they shew excellence of wit. And by how much they upon due consideration shall finde our maner of knowledge and crafts to exceede theirs in perfection, and speede for doing or execution, by so much the more is it probable that they should desire our friendship and love, and have the greater respect for pleasing and obeying us. Whereby may bee hoped, if meanes of good government be used, that they may in short time bee brought to civilitie, and the imbracing of true Religion.

... Most things they sawe with us, as Mathematicall instruments, sea Compasses, the virtue of the load-stone in drawing yron, a perspective glasse whereby was shewed many strange sights, burning glasses, wilde fireworkes, gunnes, hookes, writing and reading, springclockes that seeme to goe of themselves and many other things that wee had were so strange unto them, and so farre exceeded their capacities to comprehend the reason and meanes how they should be made and done, that they thought they were rather the workes of gods then of men, or at the leastwise they had bene given and taught us of the gods. Which made many of them to have such opinion of us, as that if they knew not the trueth of God and

Religion already, it was rather to bee had from us whom God so specially loved, then from a people that were so simple, as they found themselves to be in comparison of us. Whereupon greater credite was given unto that wee spake of, concerning such matters.

Source: Thomas Harriot, *A Briefe and True Report of the New Found Land of Virginia* (1590), in Peter Mancall, ed., *Envisioning America: English Plans for the Colonization of North America, 1580–1640* (Bedford/St. Martin's, 1995).

Study and further exploration: Harriot's rich text has been interpreted in widely different ways. Compare the use which Stephen Greenblatt makes of it in *Marvelous Possessions: The Wonder of the New World* (University of Chicago Press, 1991) and *New World Encounters* (University of California Press, 1993) with that of Joyce Chaplin, *Subject Matter: Technology, the Body, and Science on the Anglo-American Frontier, 1500–1676* (Harvard University Press, 2001).

4. John Smith's Visit to Werowocomoco

In late 1607, the new English settlers at Jamestown found themselves facing starvation. John Smith took a few men up the Chickahominy River to trade for corn but was captured by a kinsman of Powhatan, who was the paramount chief of the local Indian tribes. The Indians took Smith to Werowocomoco, meaning "village of the king." Within a few weeks they returned him to Jamestown with messages for his leaders. In early 1608, only a few weeks after the events, Smith sent a report about his experiences among the Indians to the colony's backers in London. Years later, in 1624, he wrote about the events again, this time in the third person, and he embellished them extensively. In the intervening years, the chief's daughter Pocahontas had been to London and become something of a celebrity, so Smith included her in the drama, though she would have been only about 9 years old in 1608. Moreover, in 1622, the Virginia Indians had launched a major offensive against the white colonists, thus changing their reputation in London and requiring some rewriting on Smith's part.

In 1624, Smith was free to write what he chose, as Powhatan, Pocahontas, and all the principals of the story were dead. Not long after Smith penned his famous story about Pocahontas, he wrote two other dramatic stories about his exploits elsewhere in which he was also saved at crucial moments by beautiful women; indeed, this was a favorite narrative device of his. Comparing Smith's two accounts of the same events suggests the importance of researching the full context before taking any colonist's statements concerning indigenous thoughts or actions at face value.

"A True Relation of such occurrences and accidents of note, as hath hapned in Virginia" (1608)

Arriving at Werawocomoco, their Emperour proudly lying upon a Bedstead a foote high upon tenne or twelve Mattes, richly hung with many Chaynes of great Pearles about his necke, and covered with a great Covering of rahaughcums [that is, raccoon pelts]: At his head sat a woman, at his feete another, on each side sitting upon a Matte upon the ground were raunged his chiefe men on each side the fire, tenne in a ranke, and behinde them as many young women, each a great Chaine of white Beades over their shoulders, their heades painted in redde, and [he] with such a grave and Majesticall countenance, as drove me into admiration to see such state in a naked Salvage, . . . hee kindly welcomed me with good wordes, and great Platters of sundrie Victuals, assuring mee his friendship, and my libertie within foure dayes; hee much delighted in [his kinsman] Opechancanoughs relation of what I had described to him, and oft examined me upon the same [subjects]. Hee asked me the cause of our coming; I tolde him, being in fight with the Spaniards our enemie, being over powred, near put to retreat, and by extreame weather put to his shore . . .

*

"The General Historie of Virginia" (1624)

At last they brought him to Meronocomoco [*sic*], where was Powhatan their Emperor. Here more then two hundred of those grim Courtiers stood wondering at him, as [if] he had been a monster; till Powhatan and his trayne had put themselves in their greatest braveries [that is, finest attire]. Before a fire upon a seat like a bedsted, he sat covered with a great robe, made of Rarowcun skinnes, and all the tayles hanging by. On either hand did sit a young wench of 16 or 18 yeares, and along on each side the house, two rowes of men, and behind them as many women, with all their heads and shoulders painted red; many of their heads bedecked with the white downe of Birds, but every one with something; and a great chayne of white beads about their necks. At his entrance before the King, all the people gave a great shout. The Queene of Appamatuck was appointed to bring him water to wash his hands, and another brought him a bunch of feathers, in stead of a Towell to dry them; having feasted him after their best barbarous manner they could, a long consultation was held, but the conclusion was, two great stones were brought before Powhatan; then as many as could layd hands on him, dragged him to them, and thereon laid his head, and being ready with their clubs, to beate out his braines, Pocahontas the Kings dearest daughter, when no intreaty could prevaile, got his head in her armes, and laide her owne upon his to save him from death; whereat the Emperour was contented he should live to make him hatchets, and her bells, beads, and copper...

Source: Philip Barbour, ed., *The Complete Works of John Smith* (Institute of Early American History and Culture, 1986), vol. 1, p. 53; vol. 2, pp. 150–1.

Study: Camilla Townsend, *Pocahontas and the Powhatan Dilemma* (Hill & Wang, 2004); Helen Rountree, *Pocahontas, Powhatan, Opechancanough: Three Indian Lives Changed by Jamestown* (University of Virginia Press, 2005).

Further exploration: If students consult any of the many traditional biographies of Pocahontas, they will find them full of unsubstantiated myths repeated as if they were fact. They might consider making a study of the reasons the myths have been so unshakably popular. An article that has become a classic in the field is Rayna Green, "The Pocahontas Perplex: The Image of Indian Women in American Culture," *Massachusetts Review* 16/4 (1975).

5. Edward Waterhouse's Report on the Events of 1622

By 1622, thanks to tobacco and a peace that had been made with the Indians, the English colony at Jamestown was flourishing. This was, however, bad news for the local indigenous people, who were rapidly losing all the arable land near the rivers to the well-armed colonists. In March of 1622, the Powhatans orchestrated a major attack, striking without warning at many sites up and down the James River. About a quarter of the colony's population was killed in one day. It is unclear whether the Powhatans hoped the surviving colonists would leave forever or simply be content to stay in Jamestown and operate a trading post, leaving the Indians with their lands. Most likely, the indigenous were divided among themselves as to their ultimate agenda. In any case, the settlers regrouped and sent out attack parties to wreak vengeance. Almost immediately, Edward Waterhouse sent back to London "A Declaration of the State of the Colony and Affaires in Virginia, with a Relation of the Barbarous massacre in the time of peace and League, treacherously executed by the Native Infidels upon the English."

These small and scattered Companies [of Indians] had warning given from one another in all their habitations to meete at the day and houre appointed for our destruction, at all our severall Townes and places seated upon the River; some were directed to goe to one place, some to another, all to be done at the same day and time, which they did accordingly: some entering their Houses under colour of trucking [trading], and so taking advantage, others drawing our men abroad upon faire pretences, and the rest suddenly falling upon those that were at their labours.

... Thus have you seen the particulars of this massacre, out of Letters from thence written, wherein treachery and cruelty have done their worst to us, or rather to themselves; for whose understanding is so shallow, as not to perceive that this must needs bee for the good of the Plantation after, and the losse of this blood to make the body more healthfull, as by these reasons may be manifest.

First, Because betraying of innocency never rests unpunished: And therefore *Agesilaus*,[2] when his enemies (upon whose oath of being faithfull hee rested) had deceived him, he sent them thankes, for that by their perjury, they had made God his friend, and their enemy.

Secondly, Because our hands which before were tied with gentlenesse and faire usage, are now set at liberty by the treacherous violence of the Savages, not untying the Knot, but cutting it: So that we, who hitherto have had possession of no more ground then their waste, and our purchasse at a valuable consideration to their owne contentment, gained; may now by right of Warre, and law of Nations, invade the Country and destroy them who sought to destroy us: whereby wee shall enjoy their cultivated places, turning the laborious Mattocke into the Victorious Sword (wherein there is more both ease, benefit, and glory) and possessing the fruits of others labours. Now their cleared grounds in all their villages (which are situate in the fruitfullest places of the land) shall be inhabited by us, whereas heretofore the grubbing [clearing] of woods was the greatest labour.

Thirdly, Because those commodities which the Indians enjoyed as much or rather more than we, shall now also be entirely possessed by us. The Deere and other beasts will be in safety, and finitely increase, which heretofore not onely in the generall huntings of the King (whereat foure or five hundred Deere were usually slaine) but by each particular Indian were destroied at all times of the yeare, without any difference of Male, Damme, or Young ...

Fourthly, Because the way of conquering them is much more easie then of civilizing them by faire meanes, for they are a rude, barbarous, and naked people, scattered in small companies, which are helps to Victories, but hinderances to Civilitie: Besides that, a conquest may be of many, and at once, but civility is in particular, and slow, the effect of long time, and great industry. Moreover, victorie of them may bee gained many waies; by force, by surprise, by famine in burning their Corne, by destroying and burning their Boats, Canoes and Houses, by breaking their fishing Weares, by assailing them in their huntings, whereby they get the greatest part of

[2] Agesilaus was a king of Sparta who lived from 444 BC to 360 BC. In making reference to him, Waterhouse is showing off his classical education, and thus proving his credentials as a "gentleman" to anyone who might read his work.

their sustenance in Winter, by pursuing and chasing them with our horses, and blood-Hounds to draw after them, and Mastives to teare them, which take this naked, tanned, deformed Savages, for no other then wilde beasts, and are so fierce and fell upon them, that they feare them worse then their old Devill which they worship, supposing them to be a new and worse kind of Devils then their owne. By these and sundry other wayes, as by driving them (when they flye) upon theire enemies, who are round about them, and by animating and abetting their enemies against them, may their ruine or subjection be soone effected …

Fiftly [*sic*], Because the Indians, who before were used as friends, may now most justly be compelled to servitude and drudgery, and supply the roome of men that labour, whereby even the meanest [poorest] of the Plantation may imploy themselves more entirely in their Arts and Occupations, which are more generous, whilest Savages performe their inferiour workes of digging in mynes, and the like, of whom also some may be sent for the service of the Sommer Ilands [in the Caribbean].

Sixtly, This will for ever hereafter make us more cautelous [cautious] and circumspect, as never to bee deceived more by any other treacheries, but will serve for a great instruction to all posterities there, to teach them that *Trust is the mother of Deceipt*, and to learne them that of the Italian, *Chi no fida, non s'ingamuu*, Hee that trusts not is not deceived; and make them know that kindnesses are misspent upon rude natures, so long as they continue rude; as also, that Savages and Pagans are above all other for matter of Justice ever to be suspected. Thus upon this Anvile shall wee now beate out to our selves an armour of proofe, which shall for ever after defend us from barbarous Incursions, and from greater dangers that otherwise might happen. And so we may truly say according to the French Proverb, *Aquelq chose Malheur est bon,* Ill lucke is good for something.

Source: Edward Waterhouse, "A Declaration of the State of the Colony and Affaires in Virginia, with a Relation of the Barbarous massacre in the time of peace and League, treacherously executed by the Native Infidels upon the English" (imprinted at London for Robert Mylbourne, 1622), in Susan Myra Kingsbury, ed., *The Records of the Virginia Company of London*, vol. 3 (United States Government Printing Office, 1933), pp. 541–64.

Study: Frederic Gleach, *Powhatan's World and Colonial Virginia: A Conflict of Cultures* (University of Nebraska Press, 1997); Helen Rountree, *Pocahontas's People: The Powhatan Indians of Virginia through Four Centuries* (University of Oklahoma Press, 1990).

Questions for consideration

1. Columbus is known for having envisioned the "Indians" he met as essentially naive. When you compare his account with the account of a culturally similar people given by Cabeza de Vaca, do the Indians or the Europeans end up looking more naive?
2. The documents in this chapter are presented in chronological order. How did European attitudes toward Native Americans change upon closer acquaintance? As you proceed through the documents, do you yourself conclude that the Indians were more violent than people elsewhere, less violent, or about as violent as most people?
3. In the context of what later happened at Roanoke, Thomas Harriot seems overly optimistic about the Indians' willingness to remake themselves according to European desires. Why would an intelligent man, who was in fact complimentary about the Indians' abilities, make such a serious mistake?
4. Was a policy of extermination part of the Europeans' original expectations? When does it seem to have emerged? Why?

Chapter 4 The Long Struggle for American Lands

1. A Jesuit's Story of the 1639 Smallpox Epidemic

While the English struggled to take control of Virginia and New England, the French explored the rugged Canadian territory to the north. Along with representatives of the French government went Jesuit friars, members of the Society of Jesus, who worked hard to establish missions among the Iroquoian-speaking Hurons and the Algonkian-speaking peoples of the St. Lawrence River valley. Every year from 1632 to 1673, they sent reports back to Europe which were published in Paris.

These "Jesuit Relations" are a rich source for us today. Certainly the friars were judgmental of the Indians and condescending in their perspective, but they were also immersed in the cultures of the people they were trying to "save" and astutely observant. The Jesuits were known for their high academic standards in comparison to other religious orders; they took it as a matter of course, for example, that they had to learn the language of the people among whom they lived.

Disease devastated the seventeenth-century indigenous population of the Americas. In the 1640 Relation of Father Jérôme Lalemant, living among the Huron, we can hear fleeting traces of conversations the Indians had among themselves as they tried to make sense of what they were experiencing.

It was upon the return from the journey which the Hurons had made to Kébec, that [smallpox] started in the country, – our Hurons, while again on their way up here, having thoughtlessly mingled with the Algonquins, whom they met on the route, most of whom were infected with smallpox. The first Huron who introduced it came ashore at the foote of our house, newly built on the bank of a lake, – whence being carried to his own village, about a league distant from us, he died straightaway after. Without being a great prophet, one could assure oneself that the evil would soon be spread abroad through all these regions, for the Hurons – no matter what plague or contagion they may have – live in the midst of their sick, in the same indifference, and community of all things, as if they were in perfect health. In fact, in a few days, almost all those in the cabin of the deceased found themselves infected; then the evil spread from house to house, from village to village, and finally became scattered throughout the country.

*

The villages nearer to our new house having been the first ones attacked, and most afflicted, the devil did not fail to seize his opportunity for reawakening all the old imaginations, and causing the former complaints of us, and of our sojourn in these quarters, to be renewed; as if it were the sole cause of all their misfortunes, and especially of the sick. They no longer speak of aught else, they cry aloud that the French must be massacred. These barbarians animate one another to that effect; the death of their nearest relatives takes away their reason, and increases their rage against us so strongly in each village that the best informed can hardly believe that we can survive so horrible a storm. They observed, with some sort of reason, that, since our arrival in these lands, those who had been the nearest to us, had happened to be the most ruined by the diseases, and that the whole villages of those who had received us now appeared utterly exterminated; and certainly, they said, the same would be the fate of all the others if the course of this misfortune were not stopped by the massacre of those who were the cause of it. This was a common opinion, not only in private conversation but in the general councils held on this account, where the plurality of the votes went for our death, – there being only a few elders who thought they greatly obliged us by resolving upon banishment.

What powerfully confirmed this false imagination was that, at the same time, they saw us dispersed throughout the country, – seeking all sorts of ways to enter the cabins, instructing and baptizing those most ill with a care which they had never seen. No doubt, they said, it must needs be that we had a secret understanding with the disease (for they believe that it is a demon) since we alone were all full of life and health, although we constantly breathed nothing but a totally infected air, – staying whole days close by the side of the most foul-smelling patients, for whom every one felt horror; no doubt we carried the trouble with us, since, wherever we set foot, either death or disease followed us.

In consequence of all these saying, many had us in abomination; they expelled us from their cabins, and did not allow us to approach their sick, and especially children; not even to lay eyes upon them, – in a word, we were dreaded as the greatest sorcerers on earth.

Source: Jérôme Lalemant, "Relation of What Occurred in the Mission of the Hurons, from the month of June in the year 1639, until the month of June in the year 1640," in Reuben Gold Thwaites, ed., *The Jesuit Relations and Allied Documents*, vol. 18 (Pageant Book Co., 1959 [1896]), pp. 88–93. Thwaites's translation from the French contains some archaic language, but I have chosen to leave his translation as it is, as I believe it better conveys the flavor of the times than would a modernized rendition. Students who have studied French would do well to consult the original, which is also included in Thwaites.

Study: A pathbreaking work using Jesuit sources was Bruce Trigger, *Natives and Newcomers: Canada's "Heroic Age" Reconsidered* (McGill-Queen's University Press, 1985). A more recent work is Carol Blackburn, *Harvest of Souls: The Jesuit Missions and Colonialism in North America, 1632–1650* (McGill-Queen's University Press, 2000).

Further exploration: Many research libraries house the complete set of Jesuit Relations. Students can at the very least consult an edited collection of some of the most interesting sections: Allan Greer, ed., *The Jesuit Relations: Natives and Missionaries in Seventeenth-Century North America* (Bedford/St. Martin's, 2000).

2. Gandeaktena's Decision to Become a Christian

Many native people resisted pressure brought to bear by Christian missionaries; others chose to convert. In French Canada, the most famous convert was Catherine Tegahkouita, or Kateri as she is usually called today. She lived at the mission at Kahnawake from about 1676 to the time of her death in 1680 and she insisted on maintaining her virginity. The Jesuit friars held her up as an example of the good they were doing and she has been canonized by the Catholic Church. It has traditionally been assumed that she was simply particularly susceptible to the influence of the missionaries, either for good or for ill, depending on one's perspective. In fact, however, the story is more complicated: she, like all converts, was at least partly responding to her own immediate circumstances within the indigenous world. A close reading of the Jesuit record tells us that her mother was an Algonkian captive taken by the Iroquois. When her father and his family died of smallpox, she was left without immediate kin and thus, apparently, was interested in joining a new community that would be more supportive of her. Kateri was not alone. In 1679, a Jesuit told the story of Gandeaktena, for example. She is much less well known today, but the account of her life is worth reading nonetheless, as several elements of her story are comparable to Kateri's and may put the better-known narrative in perspective.

The Queen of virtues has been wonderfully displayed in the person of a poor slave, taken prisoner by the Iroquois from the Chat nation. We shall undoubtedly be touched by the graces that God was pleased to confer upon this Captive, and by the singular virtues – and, above all, the Charity toward God and her neighbor – that she displayed before the eyes of the savages and the French at la prairie de la magdelaine. Here is the narrative:

God having permitted that Gentaienton, a village of the Chat nation, should be taken and sacked by the Iroquois, Gandeaktena, which is the name of the one of whom we are speaking, was taken into slavery together with her mother and brought to Onniout. There the misfortune of her country proved the blessing of our Captive; and her slavery was the Cause of her preparing herself to receive through baptism the liberty of the children of God. The innocency in which she had lived, even before intending to become a Christian, seemed to have prepared her to receive this grace; and it is an astonishing fact that, in the midst of the extreme Corruption of the Iroquois, she was able, before being illumined by the light of the gospel, to keep herself from participating in their debaucheries, although she was their slave.

Some years after her coming to Onneiout, father Bruyas also came thither to preach the gospel. On the day after his arrival, he made known in public the reason of his coming. Our slave was at once Inwardly influenced by God, and so keenly affected with the desire of paradise and the fear of hell, that she Immediately resolved to spare no pains in acquiring the one and avoiding the other. She showed no less Constancy in the prosecution of her purpose than promptitude in forming it; and although she encountered great obstacles, there was none that she did not succeed in overcoming. Her extreme modesty, which would not permit her to visit the father all alone; the refusal of all whom she asked to bear her company; the determination, sudden and unexpected, of her husband[1] to take her with him to the war; the work assigned to her by the woman whose slave she was, – that of going to the fishery, after her husband had sent her back from the expedition, – served only to bring to view the power of the spirit by which she was urged forward. This spirit, rendering her careful to Seek the favorable opportunity of corresponding to the divine inspiration, prevailed upon her to embrace at last what the providence of God rather than chance placed in her way. For, on her return from the fishery, she met one of her Companions who was on her way to the prayers. She went with her; and on arriving at the Cabin of the father, she repeated the prayers. The father noticed her, and judged from her modest countenance that there was something about this Young woman that was quite out of the common; this determined him to address to her some words of encouragement in private. From that time she never failed to come to pray to God in the Chapel. She learned in a very short time the prayers, and the mysteries of our faith; but,

[1] Captured girls and young women usually had the option of marrying into their new tribe.

reflecting on the Corrupt morals and licentiousness of the Iroquois, and wisely Concluding that she would experience much difficulty in securing her salvation if she lived among them, she resolved to leave them and come to live with the French. She commended the matter to God, and spoke of her plan to her mother, to her father-in-law, and to her husband, after his return from the war. She won them all over, as well as certain others of her neighbors, and came with them to Monseigneur Bishop of Canada, who, after they had been instructed, baptized them all. These blessed successes with which God had accompanied the Conversion of our Catherine – for that is the name she received at baptism – and that little band of persons whom she had attracted to the faith, and the train of events, made it apparent that he had from that time appointed her, and was Directing her, to become Instrumental in the salvation of many Iroquois; for he gave her the thought of going to dwell at la prairie de la magdelaine, where, two months ago, a settlement had been Started. She went there, in fact, together with those with whom she had been baptized – 12 in number, – and gave the first Impulse to the mission which is now so flourishing.

No advance was made in these small beginnings for 2 or 3 years; but, at length they attained much renown, especially among the Iroquois nations, so that more than 200 Iroquois have come since that time to establish themselves at la prairie de la magdelaine, in order to live there as good Christians. And it is a surprising Thing that God should have willed that they [the Iroquois] should Spare the life of Catherine in order that, afterward, she might obtain for them eternal salvation, and that thus their slave might become their instructress in the faith. She was that indeed, not only at the outset of her Conversion, but all the remainder of her life, through the rare examples of virtue which she furnished them.

Source: Vincent Bigot, revised by Claude Dablon, "Relation of What Occurred Most Remarkable in the Mission of the Fathers of the Society of Jesus in New France, in the year 1679," in Reuben Gold Thwaites, ed., *The Jesuit Relations and Allied Documents*, vol. 61 (Pageant Book Co., 1959 [1896]), pp. 195–9.

Study: On Kateri and her context, see Daniel Richter, *Facing East from Indian Country: A Native History of Early America* (Harvard University Press, 2001) and Allan Greer, *Mohawk Saint: Catherine Tekakwitha and the Jesuits* (Oxford University Press, 2005).

Further exploration: Students might research the life stories of other famous Indian women who chose to work with rather than against Europeans. Malinche (or Malintzin), for example, who translated for Hernando Cortés, had also lived as a captive among a people not her own. Sacagawea had been taken prisoner as a girl and was then sold to the Frenchman who worked as a translator for Lewis and Clark.

3. Metacom's Grievances

Massasoit, chief of the Wampanoags, chose to make peace with the English in 1621, soon after their arrival in today's Massachusetts. His people managed to hold to the peace for many years, but by the time of his death in 1661, due to the gradual loss of their land, relations with the settlers had become extremely tense. Massasoit's son Wamsutta inherited the chieftainship, and the English soon brought him to Plymouth to question him about his intentions – and to threaten him. On his way home, he died, many said by poison. A younger brother named Metacom then became high chief. He became known to the English as King Philip and he sometimes styled himself that way as well. Philip had numerous experiences with the English courts which embittered him and left him convinced that English laws always ended up working in favor of English people whenever Indians tried to use them to protect their own property or rights. Thus he was increasingly willing to consider recourse to violence.

War was to break out in 1675. But before it did, the governor of Rhode Island sent the colony's attorney general, John Eastman, to talk to Metacom and attempt to encourage peaceful negotiations. Rhode Island had a better record than Massachusetts in its history of dealings with the indigenous, and thus there was reason to hope that King Philip would speak openly to a Rhode Island representative. This is John Eastman's report of their conversation.

For forty years' time reports and jealousies of war had been very frequent that we did not think that a war was breaking forth, but about a week before it did we had cause to think it would. Then to endeavor to prevent it, we sent a man to Philip that if he would come to the ferry we would come over to speak with him. About four miles we had to come thither. Our messenger come to them, they not aware of it behaved themselves as furious but suddenly appeased when they understood who he was and what he came for he called his council and agreed to come to us came himself unarmed and about forty of his men armed. Then five of us went over. Three were magistrates. We sat very friendly together. We told him our business was to endeavor that they might not receive or do wrong. They said that was well they had done no wrong, the English wronged them, we said we knew the English said they [the Indians] wronged them and the Indians said the English wronged them but our desire was the quarrel might rightly be decided in the best way, and not as dogs decided their quarrels. The Indians owned that fighting was the worst way then they propounded how right might take place, we said by arbitration. They said all English agreed against them and so by arbitration they had had much wrong, many square miles of land so taken from them for English would have English Arbitrators, and once they were persuaded to give in their arms, that thereby jealousy might be removed and the English having their arms would not deliver them as they had promised, until they consented to pay 100 pounds, and now they had not so much land or money, that they were as good be killed as leave all their livelihood. We said they might choose a [*sic*] Indian king, and the English might choose the governor of New York that neither had cause to say either were parties of the difference. They said they had not heard of that way and said we honestly spoke so we were persuaded that if that way had been tendered they would have accepted. We did endeavor not to hear their complaints, said it was not convenient for us now to consider of, but to endeavor to prevent war, said to them when in war against English [if] blood was spilled that engaged all Englishmen for we were to be all under one king. We knew what their complaints would be, and in our colony had removed some of them in sending for Indian rulers in what the crime concerned Indian lives which they very lovingly accepted and agreed with us to their execution and said they were able to satisfy their subjects when they knew an Indian suffered duly, but said in what was only between their Indians and not in townships that we had purchased, they would not have us prosecute and that they had a great fear ... any of their Indians should be called or forced to be Christian Indians. They said that such were in everything more mischievous, only dissemblers, and then the English made them not subject to their kings, and by their lying to wrong their kings. We knew it to be true, and we promising them that however in government to Indians all should be alike and that we knew it was our king's will it should be so, that although we were weaker than other colonies, they having submitted to our king to protect them others dared not otherwise to molest them. So they expressed they took that to be well, that we had little cause to doubt but that to us under the king they would have yielded to our determinations in what any should have complained to us against them, but Philip charged it to be dishonesty in us to put off the hearing the complaints; therefore we consented to hear them. They said they had been the first in doing good to the English, and the English the first in doing wrong, said when the English first came their king's father [Massasoit] was as a great man and the English as a little child, he constrained other Indians from wronging the English and gave them corn and showed them how to plant and was free to do them any good and had let them have 100 times more land, then now the king had for his own people, but their king's brother when he was king came miserably to die by being forced to court as they judged poisoned, and another grievance was if 20 of their honest Indians testified that a Englishman had done them wrong, it was as nothing, and if but one of their worst Indians testified against any Indian or their king when it pleased the English that was sufficient. Another grievance was when their kings sold land the English would say it was more than they agreed to and a writing must be proof against all of them, and sum of their kings had done wrong to sell so much. He left his people none and some being given to drunkenness the English made them drunk and then cheated them in bargains, but now their kings were forewarned not to part with land for nothing in comparison to the value thereof. Now whom the English had owned for king or queen they would disinherit, and make another king that would give or sell them their land, that now they had no hopes left to keep any land. Another grievance the English cattle and horses still increased that when they removed 30 miles from where the English had anything to do, they could not keep their corn from being spoiled, they never being used to fence, and thought when the English bought land of them that they would have kept their cattle upon their own land. Another grievance the English were so eager to sell the Indians liquors that most of the Indians spent all in drunkenness and then ravened upon the sober Indians and they did believe often did hurt the English cattle, and their kings could not prevent it. We knew before these were their grand complaints, but then we only endeavored to persuade that all complaints might be righted without war, but could have no other answer but that they had not heard of that way for the Governor of York and an Indian king to have the hearing of it. We had cause to think if that had been tendered it would have been accepted. We endeavored that however they should lay down their arms for the English were too strong for them. They said then the English should do to them as they did when they were too strong for the English. So we departed without any discourteousness, and suddenly had letter [that is, received word] from Plimouth Governor they intended in arms to conform Philip [make him submit], but no information what that was they required or what terms he refused to have their quarrel decided, and in a weeks time after we had been with the Indians the war thus begun.

Source: John Easton, "A Relacion of the Indyan Warre" (1675), in Charles H. Lincoln, ed., *Narratives of the Indian Wars, 1675–1699* (Scribner's sons, 1913), pp. 8–12, as edited and reproduced in Neal Salisbury, ed., *The Sovereignty and Goodness of God* by Mary Rowlandson (Bedford/St. Martin's, 1997), pp. 115–18.

Study: James Drake, *King Philip's War: Civil War in New England, 1675–1676* (University of Massachusetts Press, 1999); Eric Schultz, *King Philip's War: The History and Legacy of America's Forgotten Conflict* (Norton, 1999).

4. Mary Rowlandson's Narrative

In 1675 and 1676 a brutal war was waged between the Massachusetts colonists and the New England Indians, including not only the Wampanoags but also their numerous allies. Even some of the Christian Indians turned against the English. Initially, the Indians scored some major victories, but they did not have permanent access to food, ammunition, and new recruits as did the colonists. Mary Rowlandson, a clergyman's wife and mother of four, was kidnapped from Lancaster, Massachusetts and experienced, along with her captors, the hunger that plagued the Indians as they retreated.

Rowlandson was a typical prisoner of war in the Indian world. It was common practice for Indians to refrain from killing women and children in battle; instead, they preferred to adopt them into their own tribes if they were willing or occasionally sell them for ransom. However, prisoners who could not keep up with the general pace or control their emotions faced death. If the group was to survive, they could not make room for weakness. Rowlandson experienced great trauma: her 6-year-old daughter was wounded in the initial attack and died in her arms nine days into the trek. Still she kept going, hoping to be reunited with her other children, two of whom had also been taken. Several weeks into her captivity, Mary Rowlandson learned that she had earned the respect of her enemies. In the midst of her grief and rage, she too suddenly saw them as human.

My Child being even ready to depart this sorrowful world, they bade me carry it out to another Wigwam (I suppose because they would not be troubled with such spectacles) Whither I went with a very heavy heart, and down I sat with the picture of death in my lap. About two houres in the night, my sweet Babe, like a lamb departed this life, on *Feb. 18. 1675*, it being about six years and five months old. . . . I cannot but take notice, how at another time I could not bear to be in the room where any dead person was, but now the case [was] changed; I must and could ly down by my dead Babe, side by side all the night after. I have thought since of the wonderfull goodness of God to me, in preserving me in the use of my reason and senses, in that distressed time, that I did not use wicked and violent means to end my own miserable life. In the morning . . . I went to take up my dead child in my arms to carry it with me, but they bid me let it alone: there was no resisting, but goe I must and leave it. . . . I took the first opportunity I could get, to go look after my dead child: when I came I askt them what they had done with it? Then they told me it was upon the hill: then they went and shewed me where it was, where I saw the ground was newly digged, and there they told me they had buried it. *There I left that Child in the Wilderness, and must commit it, and my self also in this Wilderness-condition, to him who is above all.* God having taken away this dear Child, I went to see my daughter *Mary*, who was [for a while] at this same *Indian Town*, at a *Wigwam* not very far off, though we had little liberty or opportunity to see one another; she was about ten years old. . . . When I came in sight, she would fall a weeping; at which they were provoked, and would not let me come near her, but bade me be gone; which was a heart-cutting word to me.

I had one Child dead, another in the Wilderness, I knew not where, the third they would not let me come near to . . .

[Two weeks later]

On the Saturday, they boyled an old Horses leg which they had got, and so we drank of the broth, as soon as they thought it was ready . . . The first week of my being among them, I hardly ate any thing; the second week, I found my stomach grow very faint for want of something; and yet it was very hard to get down their filthy trash: but the third week, though I could think how formerly my stomach would turn against this or that, and I could starve or die before I could eat such things, yet they were sweet and savory to my taste. . . . And here I cannot but take notice of the strange providence of God in preserving the heathen: They were many hundreds, old and young, some sick, and some lame, many had *Papooses* at their backs, the greatest number at this time with us, were *Squaws*, and they traveled with all they had, bag and baggage, and yet they got over the River; and on *Munday*, they set their *Wigwams* on fire, and away they went: On that very same day came the English Army after them to this River, and saw the smoak of their Wigwams, and yet this River put a stop to them . . .

On *Munday* (as I said), they set their *Wigwams* on fire, and went away. It was a cold morning, and before us there was a great Brook with ice on it; some waded through it, up to the knees & higher, but others went till they came to a Beaver dam, and I amongst them, where through the good providence of God, I did not wet my foot.[2] I went along that day mourning and lamenting, leaving farther my own Country, and traveling into the vast and howling Wilderness, and I understood something of Lot's Wife's[3] Temptations, when she looked back: We came that day to a great Swamp, by the side of which we took up our lodging that night. When I came to the brow of the hill, that looked toward the Swamp, I thought we had been come to a great Indian Town (though there were none but our own Company). The Indians were as thick as the trees; it seemed as if there had been a thousand Hatchets going at once: if one looked before one, there was nothing but Indians, and behind one, nothing but Indians, and so on either hand, I myself in the midst, and no Christian soul near me . . .

On the morrow morning we must go over the River, i.e. Connecticot, to meet with King *Philip*, two *Cannoos* full, they had carried over, the next Turn I myself was to go; but as my foot was upon the *Cannoo* to stop in, there was a

[2] Whether or not Rowlandson got wet in making the crossings became extremely important to her as the cold was almost unendurable when she was soaked.

[3] Lot's wife was warned not to look back or she would be turned to a pillar of salt. See Genesis 19:26.

sudden out-cry among them, and I must step back; and instead of going over the River, I must go four or five miles up the River farther Northward. Some of the *Indians* ran one way, and some another. The cause of this rout was, as I thought, their espying some *English Scouts*, who were thereabout. In this travel up the river, about noon the Company made a stop, and sat down; some to eat, and others to rest them. As I sate amongst them, musing of things past, my son *Joseph* unexpectedly came to me: we asked of each others welfare, bemoaning our dolefull condition, and the change that had come upon us.... I asked him whither he would read; he told me, he earnestly desired it. I gave him my Bible,[4] and he lighted upon that comfortable scripture, Psal. 118.17, 18. *I shall not dy but live, and declare the works of the Lord: the Lord hath chastened me sore, yet he hath not given me over to death.* Look here, Mother (sayes he), did you read this? ... We traveled on till night; and in the morning, we must go over the River to *Philip's* crew. When I was in the Cannoo, I could not but be amazed at the numerous crew of Pagans that were on the Bank on the other side. When I came ashore, they gathered all about me, I sitting alone in the midst: I observed they asked one another questions, and laughed, and rejoyced over their Gains and Victories. Then my heart began to fail: and I fell a weeping which was the first time to my remembrance, that I wept before them. Although I had met with so much Affliction, and my heart was many times ready to break, yet could I not shed one tear in their sight: but rather had been all this while in a maze,[5] like one astonished: but now I may say as Psal. 137.1 *By the rivers of* Babylon, *there we sat down: yea, we wept when we remembered Zion.* There one of them asked me, why I wept, I could hardly tell what to say: yet I answered, they would kill me: No, said he, none will hurt you. Then came one of them and gave me two spoon-fulls of Meal to comfort me, and another gave me half a pint of Pease; which was more worth than many Bushels at another time.[6] Then I went to see King *Philip*, he bade me come in and sit down, and asked me whether I would smoke ...

Source and study: Neal Salisbury, ed., *The Sovereignty and Goodness of God by Mary Rowlandson with Related Documents* (Bedford/St. Martin's, 1997), pp. 75–82.

Further exploration: It would be worth comparing the captivity narrative of a person (like Rowlandson) who remained committed to returning to the colonial world with one by someone who chose to be adopted and become an Indian. Mary Jemison, for example, chose to become a Seneca, but in old age she dictated her story to an interested editor. See Kathryn Zabelle Derounian-Stodola, ed., *Women's Indian Captivity Narratives* (Penguin, 1998). See also the first section in Chapter 5.

[4] Rowlandson had not been able to leave carrying anything except her child but an Indian had later given her a Bible taken in the spoils of battle.

[5] The meaning here is stunned, in a state of overwhelming confusion.

[6] It was worth so much because the company was starving.

5. The Declaration of a Rebellious Christian Indian in the Pueblo Revolt

The Spanish had established dominance over native peoples much more rapidly than the English or the French were able to do. This was because they met with sedentary cultures in the Aztec and Inca empires, people who had long been farmers and were accustomed to paying tribute to overlords. When the Spanish moved outward to conquer nomadic or semi-sedentary people, they experienced far more difficulty. The case of New Mexico, in today's southwestern United States, where some of the people were traditionally farmers and some were not, was particularly dramatic. The Spanish had been a strong presence in New Mexico since 1598; they had required Indians to labor for them for part of each year and had pressured them to become Christians. In 1680, a rebellion broke out which was so successful that the surviving Spanish were forced to flee and were unable to retake the territory for a full 12 years. The leaders of the rebellion had been well organized, orchestrating the timing across a wide region, and the movement had broad popular support.

In the midst of the events, before they decided to try to escape south to Mexico, the Spanish desperately sent out military parties to attempt to gather useful information or save certain Spanish sites. They essentially failed in both agendas, finding the damage already done and the region largely depopulated, but they did capture some straggler Indians and brought them back for questioning. They recorded their efforts in formal legal documents.

In the place of El Alamillo, jurisdiction of El Socorro, on the 6th day of the month of September, 1680, for the prosecution of this case, and so that an Indian who was captured on the road as the camp was marching may be examined, in order to ascertain the plans, designs, and motives of the rebellious enemy, his lordship, the señor-gobernador and captain-general, caused the said Indian to appear before him. He received the oath from him in due legal form, in the name of God, our Lord, and on a sign of the cross, under charge of which he promised to tell the truth concerning what he might know and as he might be questioned. Having been asked his name and of what place he is a native, his condition, and age, he said that his name is don Pedro Nanboa,[7] that he is a native of the pueblo of Alameda, a widower, and somewhat more than eighty years of age. Asked for what reason the Indians of this kingdom have rebelled, forsaking their obedience to his Majesty and failing in their obligation as Christians, he said that for a long time, because the Spaniards punished sorcerers and idolaters, the nations of the Teguas, Tao, Pecuríes, Pecos and Jemez had been plotting

[7] The use of the title "don" by a native man in this period indicates that he was of high or noble status within his own community.

to rebel and kill the Spaniards and the religious [Franciscans], and that they had been planning constantly to carry it out, down to the present occasion. Asked what he learned, saw and heard in the juntas and parleys that the Indians have held, what they have plotted among themselves, and why the Indians have burned the church and profaned the images of the pueblo of Sandia, he said that he has not taken part in any junta, nor has he harmed any one; that what he has heard is that the Indians do not want religious [friars] or Spaniards. Because he is so old he was in the cornfield[8] when he learned from the Indian rebels who came from the sierra that they had killed the Spaniards of the jurisdiction and robbed all their haciendas, sacking their houses. Asked whether he knows about the Spaniards and religious who were gathered in the pueblo of La Isleta, he said that it is true that some days ago there assembled in the said pueblo of La Isleta the religious of Sandia, Jemez, and Zia, and that they set out to leave the kingdom with those of the said pueblo of la Isleta and the Spaniards – not one of whom remained—taking along their property. The Indians did not fight with them because all the men had gone with the other nations to fight at the villa [in the capital] and destroy the governor and captain-general and all the people who were with him. He declared that the resentment which all the Indians have in their hearts has been so strong, from the time this kingdom was discovered, because the religious and the Spaniards took away their idols and forbade their sorceries and idolatries; that they have inherited successively from their old men the things pertaining to their ancient customs; and that he has heard this resentment spoken of since he was of an age to understand. What he has said is the truth and what he knows, under the oath taken, and he signs and ratifies it, it being read and explained to him in his language through the interpretation of Captain Sebastián Montaño, who signed it with his lordship, as the said Indian does not know how, before me, the present secretary. Antonio de Otermín (rubric); Sebastián Montaño (rubric); Juan Lucero de Godoy (rubric); Luis de Quintana (rubric). Before me, Francisco Xavier, secretary of government and war (rubric).

Source: "Declaration of one of the rebellious Christian Indians who was captured on the road. El Alamillo, September 6, 1680," in Charles Wilson Hackett, ed., *Revolt of the Pueblo Indians of New Mexico and Otermín's Attempted Reconquest, 1680–1682* (University of New Mexico Press, 1942), pp. 60–2.

Study and further exploration: David J. Weber, *What Caused the Pueblo Revolt of 1680?* (Bedford/St. Martin's, 1999). This book consists of selections from the most interesting studies that have been made of the revolt and places them in counterpoint

[8] Don Pedro meant that because of his advanced age, he had been left to till the fields rather than invited to join the war party.

to one another, raising issues worthy of analysis. There are about a dozen more statements taken from Indians in the Hackett collection cited above.

Questions for Consideration

1 Do these documents indicate that colonial relations between natives and newcomers were more peaceful or more violent than you had imagined?
2 In this chapter we have examples of the grievances of Indians in Canada, New England, and the southwest several decades after first contact. How are the texts different? Are there any commonalities?
3 How can European sources be surprisingly useful in our studies of Native Americans?
4 Gandeaktena was a prisoner of war, just as Kateri's mother had been. We have no testimonies left to us by native women about their experiences in captivity. To what extent can we use the words of white prisoners like Mary Rowlandson to gain insight into their feelings?

Chapter 5 Eighteenth-Century Power Shifts

1. The Refusal of Some English Prisoners to Return to English Life

As Europeans battled for control of the continent of North America, they enlisted indigenous people to fight for them. Indeed, the Indians had no choice but to form alliances with Europeans if they were to gain access to the firearms they had come to need for both hunting and self-defense. The war parties took many prisoners according to their custom, and these were usually given the opportunity to become part of the tribes. Some of the prisoners lived in hopes of being ransomed, but others became "white Indians," preferring to remain with their Indian families rather than return to colonial life.

In 1750, in the wake of King George's War, French and English authorities negotiated an exchange of prisoners who were living with Indians in the opposing territory. Here a French officer reports that he has turned over 24 (including 21 colonists and three unnamed Mohawks) to an English representative, but that 13 colonists have given reasons for refusing to leave.

General Return of the English prisoners detained in the government of New France

Prisoners' names	*Observations*
Anthony Van Schaik, Captain of the Militia of the Government of New York	Depart with Mr. Stoddert for Fort St. Frederic
John Vroman	
Peter Vosborough	
William Goff	
Christopher McGraw	
John Philips	
Edward Varen	
Benjamin Blachford	
Peter Clincton	
John Thompson	
Daniel Eden	
Albert Vedder	
Adam Mole	
Francis Conner	
Cornelius Sprong	
Elisha Stansbury	
Timothy Colbe	
Southerland Fort	
Timothy Colson	
Peter Dogaman	
Mattée Gatroup	
3 Mohawks	Total: 24
Rachel Quackenbus	Has abjured and desires to remain in the Colony. Mr. Stoddert has spoken to her repeatedly, without being able to persuade her to accompany him.
Samuel Frement, a Negro	Remains in the Colony for reasons set forth in the Minute of the 26th June, 1750 [which explained "all negroes being slaves, in whatever country they reside"]
Simon Vort, Philip Philipson, Thomas Volmer	They have declared that they wish to remain with the Iroquois of Sault St. Louis, having made abduration, as appears by Sieur Douville's letter

Jacob Suitzer	Desires to remain with the Indians of Sault St. Louis
Jacob Volmer, Joshua Nicolson, Henry Piper	Joshua Nicolson is disposed to go; the other two desire to remain with the Iroquois of the Lake of the Two Mountains and Nipissings, who, moreover, are unwilling to allow any of the said prisoners to leave at any price whatsoever, as they love them very much
Christian Volmer	Is hunting with the Iroquois of the Lake of the Two Mountains, and on his return will be set at liberty if he wish to return to New England
John	Desires to remain with the Abenakis of St. Francis, as appears by the process-verbal of the 23rd of June, 1750
Edward Cheaole	Married to a Squaw among the Hurons of Lorette, and desired to remain with them
An old man	Is hunting with the Hurons of Lorette, and will be set at liberty on his return if he be inclined to go to New England

I, the Undersigned, Lieutenant of Infantry in the troops of New-York, deputed by order of Mr. Clinton, Governor of the said New-York, to the Marquis de Jonquière, Governor-General of New France, do declare to have received from the said Marquis de la Jonquière the twenty-four prisoners mentioned in the present list, with whom I will proceed, forthwith, to Fort St. Frederic under the guidance of Sieur de Bleury, Ensign of Infantry, where arriving I promise to dispatch one or two prisoners to inform my Governor that they are at liberty, so that he may send, at the same time, all the prisoners, both French and Indians, who may be in his hands, to Mr. Lydieus, and give orders to the officer who will have charge of them to send me an express on their arrival at that place to inform me thereof, and to tarry one day so that they may be exchanged, one against another, at the foot of the great Carrying place of Lake St. Sacrament, whither I will repair in order to conclude the reciprocal exchange of the French and English prisoners. And as regards the thirteen others, also mentioned in the present list, it has not been in our power to bring them back with us, notwithstanding the facilities and orders said Sieur de la Jonquière has given, for the reasons annexed in the present list. In testimony whereof the said Marquis de la Jonquière hath signed with us, the English deputy aforesaid.

Done, in duplicate, at Montreal, the twenty-seventh of June, one thousand seven hundred and fifty.

Signed: LA JONQUIERE and B. STODDERT

Copy of the letter written by Sieur Douville, commandant of Sault St. Louis, to the Marquis de la Jonquière, Governor General of New France, 27th June, 1750

Sir,

The English prisoner, belonging to la Delislle, has come to tell me that I could have the honor to inform you he did not desire any longer to return; that the principal reason is that he has embraced our religion; that when he told the English he wished to return, he acted unreflectingly. On the other hand that his father is dead, and by the laws of his country whoever has been ransomed, if obliged to borrow the money, is bound for service until he have repaid, by his labor, the sum he cost; that he prefers being a slave with the Indians than in his country where there is no religion.

He who belongs to Ononraguete's nieces has come to tell me, also, that inasmuch as his elder brother, who is at the Lake of Two Mountains, will not return, neither will he; that his father was poor; that he must work all his life to pay his ransom; on the other hand, he has embraced our religion, which is the strongest reason.

Ononraguete said to him, in my presence: You are at liberty to go away if you like. He answered, No; that he hated too strongly the English Nation, where he was almost a slave, to give up his religion and his liberty.

I have the honor to be, etc.

Signed: DOUVILLE

Source: Edward O'Callaghan, ed., *Documents Relative to the Colonial History of the State of New York*, vol. 10: *Transcripts of Documents in the Archives of the Ministère de la Marine et des Colonies, at Paris* (Weed, Parsons & Co., 1858), pp. 214–16.

Study: There have been many interesting studies of "white Indians." A fascinating place to begin is John Demos, *The Unredeemed Captive: A Family Story from Early America* (Alfred Knopf, 1994). James Axtell includes a thorough study of the issue in *The Invasion Within: The Contest of Cultures in Colonial North America* (Oxford University Press, 1986).

2. The Abenakis' Forceful Statement to the English

The Abenaki of Maine were gradually pushed northward by encroaching American settlers. In the tense years leading up to the Seven Years War, they allied with France and thus gained direct access to arms and ammunition. From their new position of strength, they declared to the English in no uncertain terms that they were now drawing a line which no colonist should dare to cross. They used as a translator Phineas Stevens, who had been taken as a prisoner of war to live among the Abenaki when he was a boy. He still spoke their language fluently and understood their diplomatic customs. Note that the Abenaki also needed to signal that they had the support of the Iroquois in order to make their political statement effective, for the Iroquois were the largest Indian nation in the region and a powerful player. They memorialized their declaration in a wampum belt, which Indians who had been at the event would long recognize as a distillation of their speeches. That belt, unfortunately, apparently no longer exists.

Propositions of the Abenakis of St. Francis to Captain Phineas Stevens, delegate from the Governor of Boston, in presence of the Baron de Longueuil, Governor of Montreal, Commandant of Canada and of the Iroquois of the Sault Saint Louis and of the Lake of the Two Mountains, 5th of July, 1752

Atiwaneto,[1] Chief Speaker

[1.]

Brother, We speak to you as if we spoke to your Governor of Boston. We hear on all sides that this Governor and the Bostonians say that the Abenakis are bad people. 'Tis in vain that we are taxed with having a bad heart; it is you, brother, that always attack us; your mouth is of sugar but your heart of gall; in truth, the moment you begin we are on our guard.

2.

Brothers, We tell you that we seek not war, we ask nothing better than to be quiet, and it depends, Brothers, only on you English, to have peace with us.

[1] This name is given erroneously. The man was normally known at Ateawanto or Atecuando, which two variants represent different English efforts to represent the same name phonetically.

3.

We have not yet sold the lands we inhabit, we wish to keep the possession of them. Our elders have been willing to tolerate you, brothers Englishmen, on the seaboard as far as Sawakwato; as that has been so decided, we wish it to be so.

4.

But we will not cede one single inch of the lands we inhabit beyond what has been decided formerly by our fathers.

5.

You have the sea for your share from the place where you reside; you can trade there; but we expressly forbid you to kill a single Beaver, or to take a single stick of timber on the lands we inhabit; if you want timber we'll sell you some, but you shall not take it without our permission.

6.

Brothers, Who hath authorized you to have those lands surveyed? We request our brother, the Governor of Boston, to have these Surveyors punished, as we cannot imagine that they have acted by his authority.

7.

Brother, You are therefore masters of the peace that we are to have with you; on condition that you will not encroach on those lands we will be at peace, as the King of France is with the King of Great Britain.

8.

By a Belt

I repeat to you, Brothers, by this Belt, that it depends on yourselves to be at peace with the Abenakis.

9.

Our [political] Father [the French governor] who is here present has nothing to do with what we say to you; we speak to you of our own accord, and in the name of all our allies; we regard our Father, in this instance, only as a witness of our words.

10.

We acknowledge no other boundaries of yours than your settlements whereon you have built, and we will not [that is, do not desire], under any pretext whatsoever, that you pass beyond them. The lands we possess have been given us by the master of Life. We acknowledge to hold only from him.

11.

We are entirely free; we are allies of the King of France, from whom we have received the Faith and all sorts of assistance in our necessities; we love that Monarch, and we are strongly attached to his interests.

12.

Let us have an answer to the propositions we address you, as soon as possible; take this message in writing to give to your Governor; we, also, shall keep a copy of it to use in case of need.

Without stirring a step it is easy for your Governor to transmit his answer to us; he will have merely to address it to our [French] Father who will have the goodness to send it to us.

13.

[Phineas Stevens speaks.] Brothers, I shall report your Message to my Governor, and in order that it may not suffer any alternation I shall take it in writing. He will transmit his answer to the Baron de Longueuil as you desire.

The English Demand of the Abenakis

1.

Brothers Abenakis, I ask you if the attack which your Nation has made these two years [past] on the English is in consequence of encroachments by the latter on your lands?

2.

Are you satisfied with the death of your people on account of your attacks on the English?

3.

I know that it is not permitted to go on your lands; those who have been there are young fools, without any character.

The Answer of the Abenakis

1.

Brothers, When peace was concluded[2] we hoped to enjoy it, like the French, but we learned at the same time, that you English had killed one of our people, and had hid him under the ice.

We asked wherefore you killed us? You answered that you would give us satisfaction, but your ill-will having been sensibly indicated by your inaction, pending seven months, we resolved to avenge ourselves, and to pull down one house.

Since then we have missed one man and one woman belonging to our village; we learned their sad fate only from an Englishwoman, who is at present at our place, who assured us that that man and woman were killed in her presence by Englishmen, and in order to afford us a convincing proof thereof, she gave us a bag which we perfectly recognized as having belonged to those unfortunate people. We felt, as we ought to do, this murder, and avenged it last year.

The two Englishmen that we killed this year on the head waters of our river, and the two others that we have taken prisoners, must attribute their misfortunes to themselves, because they hunted Beaver on our lands, and on this point we repeat to you, with all the firmness we are capable of, that we will kill all the Englishmen we shall find on the lands in our possession.

2.

Our heart is good, and since we struck the blow our thirst for vengeance is extinguished.

3.

Listen, Brothers Englishmen, to what is our Indian custom among ourselves, with persons we would find on the lands we possess? We should take their game, and if they made any resistance, we would knock them on the head.[3]

[2] King George's War ended in 1748.
[3] Giving a lethal blow to the head was a common form of punishment for criminals.

How can you suppose, Brothers, that we should suffer you on those lands?

You have only to excite fear in your houses. We are not capable of offering the least insult, but should any of you be found on our lands, they shall die.

The Iroquois to the Abenakis

We have heard, with pleasure, what you said to the English deputy; we are charmed that you have vigorously maintained your rights. We exhort you to keep your word with the English; should the case require it, we oblige ourselves to aid you with all our might.

Source: Edward O'Callaghan, ed., *Documents Relative to the Colonial History of the State of New York*, vol. 10: *Transcripts of Documents in the Archives of the Ministère de la Marine et des Colonies, at Paris* (Weed, Parsons and Co., 1858), pp. 252–4.

Study: Colin Calloway, *The Western Abenaki of Vermont, 1600–1800: War, Migration and the Survival of an Indian People* (University of Oklahoma Press, 1990).

3. The Chickasaws' Political Vision in 1723

Mississippian cultures spread along feeders to the great river in the centuries before the arrival of the Europeans; they held many traits in common. Among these was a tendency to represent self-contained ethnic communities or political entities visually as circles, and the political or economic ties between them as different kinds of lines. Such maps were apparently a central part of political life within the region for many centuries.

In the figures below you see first a carving found on a conch shell found in Spiro, Oklahoma, among mounds dating from about 1400, constructed by migrants from the Mississippi River basin (fig. 5.3.1). Next you see a 1723 Chickasaw map drawn on parchment, which was copied from an older indigenous image inscribed on a deerskin, with the place names in the Chickasaw language then written in (figs. 5.3.2 and 5.3.3). Several such maps made by the Catawba, Chickasaw, and Alabama peoples, and clearly based on ancient traditions, have been found in archives.

This particular example was presented by Chickasaw chiefs to Francis Nicholson, governor of South Carolina, at a meeting in 1723. Nicholson was a strong believer in the importance of asking Indians for their geographical knowledge, which he understood to be extensive, so he may have solicited the document. However, the piece offers a political vision more than an "accurate" geographic overview of the region. The Chickasaw obviously considered themselves to be powerful and important players. Though they had fewer than

1,000 warriors, they placed themselves in a triangle of equals along with the populous Cherokee and the English. They saw themselves as the center of a wheel with many spires radiating outward. If the English wanted to communicate with the Choctaw, for example, they could do it through the Chickasaw. A total of 43 communities were represented, almost all of them appearing through their connections to the Chickasaw. Some would have been tribute payers to them, others merely trade partners; the Indians living then could have interpreted the map easily. Whether the Chickasaw hastened to add which communities were tied to the French (indicated with an "F") so as to underscore their own importance to the English, or whether Nichols went over the map asking about each community, we shall never know.

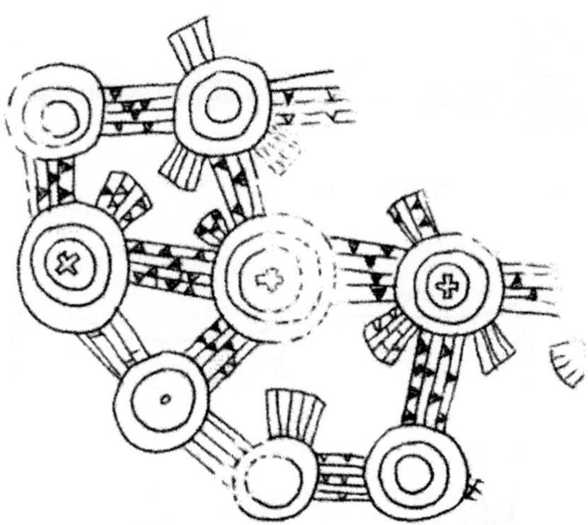

Figure 5.3.1 Conch shell engraving (c.1400) found at Spiro, Oklahoma

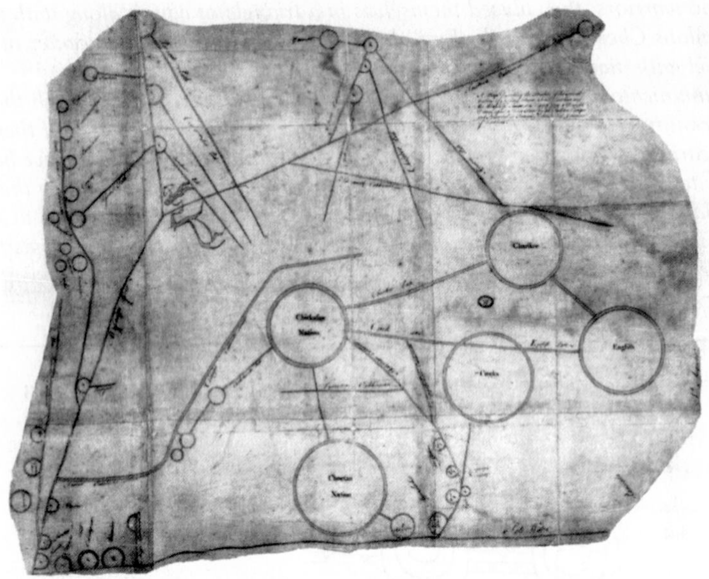

Figure 5.3.2 Chickasaw map (1723)

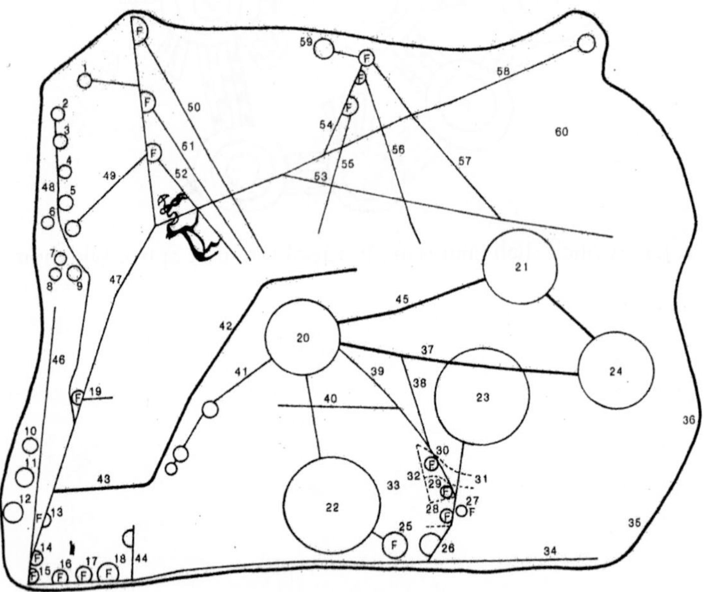

Figure 5.3.3 Line drawing of the 1723 Chickasaw map

The title reads: "A Map Describing the Situation of the several Nations of Indians between South Carolina and the Massisipi; was Copyed from a Draught Drawn upon a Deer Skin by an Indian Cacique [chief] and Presented to Francis Nicholson Esqr. Governor of Carolina."

Transcription of the place names given in the document:

1 Sauhau
2 Vossulau
3 Commaucerilau
4 Pauneassau
5 Causau
6 Carenahish
7 Sovuasau
8 Vauhu
9 Tovocolau
10 Kejos
11 Katulaucheu
12 Notauku
13 Nauchee (F)
14 Tunecau (F)
15 Humau (F)
16 Sovuasau (F)
17 Oakculapesar (F)
18 Biuculau (F)
19 Ucaupau (F)
20 Chickasaw Nation
21 Charikee [Cherokee]
22 Choctau nation
23 Creeks
24 English
25 Noe India (F)
26 Came in the Indian War
27 Tausau (F)
28 Movele (F) [Mobile]
29 Tume (F)
30 Tume (F)
31 Chocktau Benelee
32 Elav Chickasau au abbe[4]
33 Appaulachee
34 Salt Water
35 Pansecula
36 St. Augustine [Spanish]
37 Creek and English Path
38 Tongolickau Oakhinnau
39 Shaterrau Oakhinnau
40 Tyannacau Oakhinnau
41 Chockchumau Path
42 Chickasau Oakhinnau
43 Yausau Oakhinnau
44 Hoppe Oakhinnau
45 Charikee Path
46 Ucau Humer Oakhinnau
47 Massasippe River
48 Ucau Humer Oakhinnau
49 Ussaule Path
50 Pavuaule Path
51 Cow' a-keer Path
52 Cuscuskeer Path
53 Ta[...]canuck Oakhinnau
54 Yolternno Oakhinnau
55 Yoltenno Path
56 Chickabou Path
57 Kenoculu Path
58 Senottova Oakhinnau [Ohio River]
59 Yaumeer
60 title [see above]

[4] Probable translation: "Elaw, Chickasaw, killed (or was killed) here."

Explanation of certain terms used on the map:
F: connection established with the French
Oakhinnau: river
Ucau: water
Humer: red
Benelee: settlement

Source and study: Timothy R. Pauketat, *Ancient Cahokia and the Mississippians* (Cambridge University Press, 2004), p. 142; Gregroy A. Waselkov, "Indian Maps of the Colonial Southeast," in Peter H. Wood, Gregory A. Waselkov, and M. Thomas Hatley, eds., *Powhatan's Mantle: Indians in the Colonial Southeast* (University of Nebraska Press, 1989), pp. 324–9.

Further exploration: Waselkov's article (cited above) includes reproductions of several comparable maps from the era. The author also helps readers correlate the Indian place names given above with places known today, but there are still some mysteries which students from those areas might be able to help resolve.

4. Sir Jeffery Amherst Suggests the Smallpox

At the close of the "French and Indian War," now more often termed the Seven Years War (1756–63), the British were victorious and the French were forced to remove themselves from the St. Lawrence River valley and the Great Lakes region. The Indian peoples of the region, many of whom had sided with the French, were distraught. No longer could they play the two European powers off against each other, obtaining arms from the one in order to fight the other: they feared that if they did not act quickly, they would lose all their land and with it their livelihood. Warriors from numerous tribes grouped themselves around a charismatic Ottawa chieftain named Pontiac. To make the point that they would tolerate no further incursions, they struck with great violence up and down the edge of the territory settled by British families and for many months held the upper hand. Eventually, British forces overcame them since the Indians no longer had access to French supplies. In the mean time, however, the British military was desperate. Sir Jeffery Amherst, commander of the British Army in North America, corresponded with Colonel Henry Bouquet at Carlisle, Pennsylvania. Amherst was normally a level-headed man, but in this situation, hatred surfaced and he suggested to Bouquet that he try to infect the enemy with smallpox.

This exchange has been hotly debated: because we find the initial suggestion on the inside of the envelope, instead of in the body of the letter proper, it is theoretically possible that the note was a forgery added later by somebody else. However, the handwriting is in keeping with that of Amherst's clerk, and furthermore, Bouquet answered him. The exchange does seem to indicate, however, that the venture was never actually attempted, only discussed.

Bouquet, as the commander on the scene, did not want to risk infecting his own men. Given the use of detachable postscripts, both men seem to have recognized that the project would not be at all in keeping with their official mandate. It has been rumored, in addition, that much later in history the US Army did give out smallpox blankets, but there is no proof of that anywhere in the records.

New York 7th July 1763

Sir,

Last Night I received your Letter of the 29th June; and Early this morning an Express Brought me that of the 3d Instant.

The Loss of Presque' Isle (which I fear is too True, altho' it may happen that the Soldier who gives the Account may prove to be a Deserter) gives me great Concern:[5] But it must make no Alteration in my Plan: There seems to have been an Absolute Necessity for my Sending You all the Troops I could for the protection of the Inhabitants, Otherwise the Savages would have Spread their Depredations all over the Country: They will not Retire as You Advance; And I would have you Follow the same Directions I have already given You for Sending Troops forward to Presqu' Isle, Notwithstanding this Disaster, only Observing to Send them in such a manner that their March may be Secure, and that they may be able to Encounter any Body of Indians that can Attack them.

I Write Immediately to Niagara, and Shall Try to Send Troops from thence to Retake possession of Presqu' Isle: The Orders I have already Sent to Major Gladwin, of which, you have been Acquainted, are to that Purpose: I shall now Acquaint him of this Loss, and I Wish I could Send him Immediately some more Force; Should any of the Corps from the West Indies come this way, I shall Lose no time in Forwarding them to Niagara to Strengthen the Force already sent; but, in the meantime, We must Do the Best We can with the Numbers We have ...

On your Arrival at Fort Pitt,[6] You will, of Course, get Rid of the Women & Children, and all Useless Hands as fast as can be Done, with their Safety; for the Article of Provisions is a very Material one, and must be Attended to ...

Captain Ecuyer Seems to Act with great Prudence, & I Approve of Everything he mentions to have Done: A Fixed Resolution should be taken by Every Commanding Officer, whose Post is Attacked by Savages, Never to Trust to their Promises, but to Defend his Post to the Last Extremity; and to take Every Occasion he can of Putting them to Death

[5] Presqu' Isle was a fort built by the French at what is now Erie, Pennsylvania. Pontiac and his followers had indeed taken the fort shortly before this letter was written.

[6] This was a crucial fort at what is now Pittsburgh, Pennsylvania.

while they are Attempting to Take Every Life away that they can: We have so many Recent Instances of their Breach of Faith, in this Particular, that I am Surprized any Officer in his Senses would Enter into Terms with such barbarians.

I am, Sir, Your most Obedient Servant,

Jeff: Amherst

[enclosure]
J. Amherst: Memorandum

Could it not be contrived to Send the Small Pox among those Disaffected Tribes of Indians? We must, on this occasion, Use Every Stratagem in our power to Reduce them.

*

Carlisle 13th July 1763

Sir,

I had the 11th your Excellency's Letter of the 2d by Capt Grant, and the same Day that of the 7th by Express – I shall remain at F: Pitt to forward the Troops and Shipwrights to Presqu' Isle, and the Service that may be required on the Communication, and be in Readiness for going down the River when I receive your Orders. I am averse to start Difficulties so long as I can see how to get clear of them but being, for the present, totally disappointed in the Assistance I expected by the extraordinary Votes of the Assembly of Pennsylvania I must represent to you that I think it equally precarious to leave F: Pitt & its Communications too thinly guarded, or to weaken major Campbell's Detatchment, & would be obliged to you if you would order the inclosed Return to be filled as you would have the Troops disposed: Upon which I shall make the following Remarks . . .

The Extensive & open Works of F: Pitt require more Men than would otherwise be necessary against an Enemy who has no Chance but by Surprise – The Distance from F: Pitt to Presqu' Isle is 142 Miles, thro' a narrow crooked Path, difficult Creeks, & several long Defiles: The Mingoes & Delawares who live in that Part of the Country may consist of 4 or 500 Men, exclusive of the Shawnese or western Indians who may accidentally be among them: And a Body of Troops must be respectable to force all Opposition they may have to encounter that way – The Women, Children & all useless Hands may be escorted down with the Wagons & Packhorses, by the Militia, who will quit F: Pitt, & the Soldiers sent to reinforce Bedford & Cumberland – Major Campbell with the Remains of the two Regts arrived here only the 10th his Men being greatly fatigued – The Wagons will at last be here to Morrow & we shall march the 15th having sent the Remains of the two first Companies to Bedford, & the 3d to F: Loudoun as a Guard to our Cattle & Horses – I shall make the necessary Enquiry concerning the Effects belonging to the late Colonel Clapham & acquaint you of my Success – No traders or Goods shall be permitted to pass this Way till you give further Orders and we shall have no Difficulty to prevent it: Fear being sufficient to keep them at Home – The Savages have begun to kill on the upper Part of Patowmack, & within two Days have murdered or wounded upwards of 30 people from 40 to within 16 miles of this Town which is suddenly become the Frontier; all the Inhabitants to the Westward having abandoned their Plantations, with the Harvest, Cattle Horses & every thing they had – The Situation of this County is dilatery & ineffectual measures for their Protection highly blamable – They have not paid the least Regard to the Plan I proposed to them on my Arrival here, I will lose this & York Counties if the Savages push their Attacks – As the Communication will be infested I beg you will send me Duplicates of your orders, which Sr. J. St Clair, who remains here will forward by different Expresses & on different Days.

I have the Honor to be &c

Henry Bouquet

P.S. I will try to inoculate the [illegible] with Some Blankets that may fall in their Hands, and take Care not to get the disease myself. As it is [a] pity to expose good men against them [that is, the blankets] I wish we would make use of the Spanish method to hunt them [the Indians] with English Dogs, supported by Rangers and Some Light Horse, who would I think effectually extirpate or remove that Vermin.

*

New York, 16th July 1763

Sir,

Just as I had Finished my Other Letter which Accompanys this, an Express Arrived from Philadelphia, with Yours of the 13th Instant . . .

You, on the Spot, must be the Best Judge of the Numbers that can be Allotted for the Several Garrisons, as well as for Proceeding to Presqu' Isle; And therefore I Do not Fill up the Return you sent me: I Never Expected Impossibilities, Nor would I Attempt anything that Does not promise to Success: The Detachment that goes to Presqu' Isle ought certainly to be very Respectable, & Capable of Encountering any Body of Indians that can be on that Route, or We had better not Send them at all: That Detachment, as well as Every other that may be now made, should be with a Firm Resolution of acting Offensively, the only Method to Deal with Indians, and if that Detachment could Distress any of the Tribes who are in Arms, by Burning or Destroying their Towns, so much the better; their March would be the safer for it: At the same time, Fort Pitt must not be Left so thinly Garrisoned as to be in any Danger, should the Savages Renew their Attacks: This will Depend on the Number of Provincials that join you: They may be made very good men, in a few hours time, for Firing Ball, & for the Defence of a Fort Attack by Indians, particularly as you have so many Regular Officers with you, who may be of great Service on this Occasion. –

I forgot to mention to you, that I Observed in One of Captain Ecuyer's Letters to you, he had Ordered some Cannon to be Fired at the Indians: This, I think, should never be Done, for it can seldom have any other Effect but keeping the Indians out of Reach of the Fort, and the Nearer they come, the greater Chance there is to bringing them down by small Arms: Grape Shot, properly managed, may Do good Execution, but Ball fired from Cannon at an Enemy who keep so Scattered as the Indians Do, only Serves to Learn them to Endure, what they will be more afraid of, if not Accustomed to it.

The Women, Children, & those who are really Useless hands, cannot be Sent away too Soon, and they may be Escorted from Post to Post; But the Militia ought to be obliged to Remain & Do Duty, while their Services are Necessary . . .

I am extremely Sorry to Hear the Indians have Done Mischief on the Patowmack: This ought to be a Spur to the Province in Raising the Men, & Putting them under your Command, that We may be Enabled to put a Stop to the Depredations of the Savages; for they may now See, that with out Acting offensively, the Indians will Carry their Ravages into the Heart of the Country.

I shall take Care to Send you Duplicates of my Letters, as you Desire, that Sir John St Clair may Forward them by different Routes.

I am, Sir, Your most obedt Servant

Jeff: Amherst

[enclosure]

J. Amherst: Memorandum

You will Do well to try to Inoculate the Indians, by means of Blankets, as well as to Try Every other Method, that can Serve to Extirpate this Execrable Race. – I should be very glad [if] your Scheme for Hunting them down by Dogs could take Effect; but England is at too great a Distance to think of that at present.

Sources: British Museum, MSS 21634, Amherst to Bouquet, July 7, 1763, fols. 313 and 243 [envelope], and July 16, 1763, fols. 323 and 241 [envelope], printed in Louis Waddell, ed., *The Papers of Henry Bouquet*, vol. 6 (Pennsylvania Historical and Museum Commission, 1994), pp. 299–301, 313–15. Bouquet to Amherst, July 13, 1763, folio 321, printed in Sylvester Stevens and Donald Kent, eds., *The Papers of Colonel Henry Bouquet, Series 21634* (Pennsylvania Historical Commission, 1940), pp. 214–15.

Study: The build-up to and effects of the Seven Years War have been much studied. For a recent collection of contributions by numerous scholars, see David Curtis Skaggs and Larry L. Nelson, eds., *The Sixty Years' War for the Great Lakes, 1754–1814* (Michigan State University Press, 2001).

Further exploration: Some scholars see the bitterness of the Seven Years War and Pontiac's Rebellion as ending an era of mutual cooperation, and others see it as the product of years of mutual hostility. For contrasting views see Jane Merritt, *At the Crossroads: Indians and Empires on a Mid-Atlantic Frontier, 1700–1763* (University of North Carolina Press, 2003) and Peter Silver, *Our Savage Neighbors: How Indian War Transformed Early America* (Norton, 2007).

5. The Chickasaws after the Revolution

Eventually, the European wars left the Indians decimated. The endless battles caused their populations to drop precipitously, for European warfare caused higher casualty rates and greater disruption to agriculture than traditional Indian wars ever had. Even worse, as one European player after another was removed from the scene, the Indians became increasingly desperate for arms and ammunition. Eventually there remained only the young United States, and the Americans were obviously not going to arm the Indians whose territory they were interested in taking.

The Chickasaws, for example, who had maintained their alliance with the English throughout the eighteenth century, sided with the mother country when the Revolution began in 1774. They were left with virtually no power when England suddenly capitulated to the colonists and withdrew. In 1783 the sons, grandsons, and nephews of the chiefs who had been so proud in 1723 (see section 3 above) were forced to beg for supplies from the United States. Furthermore, in this era before the existence of the Constitution, they did not even know exactly which political entity to approach. They had only one card left to play: they could threaten to ally with the Spanish across the border in Florida.

To His Excellency the President of the Honorable Congress of the United American States

Friend & Brother,

This is the first talk we ever sent you – we hope it will not be the last. We desire you to open your Ears to hear, and your heart[7] to understand us, as we shall always be ready to do to your talks, which we expect will be good, as you are a great and wise man.

Brother,

When our great father the King of England called away his warriors, he told us to take your People by the hand,[8] as friends and brothers. Our hearts were always inclined to do so and as far as our circumstances permitted us, we evinced our good intentions as our Brothers the Virginians can testify – It makes our hearts rejoice to find that our great father, and his children the Americans have at length made peace, which we wish may continue as long as the Sun and Moon, And to find that our Brothers the Americans are inclined to take us by the hand and Smoke with us at the great Fire, which we hope will never be extinguished.

Brother,

Notwithstanding the Satisfaction all these things give us we are yet in confusion and uncertainty. The Spaniards are sending talks amongst us, and inviting our young Men to trade with them. We also receive talks from the Governor of Georgia to the same effect – We have had Speeches from the Illinois inviting us to a Trade and Intercourse with them – Our Brothers, the Virginians Call upon us to a Treaty, and want part of our land, and we expect our Neighbors who live on Cumberland River, will in a Little time Demand, if not forcibly take part of it from us, also as we are informed they have been marking Lines through our hunting grounds: are daily receiving Talks from one Place or other, and from People we Know nothing about. We Know not who to mind or who to neglect. We are told that the Americans have 13 Councils Compos'd of Chiefs and Warriors. We Know not which of them we are to Listen to, or if we are to hear some, and Reject others, we are at a loss to Distinguish those we are to hear. We are told that you are the head Chief of the Grand Council, which is above these 13 Councils: if so why have we not had Talks from you, – We are head men and Chiefs and Warriors also: and have always been accustomed to speak with great Chiefs & warriors – We are Likewise told that you and the Great men of your Council are Very Wise – we are glad to hear it, being assured that you

[7] For most indigenous tribes, the "heart" was not a metaphor for emotion or sympathy, but for the soul.

[8] This image implied no condescension on either side: it was an ancient metaphor for making peace between equals found in many places in the Native American world.

will not do us any Wrong, and therefore we wish to Speak with you and your Council, or if you Do not approve of our so Doing, as you are wise, you will tell us who shall speak with us, in behalf of all our Brothers the Americans, and from whare and whome we are to be supplied with necessaries in the manner our great father [the king] supplied us – we hope you will also put a stop to any encroachments on our lands, without our consent, and silence all those People who sends us Such Talks as inflame & exasperate our Young Men, as it is our earnest desire to remain in peace and friendship with our Br: the Americans forever.

Brother,

The King our Common father always left one of his beloved Men among us, to whom we told anything we had to say, and he soon obtained an answer – and by him our great Father, his Chiefs & headmen spoke to us.

Our great father always gave him goods to cover the nakedness of our old men who could not hunt, our women and our children, and he was as one mouth, and one tongue between us, and was beloved of us all. Such a man living among us particularly at this time, would rescue us from the darkness and confusion we are in. By directing us to whom we should speak, and putting us in the right Path that we should not go wrong.

We have desired our Br. Mr. Donne, who brought talks from General Clark,[9] and has been some time among us, to deliver this talk to you, and speak it in our behalf to your Grand Council, that you may know our want,[10] and as you are wise, that you may direct us what to do for the best. He has Promised, at our desire to take it to your great council fire & to bring as your answer, that you may be no more in the dark – believe what he tells you from us; we have told him all that is in our hearts.

Brothers, we are very poor for necessaries, for Amunition particularly. We can supply ourselves from the Spaniards but we are averse to hold any intercourse with them, as our hearts are always with our Brothers the Americans. We have advised our young men to wait with patience for the answer to this talk, when we rest assured of having supplies, and every thing so regulated that no further confusion may ensue. We wish that this land may never again be stained with the blood of either white or Red men, that piece [*sic*] may last forever and that both our women and children may sit down in safety under their own shade to enjoy without fear or apprehension the Blessing which the good Spirit enriches them with. Brother, we again desire you and your chiefs to Listen to what we say that

[9] General George Rogers Clark sent John Donne to the Chicksaws to negotiate a peace between them and the state of Virginia. It is not entirely clear if he spoke the language himself, but he probably did.

[10] "Want" in this case meant "need," even implying "poverty."

we shall not have to Repeat it again, and as you are all Wise, you will know what to do.

Done at Chuck-ul-issah our Great Town the 28th day of July, 1783.

Minghoma
Pyamathahaw
Kushthaputhasa
Pyamingoe of Christhautra
Pyamingo of Chuckaferah

Source: *Calendar of Virginia State Papers*, 3: 515–17, reprinted in Colin Calloway, ed., *The World Turned Upside Down: Indian Voices from Early America* (Bedford/ St. Martin's, 1994), pp. 162–6.

Study: Colin Calloway, *The American Revolution in Indian Country* (Cambridge University Press, 1995).

6. George Washington's Indian Policy

At the end of the Revolutionary War, George Washington wrote to James Duane, who was heading a committee on Indian affairs for the Continental Congress. Duane's report, which he finished in October of 1783, was a direct reflection of Washington's letter. It immediately influenced policy in the formation of the numerous Indian treaties that were promulgated in the 1780s.

To James Duane

Rocky Hill, September 7, 1783

Sir: I have carefully perused the Papers which you put into my hands relative to Indian Affairs.

My Sentiments with respect to the proper line of Conduct to be observed towards these people coincides precisely with those delivered by Genl. Schuyler, so far as he has gone in his Letter of the 29th July to Congress (which, with the other Papers is herewith returned), and for the reasons he has there assigned; a repetition of them therefore by me would be unnecessary. But independent of the arguments made use of by him the following considerations have no small weight in my Mind.

To suffer a wide extended Country to be over run with Land Jobbers, Speculators and Monopolisers or even with scatter'd settlers, is, in my opinion, inconsistent with that wisdom and policy which our true interest dictates, or that an enlightened People ought to adopt and, besides, is pregnant of disputes both with the Savages, and among ourselves, the evils of which are easier to be conceived than described; and for what? But to aggrandize a few avaricious men to the prejudice of many, and the embarrassment of Government. For the People engaged in these pursuits without contributing in the smallest degree to the support of Government, or considering themselves as amenable to its Laws, will involve it by their unrestrained conduct, in inextricable perplexities, and more than probable in a great deal of Bloodshed.

My ideas therefore of the line of Conduct proper to be observed not only towards the Indians, but for the government of the Citizens of America, in their Settlement of the Western Country (which is intimately connected therewith) are simply these.

First and as a preliminary, that all Prisoners of whatever age or Sex, among the Indians shall be delivered up.

That the Indians should be informed, that after a Contest of eight years for the Sovereignty of this Country G: Britain has ceded all the Lands of the United States within the limits described by the arte. of the Provisional Treaty.

That as they (the Indians) maugre all the advice and admonition which could be given them at the commencement; and during the prosecution of the War could not be restrained from acts of hostility, but were determined to join their Arms to those of G. Britain and to share their fortune; so, consequently, with a less generous People than Americans they would be made to share the same fate; and be compelld to retire along with them beyond the Lakes. But as we prefer Peace to a state of warfare, as we consider them as a deluded People; as we perswade ourselves that they are convinced, from experience, of their error in taking up the Hatchet against us, and that their true Interest and safety must now depend upon *our* friendship; as the Country is large enough to contain us all; and as we are disposed to be kind to them and to partake of their Trade, we will from these considerations and from motives of Cmpn., draw a veil over what is past and establish a boundary line between them and us beyond which we will *endeavor* to restrain our People from Hunting or Settling, and within which they shall not come, but for the purposes of Trading, Treating, or other business unexceptionable in its nature.

In establishing this line, in the first instance, care should be taken neither to yield nor to grasp at too much. But to endeavor to impress the Indians with an idea of the generosity of our disposition to accommodate them, and with the necessity we are under, of providing for our Warriors, our Young People who are growing up, and strangers who are coming from other Countries to live among us. And if they should make a point of it, or appear dissatisfied at the line we may find it necessary to establish, compensation should be made them for their claims within it.

It is needless for me to express more explicitly because the tendency of my observns. evinces in my opinion that if the Legislature of the State of New York should insist upon expelling the Six Nations [of the Iroquois] from all the Country they Inhabited previous to the War, within their Territory (as General Schuyler seems to be apprehensive of) that it will end in another Indian War. I have every reason to believe from my enquiries, and the information I have received, that they will not suffer their Country (if it was our policy to take it before we could settle it) to be wrested from them without another struggle. That they would compromise for a part of it I have very little doubt, and that it would be the cheapest way of coming at it, I have no doubt at all. The same observations, I am perswaded, will hold good with respect to Virginia, or any other state which has powerful Tribes of Indians on their Frontiers; and the reason of my mentioning New York is because General Schulyer has expressed his opinion of the temper of its Legislature; and because I have been more in the way of learning the Sentimes. of the Six Nations, than of any other Tribes of Indians on this Subject.

The limits being sufficiently extensive (in the New Ctry.) to comply with all the engagements of Government and to admit such emigrations as may be supposed to happen within a given time not only from the several States of the Union but from Foreign Countries, and moreover of such magnitude as to form a distinct and proper Government; a Proclamation in my opinion, should issue, making it Felony (if there is power for the purpose and if not imposing some very heavy restraint) for any person to Survey or Settle beyond the Line; and the Officers Commanding the Frontier Garrison should have pointed and peremptory orders to see that the Proclamation is carried into effect.

Measures of this sort would not only obtain Peace from the Indians, but would, in my opinion, be the surest means of preserving it. It would dispose of the Land to the best advantage; People the Country progressively [gradually], and check Land Jobbing and Monopolizing (which is now going forward with great avidity) while the door would be open, and the terms known for every one to obtain what is reasonable and proper for himself upon legal and constitutional ground.

Every advantage that could be expected or even wished for would result from such a mode of procedure our Settlements would be compact, Government well established, and our Barrier formidable, not only for ourselves but against our Neighbours, and the Indians as has been observed in Genl Schuylers Letter will ever retreat as our Settlements advance upon them and they will be as ready to sell, as we are to buy; That it is the cheapest as well as the least distressing way of dealing with them, none who are acquainted with the Nature of Indian warfare, and has ever been at the trouble of estimating the expence of one, and comparing it with the cost of purchasing their Lands, will hesitate to acknowledge.

Unless some such measures as I have here taken the liberty of suggesting are speedily adopted one of two capital evils, in my opinion, will inevitably result, and is near at hand; either that the settling, or rather overspreading the Western Country will take place, by a parcel of Banditti, who will bid defiance to all Authority while they are skimming and disposing of the Cream of the Country at the expence of many suffering Officers and Soldiers who have fought and bled to obtain it, and are now waiting the decision of Congress to point them to the promised reward of their past dangers and toils, or a renewal of hostilities with the Indians, brought about more than probably, by this very means ...

[Washington goes on to outline the territories that might possibly be allotted to certain tribes.]

At first view, it may seem a little extraneous, when I am called upon to give an opinion upon the terms of a Peace proper to be made with the Indians, that I should go into the formation of New States; but the Settlemt of the Western Country and making a Peace with the Indians are so analogous that there can be no definition of the one without involving considerations of the other. For I repeat it, again, and I am clear in my opinion, that policy and economy point very strongly to the expediency of being upon good terms with the Indians, and the propriety of purchasing their Lands in preference to attempting to drive them by force of arms out of their Country; which as we have already experienced is like driving the Wild Beasts of the Forest which will return as soon as the pursuit is at an end and fall perhaps on those that are left there; when the gradual extension of our Settlements will as certainly cause the Savage as the Wolf to retire; both being beasts of prey tho' they differ in shape. In a word there is nothing to be obtained by an Indian War but the Soil they live on and this can be had by purchase at less expence, and without that bloodshed, and those distresses which helpless Women and Children are made partakers of in all kinds of disputes with them.

If there is any thing in these thoughts (which I have fully and freely communicated) worthy attention I shall be happy and am Sir Yr. etc.

P.S. A formal Address, and memorial from the Oneida Indians [of the Six Nations of the Haudenosaunee or Iroquois][11] when I was on the Mohawk River, setting forth their Grievances and distresses and praying

[11] The Oneida, unlike most of the Iroquois or Haudenosaunee, had sided with the Americans rather than the British, probably because of their proximity to American settlements. After the war, they received almost nothing in exchange for their efforts.

relief, induced me to order a pound of Powder and 3lbs. of Lead to be issued to each Man, from the Military magazines in the care of Colo. Willet; this, I presume, was unknown to Genl. Schuyler at the time he recommended the like measure in his Letter to Congress.

Source: John C. Fitzpatrick, ed., *The Writings of George Washington from the Original Manuscript Sources, 1745–1799*, vol. 27 (US Government Printing Office, 1938), pp. 133–40.

Study: Francis Paul Prucha, *The Great Father: The United States Government and the American Indian* (University of Nebraska Press, 1984).

Further exploration: Most of us are familiar with accounts of George Washington's life and deeds which make him out to be a great hero. There are people, however, who tell his story very differently. See Glenn Williams, *The Year of the Hangman: George Washington's Campaign against the Iroquois* (Westholme, 2005), and Barbara Alice Mann, *George Washington's War on Native America* (Praeger, 2005).

Questions for consideration

1. Why do you think so many settlers taken prisoner by the Indians during the colonial era ended up choosing to stay with them?
2. What factors gave the Abenaki their confidence in speaking to the English? When do you think they lost such confidence?
3. Imagine the Chickasaw headmen explaining their map to Governor Nicholson in 1723. Which part of their message do you find most interesting? What was different about the dynamic of their meeting with Mr. Donne in 1783? How do we know that, despite their losses, the Chickasaw were still proud of their prowess as warriors?
4. What explains the level of hostility evinced by Jeffery Amherst? Does it surprise you?
5. At the end of the Revolutionary War, George Washington insisted on the importance of the Indians being allowed to keep some of their land. Why did he believe this was important? Did he believe their stay on the land would be permanent?

Chapter 6 What the New Nation Portended for Indians

1. Lewis and Clark in the Pacific Northwest

From the time the United States came into being, the country's leaders assumed it was their duty to oversee territorial expansion. France, desperate for cash at the end of the Napoleonic Wars, sold the new nation the Louisiana territory (over 800,000 square miles between the Mississippi and the Rocky Mountains) in 1803. President Thomas Jefferson, concerned that the Russians and Spaniards and even some English merchants were making inroads from the Pacific coast, rapidly organized an exploratory expedition led by Meriwether Lewis and William Clark. All along the way to the western shore they depended on Indians for information, horses, and part of their food, but they never acknowledged this. Nor did those back east who avidly waited for news of the explorers. Instead, the Indians seemed to become more and more invisible to the American public, whose enthusiasm for settling the west was aroused by the famous expedition.

By the winter of 1804–5, the explorers were temporarily settled with the Mandan in today's South Dakota, collecting supplies and waiting for spring. By the winter of 1805–6, they had reached the Pacific, and after staying with the Clatsop Indians for a while, constructed a flimsy fort in their territory, in today's Oregon. Over the course of weeks, William Clark's journal reveals the tension he experienced when the indigenous people refused to be awed by him while they were serving as his hosts. When it became obvious that they were accustomed to driving hard bargains with visiting Europeans, he condemned them as "close dealers".

Tuesday, 10th December, 1805

A Cloudy rainey morning verry early I rose and walked on the Shore of the Sea coast and picked up Several Curious Shells. I saw Indians walking up and down the beech which I did not at first understand the Cause of, one man came to where I was and told me that he was in Serch of fish which is frequently thrown up on Shore and left by the tide, and told me [in English] the "Sturgion was verry good" and that the water when it retired left fish which they eate this was Conclusive evedance to me that this Small band depended in Some Measure for their winters Subsistance on the fish which is thrown on Shore and left by the tide – after amuseing my Self for about an hour on the edge of the rageing Seas I returned to the houses, one of the Indians pointed to a flock of Brant sitting in the creek at Short distance below and requested me to Shute one, I walked down with my Small rifle and killed two at about 40 yds distance, on my return to the houses two Small ducks Set at about 30 steps from me the Indians pointed at the ducks they were near together, I Shot at the ducks and accidentally Shot the head of one off, this Duck and brant was Carried to the house and every man Came around examined the Duck looked at the gun the Size of the ball which was 100 to the pound and Said in their own language *Couch Musket wake, com ma-tax Musket*, which is, a good Musket, do not under Stand this kind of Musket, &c. I entered the Same house I Slept in, they immediately Set before me their best roots, fish and Surup —, I attempted to purchase a Small Sea otter Skin for read [red] beeds which I had in my pockets, they would not trade for those beeds not priseing any other Colour than Blue or White, I purchased a little of the berry bread and a fiew of their roots for which I gave Small fish hooks, which they appeared fond of – I then Set out on my return by the Same rout I had Come out accompanied by *Cus-ka-lah* [the chief] and his brothers as far as the 3d Creek, for the purpose of Setting me across, from which place they returned, and I proceeded on through a heavy rain to the Camp at our intended fort, Saw a bears track & the tracks of 2 Elk in the thick woods – found Capt. Lewis with all the men out Cutting down trees for our huts &c. in my absence the Men brought in the Six Elk which was killed Several days ago —. 4 men Complaining of violent Coalds. Three Indians in a Canoe Came up from the *Clat Sop* Village yesterday and returned to day. The Sea Coast is about 7 miles distant Nearly West about 5 miles of the distance through a thick wood with reveens hills and Swamps the land, rich black moald 2 miles in a open wavering Sandy prairie, ridge runing parrelal to the river, Covered with Green Grass.

Wednesday 11th December

Rained all the last night moderately we are all employed putting up huts or Cabins for our winters quarters. Sergeant Pryor unwell from a dislocation of his Sholder, Gibson with the disentary, Jo. Fields with biles on his legs, & Werner with a Strained Knee. The rain Continued moderately all day.

Thursday 12th December

All hands that are well employ'd in Cutting logs and raising our winter Cabins, detached two men to Split boards – Some rain at intervals all last night and to day – the flees were So troublesome last night that I made but a broken nights rest, we find great dificuelty in getting those trouble insects out of our robes and blankets – in the evening two Canoes of *Clât Sops* Visit us they brought with them *Wap pa to*, a black Sweet root they Call *Sha-na toe qua*, and a Small Sea otter Skin, all of which we purchased for a fiew fishing hooks and a Small Sack of Indian tobacco which was given [to us before] by the Snake Inds.

Those Indians appear well disposed we gave a Medal to the principal Chief named *Con-ny-au* or *Con mo-wol* and treated those with him with as much attention as we could – I can readily discover that they are Close deelers, & Stike for a verry little, never close a bargain except they think they have the advantage Value Blue beeds highly, white they also prise but no other Colour do they Value in the least – the *Wap pa* they Sell high, this root the[y] purchase at a high price from the natives above [to the north].

Source: Gary E. Moulton and Thomas W. Dunlay, eds., *The Journals of the Lewis and Clark Expedition*, vol. 6 (University of Nebraska Press, 1990), pp. 121–3.

Study: Many recent studies of Lewis and Clark persist in ignoring the centrality of the Indians. A book which overturns many of our expectations is Thomas P. Slaughter, *Exploring Lewis and Clark: Reflections on Men and Wilderness* (Knopf, 2003).

Further exploration: Because we do not have records of the Indians' thoughts about Lewis and Clark, it is difficult to study their reactions to the expedition. Scholars have taken varying approaches. See James Ronda, *Lewis and Clark among the Indians* (University of Nebraska Press, 1984); Alvin Josephy, ed., *Lewis and Clark through Indian Eyes* (Knopf, 2006); and Frederick E. Hoxie and Jay Nelson, eds., *Lewis and Clark and the Indian Country: The Native American Perspective* (University of Illinois Press, 2007).

2. Russian Settlements in Alaska

While Lewis and Clark and their men may have prided themselves on being the first white people to stand on the northwest coast and survey the Pacific, they were not really the first. In 1805, while the expedition camped among the Clatsop, Russian traders left their settlements in Alaska and tooled southward along the coast looking for sea otter and other goods. A German who was among them wrote of what he saw. Georg Heinrich von Langsdorff had trained as a medical doctor at the University of Göttingen, and later took a position as a naturalist on a Russian voyage to Brazil and Japan. As soon as the voyage was finished, he accepted a position on an expedition to the Russian coast of America. He planned to publish his findings for a Russian audience, so his criticism of what he observed is noteworthy.

On the evening of June 13, 1805, our belongings were taken aboard the brig *Maria* and we sailed very early the next morning from Awatscha Bay [on the coast of Kamtschatka in eastern Siberia] ...

Instead of sailors we found sixty men on board who had worked as trappers or hunters (Russian *promyshlenniks*) for the Russian-American Company. Our crew was made up of adventurers, drunkards, bankrupt, depraved merchants and craftsmen and, in addition, several criminals who had been flogged and branded. All were in search of their fortunes. Most of them had sailed for the first time the previous year from Ochotsk to Kamtschatka. ... They got in each other's way and, if the wind changed, fifty men could not do what ten ordinary sailors would have taken care of easily. Furthermore, the ship was so filled with cargo that most of the men had to take turns spending time on deck. Considering the fact that the Russian-American Company had fed the men very sparingly all winter in Kamtschatka – i.e. bread, dried and frozen fish, seal and whale blubber – but only in meager portions – no one should be surprised to hear that most of them had been suffering from scurvy, from which most had not yet recovered by eating wild Kamtschatkan garlic and fresh fish ... The crew was not only badly fed but also even more poorly and wretchedly clothed. Especially because of their lack of linens, the quantity of vermin on the men had to have increased mightily. It was virtually impossible to go out on the small deck – the only place one could breathe some fresh air – because those disgustingly dirty men continually sat there picking vermin off each other...

*

Kodiak is a collection point for furs taken in the area, i.e., Alaska – the Cook River, Prince William Sound, etc. That is why the storehouse sometimes contains a stock of very valuable furs. In 1802 the number of sea otter pelts collected in the five preceding years came to 18,000 ...

The management of every single company outpost is completely despotic. The agents under the business office in Kodiak do exactly as they wish without being responsible to or supervised by anyone.

The Aleuts living on distant islands and areas are supervised by some kind of promyshlennik, or, in other words, an ignorant, evil man, who suppresses and intimidates those placid and now defenseless natives in every way possible and, I am not saying too much, sucks them dry. ... I have examples of how several Russian fur hunters or promyshlenniks rule over the lives of natives according to whim. They have tortured those defenseless creatures to death in the cruelest manner and gone unpunished. That is why the natives hate the Russians, including their wives and children, and kill them whenever an opportunity presents itself . . .

The injustice and raw violence perpetuated by the assistant overseers and agents of the company go so far that the natives have lost all their possessions and own barely more than the clothing on their backs. One of the main reasons for their total suppression . . . is the Company's having taken possession of their bairdarkas or leather boats. If they steal the boats from people who have to get all of their food and clothing from the sea, they have then cut them off from all means of livelihood. At present the Aleuts are so enslaved to the Company that they get bairdarkas, the bones for their arrows, and indeed, even their clothing from the Company. The entire take of a hunt has to be turned over to the Company for disposition. . . . In other words, the Aleuts have lost all powers to make decisions for themselves, even in the use of their time. It is disgraceful to see these people going hungry and almost naked and working as in a prison, while the Company's warehouses are full of provisions and clothing . . .

The decline in the numbers of sea otters, more apparent with each passing year, and the interest in trading in their valuable fur has caused the Russians to expand farther and farther eastward from Kamtschatka. The number of sea otters on the Aleutian Islands diminished noticeably after they began being pursued and killed in ever greater numbers. This has caused the Russians to move farther and farther, first to Kodiak, from there to Cook's River, to Prince William Sound, and then to the bays and inlets farther south and then to the Northwest Coast of America. They have killed so many sea otters of every age that they are now either almost totally extinct or have moved farther south. It is now hardly worth financing hunting parties at the northern outposts.

The Company has decided to explore more and more country for sea otters in order not to lose a source of wealth and to maintain the reputation and patent of a respectable Imperial trading company. Norfolk Sound seemed like a good location for an outpost since large numbers of sea otters lived there. Therefore Mr. Von Baranoff laid claim to it several years ago. That courageous conqueror drove out the natives – the Russians usually call them Kalusch but they call themselves Schitchachan, ie, inhabitants of Sitcha or Schitcha – and established a new outpost called Sitcha.

After spending some time there while living quarters and a storehouse were being built, Mr. Von Baranoff returned to Kodiak in the belief that the Kalusch had been relatively placated by gifts. He entrusted that newly conquered area to about 30 promyshlenniks along with an overseer and several Aleuts. Several years later when most of these people were at scattered activities – fishing, felling trees, etc. – the Kalusch attacked and killed all of them except for a few Aleuts, who saved themselves by fleeing in their bairdarkas along the coast to Kodiak. They spread the frightening news of the destruction of the outpost.

Because of the importance of the outpost and the numbers of sea otters in the vicinity, Mr. Von Baranoff decided to reconquer the area and succeeded.

Source and study: Georg Heinrich von Langsdorff, *Remarks and Observations on a Voyage around the World from 1803 to 1807*, vol. 2, ed. Victoria Joan Moessner and Richard A. Pierce (Limestone, 1993 [1811]), pp. 1–2, 35–8, 45–6.

Further exploration: There are a number of published journals kept by settlers who lived in Alaska later in the nineteenth century. See, for example, S. A. Mousalimas, ed., *Journals of the Priest Ioann Veniaminov in Alaska, 1823–1836* (University of Alaska Press, 1993) and Jane Jacobs, ed., *A Schoolteacher in Old Alaska: The Story of Hannah Breece* (Random House, 1995). The story of what the hunting of the sea otters did to the Native Americans along the coast has been explored in a thought-provoking novel intended for young adults but well worth reading by anybody: Scott O'Dell's *Island of the Blue Dolphins* (Dell, 1960). O'Dell researched the life of the "Lost Woman of San Nicolas" as she was called, a woman who lived alone for many years on one of the Channel Islands (off the coast of California) after her people were destroyed by Russian fur traders. In 1853, she was found and brought to the Catholic mission in Santa Barbara, where she died and is buried.

3. Tecumseh's Demands

Native Americans were well aware of the young United States' aims to spread westward across the continent, and after the disappearance of the French from the scene, they felt particularly vulnerable. In the early nineteenth century, various pan-Indian movements formed. This meant that multiple tribes worked together to try to stop the westward expansion of white settlement. Tecumseh, a Shawnee chief, and his brother Tenskwatawa, a prophet, led a coalition of Delawares, Kickappoos, Ottawas, Potawatomis, Anishinabe, and others. Together, they founded Prophetstown on the Tippecanoe River in Indiana. Tecumseh was known in his own time as a great orator, but most of the records we have of his speeches come from newspapers and semi-fictional narratives. White writers remembered and changed his words as they saw fit; sometimes they even reported from hearsay. In one instance, however, we can come close to what Tecumseh actually said. In August of 1810, William Henry Harrison, governor of the Indiana Territory (and later president of the United States), met with Tecumseh in the presence of an interpreter and scribe. The record of what transpired was then sent to Washington and archived, and so we have it today.

To the Secretary of War

Vincennes 22nd August 1810

Sir:

If the information which I have heretofore given you on the subject of the designs of the Prophet [Tenskwatawa] and his followers has been vague and in some respects contradictory the consequence of my having derived it from various sources, not always the most intelligent, that which I have now the honor to communicate has at least the advantage of authenticity, coming from the brother of the Prophet who as I have before informed you is the great man of the party. This personage, who is called Tecumseh, arrived here on the 12th Inst., and excepting the intervening Sunday and one bad day I have been constantly engaged with him until the last evening. His speeches the two first days were sufficiently insolent and his pretensions arrogant, but that of Monday [August 20] I enclose to you entire, as it was taken down by a Gentleman whom I employed for that purpose, and is as correct as could be expected, considering that the Interpreter speaks bad English and is not very remarkable for clearness of intilect, although faithfull in the highest degree and for knowledge of the Indian languages unrivalled. The facts avowed by Tecumseh in the broadest manner are: That it was the object of his brother and himself from the commencement to form a combination of all the Indian Tribes in this quarter to put a stop to the encroachments of the white people and to establish a principle that the lands should be considered common property and none sold without the consent of all, that it was their intention to put to death all the chiefs who were parties to the late Treaty,[1] and never more to suffer any village chiefs to manage the arrears of the Indians, but that everything should be put into the hands of the warriors.[2] That the Americans had driven them from the sea coast, and would shortly if not stopped, push them into the Lakes, that they were determined to make a stand, where they were. He still however with strange inconsistency, asserted that it was not his intention to go to war, and that the persons who had given me that information were liars ... Every instance of injustice and injury which have been committed by our citizens upon the Indians from the commencement of the revolutionary war (There are unfortunately too many of them) were brought forward and exaggerated, and everything said which was likely to inflame the mind of the

[1] He is referring to the 1809 Treaty of Fort Wayne, at which certain chiefs were wined, dined, and pressured. They ended by giving up over 3 million acres to the US government. Many Indians quarreled with the notion that any chiefs had the right to do this. According to their traditions, chiefs held land on behalf of all the people, not as private fiefdoms.

[2] By "warriors" he meant councils of all the leading men. He is implicitly contrasting an open council to the idea of hereditary chiefs making decisions on their own on behalf of their people.

Indians against us. When he finished his harangue, I began to answer him and was contrasting the conduct of the United States towards Indians with that of other civilized powers, showing their uniform regard to justice in their transactions with the most significant tribe, when he interrupted me before the interpreter could explain what I had said to the Potawatomies and Miamis and with the most violent gesticulations and indications of anger began to contradict what I had said in the most indecent manner. When he first rose, a number of his party also sprung up, arm'd with war clubs, tomahawks and spears and stood in a threatening attitude. Not understanding his language I did not know what he had said, until the Interpreter explained it to me ... As soon as his speech was interpreted to me, I reproached him for his conduct and required him instantly to depart his camp, declaring that I was determined to extinguish the council fire, and no longer have any communication with him, that my answer to that part of his speech which related to the lands lately purchased would be communicated to the Tribes which he said he represented, in a written message, and if he had anything further to say to me, he must send the Huron or some other chief to me. When the Interpreter visited him in the morning, he earnestly requested me to give him another interview and protested that he meant no harm by his conduct the day before, and that he wished everything to be amicably settled ...

I have promised Tecumseh to send on the President his speech[es] and to procure the President's answer and I should be glad to receive a speech signed by the President or yourself informing him that the land would not be given up [to them]. ... It will [also] assist the cause greatly to let them see that we are ready to support our rights with the sword ...

I have the honor to be with greatest respect Sir

Your Humble Servt.

Willm. Henry Harrison

Tecumseh's Speech to Governor Harrison, August 20, 1810

Brother When we were first discover'd it was by the French who told us that they would adopt us as their children and gave us presents without asking anything in return but our considering them our fathers. Since we have changed our fathers we find it different.

Brother. This is the manner that the treaty was made by us with the French. They gave us many presents and treated us well. They asked us for a small piece of country to live on which they were not to leave and continue to treat us as their children after some time the British and French came to quarrel the British were victorious yet the French promised to think of us as their child and if they ever could serve us to do it. Now my red children I know I was obliged to abandon you in disagreeable circumstances, but we have never ceased to look upon you and if we could now be of service to you we would still be your friends.

The next father we found was the British who told us that they would now be our fathers and treat us in the same manner as our former fathers the French – they would occupy the same land they did and not trouble us on ours; but would look on us as their children.

Brother. We were very glad to hear the British promise to treat us as our fathers the French had done they began to treat us in the same way but at last they changed their good treatment by raising the Tomahawk against the Americans and put it into our hands, by which we have suffered the loss of a great many of your young men etc.

Brother. Now we began to discover the treachery of the British they never troubled us for our land but they have done worse by inducing us to go to war. The Hurons have particularly suffered during the war and have at length become certain of it. They have told us that we must bury the British Tomahawk entirely that if we did not they (the B.) would ere long ask us to take it up.

You ought to know that after we agreed to bury the Tomhawk [*sic*] at Greenville we then found their new fathers in the Americans who told us that would treat us well, not like the British who gave us but a small piece of pork every day. I want now to remind you of the promises of the white people. You recollect that the time the Delawares lived near the white people (Americans) and satisfied with the promise of friendship and remained in security yet one of their towns was surrounded and the men women and children murdered.

The same promises were given to the Shawonese, flags were given to them and [they] were told by the Americans that they were now the children of the Americans. Their flags will be as security for you, if the white people intend to do you harm hold up your flags and no harm will be done you. This was at length practiced and the consequence was that the person bearing the flag was murdered with others in their village. Know my Bro. after this conduct can you blame me for placing little confidence in the promises of our fathers the Americans.

Brother. Since the peace was made you have kill'd some of the Shawanese, Winebagoes, Delawares and Miamies and you have taken our lands from us and I do not see how we can remain at peace with you if you continue to do so. You have given goods to the Kickapoos for the sale of their lands to you which has been the cause of many deaths amongst them. You have promised us assistance but I do not see that you have given us any.

You try to force the red people to do some injury. It is you that is pushing them on to do mischief. You endeavor to make destructions, you wish to prevent the Indians to do as we wish them to unite and let them consider their land as the common property of the whole you take tribes aside and advise them not to come into this measure and until our design is accomplished we do not wish to accept of your invitation to go and visit the President.

The reason I tell you this is – You want by your distinctions of Indian tribes in allotting to each a particular track of land to make them to war with each other. You never see an Indian come and endeavor to make the white people do so. You are continually driving the red people when at last you will drive them into the great lake where they can't either stand or work.

Brother. You ought to know what you are doing with the Indians. Perhaps it is by the direction of the President to make those distinctions. It is a very bad thing and we do not like it. Since my residence at Tippecanoe we have endeavored to level all distinctions to destroy village chiefs by whom all mischief is done; it is they who will our land to the Americans our object is to let all our affairs be transacted by Warriors.

Brother. This land that was sold and the goods that was given for it was only done by a few. The treaty was afterwards brought here and the Weas were induced to give their consent because of their small numbers. The treaty at Fort Wayne was made through the threats of [the chief] Winamac but in future we are prepared to punish those chiefs who may come forward to propose to sell their land. If you continue to purchase of them it will produce war among the different tribes and at last I do not know what will be the consequence to the white people.

Brother. I was glad to hear your speech you said if we could show that the land was sold by persons that had no right to sell you would restore it, that [they who] did sell did not own it, it was [asserted by] *me*. These tribes set up a claim but the tribes with me will not agree to their claim, if the land is not restored to us you will soon see when we return to our homes how it will be settled. We shall have a great council at which all the tribes shall be present when we will show to those who sold that they had no right to sell the claim they set up and we will know what will be done with those Chiefs that did sell the land to you. I am not alone in this determination it is the determination of all the warriors and red people that listen to me.

I now wish you to listen to me. If you do not it will appear as if you wished me to kill all the chiefs that sold you this land. I tell you so because I am authorized by all the tribes to do so. I am at the head of them all. I am a Warrior and all the Warriors will meet together in two or three moons from this. Then I will call for those chiefs that sold the land and shall know what to do with them. If you do not restore the land you will have a hand in killing them.

Brother. Do not believe that I came here to get presents from you if you offer us anything we will not take it. By taking goods from you, you will hereafter say that with them you purchased another piece of land from us. If we want anything we are able to buy it, from your traders. Since the land was sold to you no traders come among us. I now wish you would clear all the roads and let the traders come among us. Then perhaps some of our young men will occasionally call upon you to get their guns repaired. This is all the assistance we ask of you ...

Brother. I wish you could take pity on all the red people and do what I have requested. If you will not give up the land and do cross the boundary of your present settlement it will be very hard and produce great troubles among us. How can we have confidence in the white people when Jesus Christ came upon the earth you kill'd and nail'd him on a cross, you thought he was dead but you were mistaken. You have shaken among you and you laugh and make light of their worship.

Everything I have said to you is the truth the great spirit has inspired me and I speak nothing but the truth to you ...

Source: Logan Esarey, ed., *Messages and Letters of William Henry Harrison*, vol. 1 (Arno, 1975 [1922]), pp. 459–67.

Study: Tecumseh and his period have recently received a great deal of attention. Colin Calloway, *The Shawnees and the War for America* (Viking, 2007); Alfred Cave, *Prophets of the Great Spirit: Native American Revitalization Movements in Eastern North America* (University of Nebraska Press, 2006); R. David Edmunds, *Tecumseh and the Quest for Indian Leadership* (Pearson Longman, 2007).

4. The Cherokee Syllabary and Newspaper

By the early years of the Republic, many southeastern Indians had adopted aspects of United States culture, most especially agriculture. A Cherokee silversmith named Sequoyah, whose English name was George Gist, believed it was also important for Indians to develop their own writing system in order to communicate with each other and defend their interests. He spoke only Cherokee and had never been educated in English or any other written language, but he had an extraordinary linguistic aptitude. In 1821, after several years of trial and error, he produced a highly efficient syllabary, the effectiveness of which he quickly demonstrated by training first his own daughter and then several boys. Educated Cherokees responded with enthusiasm and arranged to teach the new writing system. Within a few months, most Cherokee adults had learned to use it. In the late 1820s, having obtained a printing press, the Cherokee started their own bilingual newspaper, the Cherokee Phoenix.

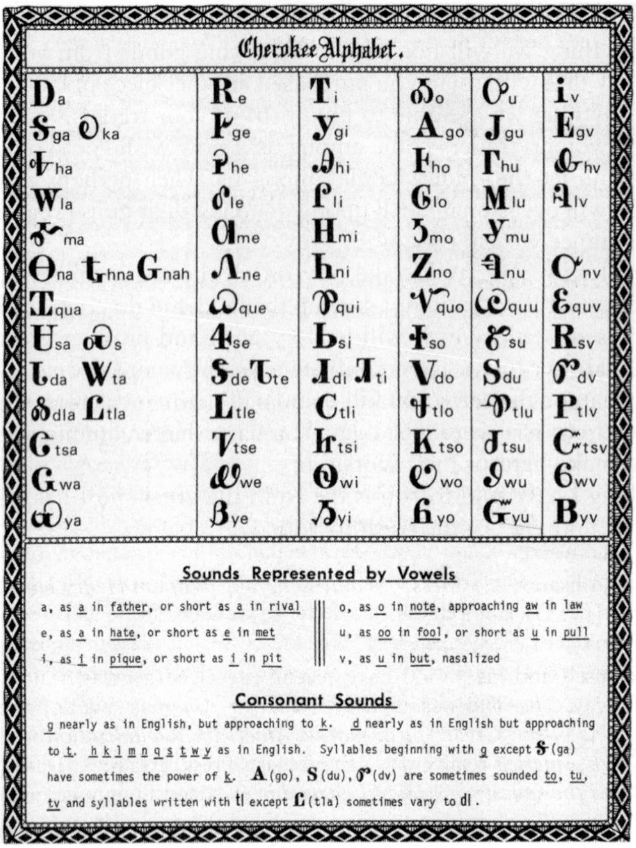

Cherokee Alphabet.

Ꭰ a	Ꭱ e	Ꭲ i	Ꭳ o	Ꭴ u	Ꭵ v
Ꭶ ga Ꭷ ka	Ꭸ ge	Ꭹ gi	Ꭺ go	Ꭻ gu	Ꭼ gv
Ꭽ ha	Ꭾ he	Ꭿ hi	Ꮀ ho	Ꮁ hu	Ꮂ hv
Ꮃ la	Ꮄ le	Ꮅ li	Ꮆ lo	Ꮇ lu	Ꮈ lv
Ꮉ ma	Ꮊ me	Ꮋ mi	Ꮌ mo	Ꮍ mu	
Ꮎ na Ꮏ hna Ꮐ nah	Ꮑ ne	Ꮒ ni	Ꮓ no	Ꮔ nu	Ꮕ nv
Ꮖ qua	Ꮗ que	Ꮘ qui	Ꮙ quo	Ꮚ quu	Ꮛ quv
Ꮜ sa Ꮝ s	Ꮞ se	Ꮟ si	Ꮠ so	Ꮡ su	Ꮢ sv
Ꮣ da Ꮤ ta	Ꮥ de Ꮦ te	Ꮧ di Ꮨ ti	Ꮩ do	Ꮪ du	Ꮫ dv
Ꮬ dla Ꮭ tla	Ꮮ tle	Ꮯ tli	Ꮰ tlo	Ꮱ tlu	Ꮲ tlv
Ꮳ tsa	Ꮴ tse	Ꮵ tsi	Ꮶ tso	Ꮷ tsu	Ꮸ tsv
Ꮹ wa	Ꮺ we	Ꮻ wi	Ꮼ wo	Ꮽ wu	Ꮾ wv
Ꮿ ya	Ᏸ ye	Ᏹ yi	Ᏺ yo	Ᏻ yu	Ᏼ yv

Sounds Represented by Vowels

a, as a in father, or short as a in rival
e, as a in hate, or short as e in met
i, as i in pique, or short as i in pit
o, as o in note, approaching aw in law
u, as oo in fool, or short as u in pull
v, as u in but, nasalized

Consonant Sounds

g nearly as in English, but approaching to k. d nearly as in English but approaching to t. h k l m n q s t w y as in English. Syllables beginning with g except Ꭶ (ga) have sometimes the power of k. Ꭺ (go), Ꮪ (du), Ꮫ (dv) are sometimes sounded to, tu, tv and syllables written with tl except Ꮭ (tla) sometimes vary to dl.

Figure 6.4.1 Cherokee syllabary

Sources: Ruth Bradley Holmes and Betty Sharp Smith, *Beginning Cherokee*, 2nd edn. (University of Oklahoma Press, 1977), p. 2 (the chart, still in common use, is based on one originally published by Samuel Worcester in 1828); *The Cherokee Phoenix*, March 13, 1828.

Study: A particularly thoughtful study of Sequoyah's mindset and motivations appears in Jill Lepore's *A is for American: Letters and Other Characters in the Newly United States* (Knopf, 2002). The best study of the producer of *The Phoenix* is Thedu Perdue, ed., *Cherokee Editor: The Writings of Elias Boudinot* (University of Tennessee Press, 1983).

Further exploration: The entire run of *The Cherokee Phoenix* has been scanned and indexed and is available on the website of the American Native Press Archives, based at the University of Arkansas. There students will find numerous other Cherokee writings as well.

ᏣᎳᎩ PROTECTION. ᏧᎴᎯᏌᏅᎯ.

CHEROKEE PHŒNIX.

VOL. I. NEW ECHOTA, THURSDAY MARCH 13, 1828. NO. 4.

EDITED BY ELIAS BOUDINOTT.
PRINTED WEEKLY BY
ISAAC H. HARRIS,
FOR THE CHEROKEE NATION.

At $2 50 if paid in advance, $3 in six months, or $3 50 if paid at the end of the year.

To subscribers who can read only the Cherokee language the price will be $2,00 in advance, or $2,50 to be paid within the year.

Every subscription will be considered as continued unless subscribers give notice to the contrary before the commencement of a new year.

The Phœnix will be printed on a Super-Royal sheet, with type entirely new procured for the purpose. Any person procuring six subscribers, and becoming responsible for the payment, shall receive a seventh gratis.

Advertisements will be inserted at seventy-five cents per square for the first insertion, and thirty-seven and a half cents for each continuance; longer ones in proportion.

☞All letters addressed to the Editor, post paid, will receive due attention.

[illegible]

Be it known, That this day, the various clans or tribes which compose the Cherokee Nation, have unanimously passed an act of oblivion for all lives for which they may have been indebted, one to the other, and have mutually agreed that after this evening the aforesaid act shall become binding upon every clan, or tribe; and the aforesaid clans or tribes have also agreed that if in future, any life should be lost without malice intended, the innocent aggressor shall not be accounted guilty.

Be it known also, That should it so happen that a brother, forgetting his natural affection, should raise his hand in anger and kill his brother, he shall be accounted guilty of murder and suffer accordingly. And if a man has a horse stolen, and overtakes the thief, and should his anger be so great as to cause him to kill him, let his blood remain on his own conscience, but no satisfaction shall be demanded for his life from his relatives or the clan he may belong to.

By order of the seven clans.
TURTLE AT HOME,
Speaker of Council.

Approved.
BLACK FOX, Principal Chief.
PATH KILLER, Sec'd.
TOOCHALAR.

CHARLES HICKS, Sec'y to the Council.
Oostanallah, April 10, 1810.

WHEREAS, fifty-four towns and villages having convened in order to de-

[illegible]

1817.

SCANDAL.

'There are people,' continued the corporal, 'who can't even breathe, without slandering a neighbor.'

'You judge too severely,' replied my

Figure 6.4.2 Cherokee Phoenix

5. The Cherokee Debate in Washington

Despite the enthusiastic adoption on the part of the Cherokee of agriculture, literacy, and even representative government, white citizens of Georgia and the Georgia state government continued to insist that the Cherokee be removed from their valuable lands within the state and resettled further west. Their defense became a cause celèbre. *If even the Cherokee could be forcibly removed, then certainly none of the Indians who continued to live by hunting stood a chance of defending their territory.*

John Ross, the elected chief of the Cherokee, traveled to Washington, DC to plead his people's case. Staying at Williamson's Hotel, he and several close colleagues drafted a letter to the Senate and House of Representatives. Their pleas did not fall on deaf ears. Many US citizens believed the Indians had inalienable rights. Senator Theodore Frelinghuysen of New Jersey became a champion of their cause. In April of 1830, he made a long and impassioned speech. However, the recently elected president, Andrew Jackson, was a firm believer in a state's right to insist on full sovereignty over all territory within its borders, and he was also convinced that the Indians stood in the way of progress. In December of 1829, he said as much in his first annual message to Congress.

The following year, despite the efforts of people like Chief John Ross and Senator Frelinghuysen, the legislature passed the Indian Removal Act of 1830. The Cherokee resorted to the Supreme Court but they were eventually forced by the Georgia state militia to move to Oklahoma. A large percentage of their population died of hunger and exposure as they walked the many miles; they remembered their passage as "the Trail of Tears." Many historians consider this period to have been a defining decade in the history of the United States.

Washington City, February 27, 1829

We, the undersigned, Representatives of the Cherokee nation, beg leave to present before your honorable bodies a subject of the deepest interest to our nation, as involving the most sacred rights and privileges of the Cherokee People. The Legislature of Georgia, during its late session, passed an act to add a large portion of our Territory to that State, and to extend her jurisdiction over the same, and declaring "all laws and usages, made and enforced in said Territory by the Indians, to be null and void after the first of June, 1830. No Indian, or descendant of an Indian, to be a competent witness, or a party to any suit to which a white man is a party." This act involves a question of great magnitude and of serious import, and which calls for the deliberation and decision of Congress. It is a question upon which the salvation and happiness or the misery and destruction of *a nation* depends, therefore it should not be trifled with. The anxious solicitude of Georgia to obtain our lands through the United States by treaty was known to us, and after having accommodated her desires (with that of other States bordering on our territory) by repeated cession of lands, until no more can be reasonably spared, it was not conceived, much less believed, that *a State*, Proud of *Liberty*, and tenacious of the *rights of man*, would condescend to have placed herself before the world, in the imposing attitude of a usurper of the most sacred rights and privileges of a weak, defenceless and innocent nation of people, who are in perfect peace with the United states, and to whom the faith of the United States is solemnly pledged to protect and defend them against the encroachments of their citizens.

In acknowledgment for the protection of the United States and the consideration of guaranteeing to our nation forever the security of our land &c, the Cherokee nation ceded by treaty a large tract of country to the United States, and stipulated that the said Cherokee nation "will not hold any treaty with any *foreign power, individual State* or with *individuals of any State*." These stipulations on our part have been faithfully observed, and ever shall be.

The right of regulating our own internal affairs is a right which we have inherited from the Author of our existence, which we have always exercised, and have never surrendered. Our nation had no voice in the formation of the Federal compact between the States; and if the United States have involved themselves by an agreement with Georgia relative to the purchase of our lands, and have failed to comply with it in the strictest letter of their compact, it is a matter to be adjusted between themselves; and on no principle of justice can an innocent people, who were in no way a party to that compact, be held responsible for its fulfillment; consequently they should not be oppressed, in direct violation of the solemn obligations pledged by treaties for their protection.[3]

It is with pain and deep regret we have witnessed the various plans which have been advised within a few years past of some of the officers of the General Government, and the measures adopted by Congress in conformity to those plans, with the view of effecting the removal of our nation beyond the Mississippi, for the purpose, as has been expressed, to promote our interest and permanent happiness, and save us from the impending fate which has swept others into oblivion.[4] Without presuming to doubt the sincerity and good intentions of the advocates of this plan, we, as the descendants of the Indian race, and possessing both the feelings of the Indian and the white man cannot but believe that this system to perpetuate our happiness is visionary, and that the anticipated blessings can never be realized. The history of the prosperous and improving condition of our people in the arts of civilized life and Christianization, is before the world, and not unknown to you. The causes which have produced this great change and state of things are to be traced from the

[3] Georgia asserted that, in comparison to other territories, it had lost out in the settlement of certain border disputes and also that the United States owed them money for reserving lands within their territory for Indians.

[4] For an example of the way in which relocation was often represented as a charitable act, see Andrew Jackson's speech below.

virtue, honor and wisdom in the policy of the Administration of the Great [George] Washington, the Congress of the United States and the American People; the relationship and intercourse established by treaties, and *our location* in the immediate neighborhood of a civilized community – and withal occupying a country remarkable for its genial and salubrious climate; affording abundance of good water, timber, and a proportionate share of good lands for cultivation. If, under all these advantages, the permanent prosperity and happiness of the Cherokee people cannot be realized, they never can be realized under any other location within the limits of the United States.

We cannot but believe, that, if the same zeal and exertion were to be used by the General Government and the State of Georgia, to effect a mutual compromise in the adjustment of their compact, as has been, and is now, used to effect our removal, it could be done to the satisfaction of the people of Georgia, and without any sacrifice to the United States. We should be wanting in liberal and charitable feelings were we to doubt the virtue and magnanimity of the People of Georgia, and we do believe that there are men in that State whose moral and religious worth stands forth inferior to none within the United States. Why, then, should the power that framed the Constitution of Georgia and made the compact with the United States be not exercised for the honor of the country and the peace, happiness, and preservation of a people, who were the original proprietors of a large portion of the country now in the possession of that State? And whose title to the soil they now occupy, is lost in the ages of antiquity, whose interests are becoming identified with those of the United States, and at whose call they are ever ready to obey in the hour of danger.

In the treaty made with the Cherokees west of the Mississippi, in May last, an article was inserted with the view of inducing our citizens to emigrate, which we cannot but view as an unprecedented policy in the General Government; and whilst we admit the liberty of the Cherokees as freemen to exercise their own choice in removing where they may think proper, we cannot admit the right of the Cherokees west of the Mississippi more than any other nation, to enter into a treaty with the United States to affect our national rights and privileges in any respect whatever, and against which we would most solemnly protest. It is with no little surprise that we have seen in a document printed for the use of Congress, connected with the subject of Indian emigration, the followings statements: "from the ascertained feelings of *the Chiefs* of the *Southern Indians* there is *a fixed purpose, by threats or otherwise, to keep their people from emigrating*." Again: "*There is no doubt but these people fear their chiefs, and on that account keep back*." If we are to understand that these remarks were intended to apply to the people and chiefs of our nation, we do not hesitate in saying, that the informant betrays either an entire ignorance of the subject, or a wanton disposition to misrepresent the facts. The chiefs of our nation are the immediate representatives of the people, by whose voice they are elected; and with equal propriety it may be said, that the people of the Unites States are afraid of their representatives in Congress, and other public officers of their Government.

We cannot admit that Georgia has the right to extend her jurisdiction over our territory, nor are the Cherokee people prepared to submit to her persecuting edict. We would therefore respectfully and solemnly protest, in behalf of the Cherokee nation, before your honorable bodies, against the extension of the laws of Georgia over any part of our Territory, and appeal to the Unites States' Government for justice and protection. The great Washington advised a plan and afforded aid for the general improvement of our nation, in agriculture, science, and government. President Jefferson followed the noble example, and concluded an address to our delegation in language as follows: "I sincerely wish you may succeed in your laudable endeavors to save the remnant of your nation by adopting industrious occupations and government of regular law. *In this you may always rely on the counsel and assistance of the United States*." This kind and generous policy to meliorate our condition, has been blessed with the happiest results: our improvement has been without a parallel in the history of all Indian nations. Agriculture is every where pursued, and the interests of our citizens are permanent in the soil. We have enjoyed the blessings of a Christian instruction; the advantages of education and merit are justly appreciated, a Government of regular law has been adopted, and the nation, under a continuance of the fostering care of the United States, will stand forth as a living testimony, that all Indian nations are not doomed to the fate which has swept many from the face of the earth. Under the parental protection of the United States, we have arrived at the present degree of improvement, and they are now to decide whether we shall continue as a people or be abandoned to destruction.

In behalf, and under the authority of the Cherokee nation, this protest and memorial is respectfully submitted.

Jno Ross — Edward Gunter
R. Taylor — William S. Coodey

*

The President's First Annual Message to Congress, December 8, 1829

Fellow Citizens of the Senate and House of Representatives:

. . . The condition and ulterior destiny of the Indian tribes within the limits of some of our States have become objects of much interest and importance. It has long been the policy of Government to introduce among them the arts of civilization, in the hope of gradually reclaiming them from a wandering life. This policy has, however, been coupled with another wholly incompatible with its success. Professing a desire to civilize and settle them, we have at the same time lost no opportunity to purchase their lands and thrust them farther into the wilderness. By this means they have not only been kept in a wandering state, but been led to look upon us as unjust and indifferent to their fate. Thus, though lavish in its expenditures upon the subject, Government has constantly defeated its own policy, and the Indians in general, receding farther and farther to the west, have retained their savage habits. A portion, however, of the Southern tribes, having mingled much with the whites and made some progress in the arts of civilized life, have lately attempted to erect an independent government within the limits of Georgia and Alabama. These States, claiming to be the only sovereigns within their territories, extended their laws over the Indians, which induced the latter to call upon the United States for protection.

Under these circumstances, the question presented was whether the General Government had a right to sustain those people in their pretensions. The Constitution declares that "no new State shall be formed or erected within the jurisdiction of another State" without the consent of its legislature. If the General Government is not permitted to tolerate the erection of a confederate State within the territory of one of the members of this Union against her consent, much less could it allow a foreign and independent government to establish itself there. Georgia became a member of the Confederacy which eventuated in our Federal Union as a sovereign State, always asserting her claim to certain limits, which, having been originally defined in her colonial charter and subsequently recognized in the treaty of peace, she has ever since continued to enjoy, except as they have been circumscribed by her own voluntary transfer of a portion of her territory to the United States in her article of cession of 1802. Alabama was admitted into the Union on the same footing with the original States, with boundaries which were prescribed by Congress. There is no constitutional, conventional or legal provision which allows them less power over the Indians within their borders than is possessed by Maine or New York. Would the people of Maine permit the Penobscot tribe to erect an independent government within their State? And unless they did would it not be the duty of the general Government to support them in resisting such a measure? Would the people of New York permit each remnant of the Six Nations within her borders to declare itself an independent people under the protection of the United States? Could the Indians establish a separate republic on each of their reservations in Ohio? And if they were so disposed would it be the duty of this Government to protect them in the attempt? If the principle involved in the obvious answer to these questions be abandoned, it will follow that the objects of this Government are reversed and that it has become a part of its duty to aid in destroying the States which it was established to protect.

Actuated by this view of the subject, I informed the Indians inhabiting parts of Georgia and Alabama that their attempt to establish an independent government would not be countenanced by the Executive of the United States, and advised them to emigrate beyond the Mississippi or submit to the laws of those States.

Our conduct toward these people is deeply interesting to our national character. Their present condition, contrasted with what they once were, makes a more powerful appeal to our sympathies. Our ancestors found them the uncontrolled possessors of these vast regions. By persuasion and force they have been made to retire from river to river and from mountain to mountain, until some of the tribes have become extinct and others have left but remnants to preserve for a while their once terrible names. Surrounded by the whites with their arts of civilization, which by destroying the resources of the savage doom him to weakness and decay, the fate of the Mohegan, the Narraganset, and the Delaware is fast overtaking the Choctaw, the Cherokee, and the Creek. That this fate surely awaits them if they remain within the limits of the States does not admit of a doubt. Humanity and national honor demand that every effort should be made to avert so great a calamity. It is too late to inquire whether it was just in the United States to include them and their territory within the bounds of the new States, whose limits they could control. That step can not be retraced. A State can not be dismembered by Congress or restricted in the exercise of her constitutional power. But the people of those States and of every State, actuated by feelings of justice and a regard for our national honor, submit to you the interesting question whether something can not be done, consistently with the rights of the States, to preserve this much-injured race.

As a means of effecting this end I suggest for your consideration the propriety of setting apart an ample district west of the Mississippi, and without the limits of any State or territory now formed, to be guaranteed to the Indian tribes as long as they shall occupy it, each tribe having a distinct control over the portion designated for its use. There they may be secured in the enjoyment of governments of their own choice, subject to no other control from the Unites States than such as may be necessary to preserve peace on the frontier and between the several tribes. There the benevolent may endeavor to teach them the arts of civilization, and, by promoting union and harmony among them, to raise up an interesting commonwealth, destined to perpetuate the race and to attest the humanity and justice of this Government.

This emigration should be voluntary, for it would be as cruel as [it is] unjust to compel the aborigines to abandon the graves of their fathers and seek a home in a distant land. But they should be distinctly informed that if they remain within the limits of the States they must be subject to their laws. In return for their obedience as individuals, they will without doubt be protected in the enjoyment of those possessions which they have improved by their industry. But it seems to me visionary to suppose that in this state of things claims can be allowed on tracts of country on which they have neither dwelt nor made improvements, merely because they have seen them from the mountain or passed them in the chase. Submitting to the laws of the States, and receiving, like other citizens, protection in their person and property, they will ere long become merged in the mass of our population . . .

Andrew Jackson

*

Register of Debates in Congress, April 9, 1830

. . . God, in his providence, planted these tribes on this Western continent, so far as we know, before Great Britain herself had a political existence. I believe, sir, it is not now seriously denied that the Indians are men, endowed with kindred faculties and powers with ourselves; that they have a place in human sympathy, and are justly entitled to a share in the common bounties of a benignant Providence. And, with this conceded, I ask in what code of the law of nations, or by what process of abstract deduction, their rights have been extinguished?

Where is the decree or ordinance that has stripped these early and first lords of the soil? Sir, no record of such measure can be found. And I might triumphantly rest the hopes of these feeble fragments of once great nations upon this impregnable foundation. However mere human policy, or the law of power, or the tyrant's pleas of expediency, may have found it convenient at any or in all times to recede from the unchangeable principles of eternal justice, no argument can shake the political maxim, that, where the Indian always has been, he enjoys an absolute right still to be, in the free exercise of his own modes of thought, government and conduct.

In the light of natural law, can a reason for a distinction exist in the mode of enjoying that which is my own? If I use it for hunting, may another take it because he needs it for agriculture? I am aware that some writers have, by a system of artificial reasoning, endeavored to justify, or rather excuse the encroachments made upon Indian territory; and they denominate these abstractions the law of nations, and, in this ready way, the question is despatched. Sir, as we trace the sources of this law, we find its authority to depend either upon the conventions or common consent of nations. And when, permit me to inquire, were the Indian tribes ever consulted on the establishment of such a law? Whoever represented them or their interests in any congress of nations, to confer upon the public rules of intercourse, and the proper foundations of dominion and property? The plain matter of fact is, that all these partial doctrines have resulted from the selfish plans and pursuits of more enlightened nations; and it is not matter of any great wonder, that they should so largely partake of a mercenary and exclusive spirit toward the claims of the Indians.

It is, however, admitted, sir, that, when the increase of population and the wants of mankind demand the cultivation of the earth, a duty is thereby devolved upon the proprietors of large and uncultivated regions, of devoting them to such useful purposes. But such appropriations are to be obtained by fair contract, and for reasonable compensation. It is, in such a case, the duty of the proprietor to sell: we may properly address his reason to induce him; but we cannot rightfully compel the cession of his lands, or take them by violence, if his consent be withheld. It is with great satisfaction that I am enabled, upon the best authority, to affirm, that this duty has been largely and generously met and fulfilled on the part of the aboriginal peoples of this continent. Several years ago, official reports to Congress stated the amount of Indian grants to the United States to exceed 214 millions of acres. Yes, sir, we have acquired, and now own more land as the fruits of their bounty th[a]n we shall dispose of at the present rate to actual settlers in two hundred years. For, very recently, it has been ascertained, on this floor, that our public sales average not more than about one million of acres annually. It greatly aggravates the wrong that is now meditated against these tribes, to survey the rich and ample districts of their territories, that either force or persuasion have incorporated then our pubic domains. As the tide of our population rolled on, we have added purchase to purchase. The confiding Indian listened to our professions of friendship: we called him brother, and he believed us. Millions after millions he has yielded to our importunity, until we have acquired more than can be cultivated in centuries – and yet we crave more. We have crowded the tribes upon a few miserable acres on our southern frontier: it is all that is left to them of their once boundless forests: and still, like the horse-leech, our insatiated cupidity cries, give! give!

Before I proceed to deduce the collateral confirmations of this original title, from all our political intercourse and conventions with the Indian tribes, I beg leave to pause a moment and view the case as it lies beyond the treaties made with them; and aside also from all conflicting claims between the confederation, and the colonies, and the Congress of the States. Our ancestors found these people, far removed from the commotions of Europe, exercising all the rights, and enjoying all the privileges, of free and independent sovereigns of this new world. They were not a wild and lawless horde of banditti, but lived under the restraints of government, patriarchal in its character, and energetic in its influence. They had chiefs, head men, and councils. The white men, the authors of all their wrongs, approached them as friends – they extended the olive branch; and, being then a feeble colony and at the mercy of the native tenants of the soil, by presents and professions, propitiated their good will. The Indian yielded a slow, but substantial confidence; granted to the colonists an abiding place; and suffered them to grow up to man's estate beside him. He never raised the claim of elder title: as the white man's wants increased, he opened the hand of his bounty wider and wider. By and by, conditions are changed. His people melt away; his lands are constantly coveted; millions after millions are ceded. The Indian bears it all meekly; he complains, indeed, as well he may; but suffers on: and now he finds that this neighbor, whom his kindness had nourished, has spread an adverse title over the last remains of his patrimony, barely adequate to his wants, and turns upon him, and says, "Away, we cannot endure you so near us! These forests and rivers, these groves of your fathers, these firesides and hunting grounds, are ours by the right of power, and the force of numbers." Sir, lf every treaty be blotted from our records, and in the judgment of natural and unchangeable truth and justice, I ask, who is the injured, and who is the aggressor? Let conscience answer, and I fear not the result. Sir, let those who please, denounce the public feeling on this subject as the morbid excitement of a false humanity; but I return with the inquiry, whether I have not presented the case truly, with no feature of it overcharged or distorted? And in view of it, who can help feeling, sir? Do the obligations of justice change with the color of the skin? Is it one of the prerogatives of the white man, that he may disregard the dictates of moral principles, when an Indian shall be concerned? No, sir. In that severe and impartial scrutiny, which futurity will cast over this subject, the righteous award will be, that those very causes which are now pleaded for the relaxed enforcement of the rules of equity, urged upon us not only a rigid execution of the highest justice, to the very letter, but claimed at our hands a generous and magnanimous policy.

Standing here, then, on this unshaken basis, how is it possible that even a shadow of claim to soil, or jurisdiction, can be derived, by forming a collateral issue between the State of Georgia and the General Government? Her complaint is made against the United States, for encroachments on her sovereignty. Sir, the Cherokees are no parties to this issue; they have no part in this controversy. They hold by better title than either Georgia or the Union. They have nothing to do with State sovereignty, or United States sovereignty. They are above and beyond both. True, sir, they have made treaties with both, but not to acquire title or jurisdiction; these they had before – ages before the evil hour to them, when their white brothers fled to them for an asylum. They treated to secure protection and guarantee for subsisting powers and privileges; and so far as those conventions raise obligations, they are willing to meet, and always have met, and faithfully performed them; and now expect from a great people, the like fidelity to plighted covenants ...

It is a subject full of grateful satisfaction, that, in our public intercourse with the Indians, ever since the first colonies of white men found an abode on these Western shores, we have distinctly recognized their title; treated with them as owners, and in all our acquisitions of territory, applied ourselves to these ancient proprietors, by purchase and cession alone, to obtain the right of soil. Sir, I challenge the record of any other or different pretension. When, or where, did any assembly or convention meet which proclaimed, or even suggested to these tribes, that the right of discovery contained a superior efficacy over all prior titles?

And our recognition was not confined to the soil merely. We regarded them as nations – far behind us indeed in civilization, but still we respected their forms of government – we conformed our conduct to their notions of civil policy. We were aware of the potency of any edict that sprang from the deliberations of the council fire, and when we desired lands, or peace, or alliance, to this source of power and energy, to this great level of Indian government we addressed our proposals – to this alone did we look; and from this alone did we expect aid or relief ...

Every administration of this Government, from President Washington's, have, with like solemnities and stipulations, held treaties with the Cherokees; treaties, too, by almost all of which we obtained further acquisitions of their territory. Yes, sir, whenever we approached them in the language of friendship and kindness, we touched the chord that won their confidence; and now, when they have nothing left with which to satisfy our cravings, we propose to annul every treaty – to gainsay our word – and by violence and perfidy, drive the Indian from his home ...

[Here Frelinghuysen outlined in detail the treaties and agreements previously made with the Cherokee.]

I trust, sir, that this brief exposition of our policy, in relation to Indian affairs, establishes, beyond all controversy, the obligation of the United States to protect these tribes in the exercise and enjoyment of their civil and political rights. Sir, the question has ceased to be – What are our duties? An inquiry much more embarrassing is forced upon us: How shall we most plausibly, and with the least possible violence break our faith? Sir, we repel the inquiry – we reject such an issue – and point the guardians of public honor to the broad, plain ... [path] of faithful performance, and to which they are equally urged by duty and interest ...

Senator Frelinghuysen of New Jersey

Sources: Gary E. Moulton, ed., *The Papers of Chief John Ross*, vol. 1 (University of Oklahoma Press, 1985), pp. 154–7; James D. Richardson, ed., *A Compilation of the Messages and Papers of the Presidents, 1789–1897* (US Government Printing Office, 1896), pp. 456–9; *Register of Debates in Congress*, 6: 311–16, in Francis Paul Prucha, ed., *Documents of United States Indian Policy* (University of Nebraska Press, 2000 [1975]), pp. 48–52.

Study and further exploration: The best short study of the Cherokee crisis also introduces students to the kinds of documents that are available for its study: Theda Perdue and Michael D. Green, eds., *The Cherokee Removal: A Brief History with Documents* (Bedford/St. Martin's, 2005). People from many walks of life were involved in the debate in their newspapers, magazines, diaries, and letters; it was indeed a crucial moment in American history. Other related documents are available on the website of the American Native Press Archives, based at the University of Arkansas.

6. Black Hawk's Autobiography

The Cherokee resisted forced removal through their newspaper, visits to Washington, DC and legal cases brought to the Supreme Court. Indians with less capital and education resisted in other ways. The Sauk, who lived at the confluence of the Rock and Mississippi Rivers, resisted pressure to remove to the west side of the great river as long as they could. Some bands signed a treaty ceding their territory, but other bands refused. Eventually, in late 1831, even they left at gunpoint. But early the next spring, one band returned under the leadership of a man named Black Hawk. Traditionally, the Sauk had lived at their great town of Saukenuk in the spring and summer, planting and harvesting their corn. When winter came they dispersed into much smaller bands and headed out to hunt. On the other side of the Mississippi, Black Hawk's band found that they could not obtain enough to eat and so they decided to return home to plant their corn. Black Hawk had been convinced by a prophet that the settlers would not hurt them because the British up in Canada would provide arms and numerous other tribes would join them in their peaceful (yet menacing) protest.

The US sent the military against the Indians; many of them were killed as they desperately attempted to recross the Mississippi. Black Hawk was captured and taken east. Later, at Fort Armstrong, he told his life story to Antoine LeClaire, who was part French, part Potawatomi, and spoke Sauk. Then the text was edited and published by John Patterson. It is not certain how Black Hawk's words may have been altered by the two intermediaries, but scholars agree that the narrative is typically indigenous both in the nature of the events it includes and in its general perspective. In a series of what at first seem to be digressions, Black Hawk ultimately explains to the world what he and his fellows were thinking. He had been deeply happy and proud as a warrior in his youth. During the time of the War of 1812, he had learned to trust the British more than the Americans. When he was at last induced to leave his people's farmlands, he was promised corn on the other side of the river, but only a small proportion of the corn ever materialized. Thus when a prophet whom he trusted said it would be effective simply to march home with his people, he chose to believe him. In this excerpt, Black Hawk describes how he was pressured to leave in the first place, making it clear – to an Indian audience, at least – why he did not consider the arrangement binding.

... Our pastimes and sports had been laid aside for two years. We were a divided people, forming two parties Ke-o-cuck being at the head of one, willing to barter our rights merely for the good opinion of the whites; and cowardly enough to desert our village to them. I was at the head of the other party, and was determined to hold on to my village, although I had been *ordered* to leave it. But, I considered, as myself and band had no agency in selling our country – and that as provision had been made in the treaty, for us all to remain on it as long as it belonged to the United States [and not to an individual buyer], that we could not be *forced* away. I refused, therefore, to quit my village. It was here, that I was born – and here lie the bones of many friends and relations. For this spot I felt a sacred reverence, and never could consent to leave it, without being forced therefrom.

When I called to mind the scenes of my youth, and those of later days – and reflected that the theatre on which these were acted, had been so long the home of my fathers, who now slept on the hills around it, I could not bring my mind to consent to leave this country to the whites for any earthly consideration.

The winter passed off in gloom. We made a bad hunt, for want of guns, traps, etc that the whites had taken from our people for whiskey! The prospect before us was a bad one. I fasted, and called upon the Great Spirit to direct my steps to the right path. I was in great sorrow – because all the whites with whom I was acquainted, and had been on terms of friendship, advised me so contrary to my wishes, that I began to doubt whether I had a *friend* among them.

Ke-o-kuck, who has a smooth tongue, and is a great speaker, was busy in persuading my band that I was wrong – and thereby making many of them dissatisfied with me. I had one consolation – for all the women were on my side, on account of their corn-fields.

On my arrival again [that spring] at my village, with my band increased, I found it worse than before [with more white settlers]. I visited Rock Island. The *agent* [of the federal government] then ordered me to quit my village, he said, that if we did not, troops would be sent to drive us off. He reasoned with me, and told me, it would be better for us to be with the rest of our people, so that we might avoid difficulty, and live in peace The *interpreter* joined him, and gave me so many good reasons, that I almost wished I had not undertaken the difficult task that I had pledged myself to my brave band to perform [in resisting]. In this mood, I called upon the trader, who is fond of talking, and had long been my friend, but now amongst those advising me to give up my village. He received me very friendly, and went on to defend Ke-o-kuck in what he had done, and endeavored to show me that I was bringing distress on our women and children. He inquired, if some terms could not be made, that would be honorable to me, and satisfactory to my braves, for us to remove to the west side of the Mississippi? I replied, that if our Great Father [in Washington] would do us justice, and would make the proposition, I could then give up honorably. He asked me, "if the great chief at St. Louis would give us six thousand dollars to purchase provisions and other articles [to get started in a new home], if I would give up peaceably, and remove to the West side of the Mississippi?" After thinking some time, I agreed that I could honorably give up, by being paid for it, according to our customs; but told him, that I could not make the proposal myself, even if I wished, because it would be dishonorable in me to do so. He said he would do it, by sending word to the great chief at St. Louis, that he could remove us peaceably, for the amount stated, to the west side of the Mississippi. A steam-boat arrived at the island during my stay. After its departure, the trader told me that he had requested a war chief, who was stationed at Galena, and was on board the steam-boat, to make the offer to the great chief at St. Louis, and that he would soon be back, and bring his answer. I did not let my people know what had taken place, for fear they would be displeased. I did not like what had been done, and tried to banish it from my mind.

After a few days had passed, the war chief returned, and brought for answer, that "the great chief at St. Louis would give us nothing! – and said if we did not remove immediately we should be *drove* off!"

I was not much displeased with the answer brought by the war chief, because I would rather have laid my bones with my forefathers than remove for any consideration. Yet if a friendly offer had been made, as I expected, I would, for the sake of my women and children, have moved peaceably.

I now resolved to remain in my village, and make no resistance, if the military came, but submit to my fate! I impressed the importance of this course on all my band, and directed them, in case the military came, not to raise an arm against them . . .

Our women had planted a few patches of corn, which was growing finely, and promised a subsistence for our children – *but the white people again commenced plowing it up!* I now determined to put a stop to it, by clearing our country of the *intruders*. I went to the principal men [among the settlers] and told them that they must and should leave our country – and gave them until the middle of the next day, to remove it.[5] The worst left within the time appointed – but the one who remained, represented, that his family, (which was large,) would be in a starving condition, if he went and left his crop – and promised to behave well, if I would consent to let him remain until fall, in order to secure his crop. He spoke reasonably, and I consented.

We now resumed our games and pastimes – having been assured by the prophet [who lived upriver] that we would not be removed. But in a little while it was ascertained, that a great war chief [General Gaines] with a large number of soldiers was on his way to Rock river. I again called upon the prophet, who requested a little time to see into the matter, early next morning he came to me, and said he had been *dreaming*. "That he saw nothing bad in this great war chief, who was now near Rock river. That the *object* of his mission was to *frighten* us from our village, that the great white people might get our land for *nothing*!" He assured us that this "great war chief dare not, and would not hurt any of us. That the Americans were at peace with the British, and when they made peace, the British required, (which the Americans

[5] Black Hawk means that he threatened them with violence if they did not leave.

agreed to,) that they should never interrupt any nation of Indians that was at peace – and that all we had to do to retain our village, was to *refuse* any, and every offer that might be made by this war chief.

The war chief arrived, and convened a council at the agency. Ke-o-kuck and Wa-pe-lo were sent for, and came with a number of their band. The council house was opened, and they were all admitted. Myself and band were then sent for to attend the council. When we arrived at the door, singing a *war song*, and armed with lances, spears, war clubs and bows and arrows, as if going to battle, I halted, and refused to enter – as I could see no necessity or propriety in having the room crowded with those who were already there. If the council was convened for us, why have others in the room? The war chief having sent all out, except Ke-o-kuck, Wa-pel-lo, and a few of their chiefs and braves, we entered the council house in this war-like appearance, being desirous to show the war chief that we were *not afraid*! He then rose and made a speech. He said:

"The president is very sorry to be put to the trouble and expense of sending a large body of soldiers here, to remove you from the land you have long since ceded to the United States. Your Great Father has already warned you repeatedly, through your agent, to leave the country; and he is very sorry to find that you have disobeyed his orders. Your Great Father wishes you well; and asks nothing from you but what is reasonable and right. I hope you will consult your own interests, and leave the country you are occupying, and go to the other side of the Mississippi."

I replied, "That *we* had never sold our country. *We* never received any annuities from our American father! And *we* are determined to hold onto our village!"[6]

The war chief, apparently angry, rose and said: – "Who is *Black Hawk*? Who is *Black Hawk*?"[7]

I responded: "I am *Sak* [Sauk]! My forefather was a SAC! And all the nations call me a SAC!"[8]

The war chief said: "I came here, neither to *beg* nor *hire* [pay] you to leave your village. My business is to remove you, peaceably if I can, but *forcibly*

[6] The Sauks who had signed a treaty were receiving an annuity, but Black Hawk pointed out that his band had never been consulted or included in these arrangements.

[7] The officer was questioning Black Hawk's authority to make demands as he was not descended from a chiefly line nor was he a medicine man. Rather his prowess as a warrior and charismatic personality had combined to render him the de facto leader of a large band. Matatas was the political chief and Black Hawk was, in effect, war chief.

[8] This was a legitimate line of political reasoning according to indigenous tradition. The corporate identity of an ethnic group was a composite bundle of the bands and individuals within it; any person could speak for the group as long as others agreed that he could speak on their behalf.

if I must! I will give you two days to remove in – and if you do not cross the Mississippi within that time, I will adopt measures to *force* you away."

I told him that I never could consent to leave my village and was determined not to leave it!

The council broke up, and the war chief retired to the fort. I consulted the prophet again! He said he had been dreaming, and that the Great Spirit had directed that a woman, the daughter of Mat-ta-tas, the old chief of the village, should take a stick in her hand and go before the war chief, and tell him that she is the daughter of Mat-ta-tas, and that he had always been the *white man's friend*! That he had fought their battles – been wounded in their service – and had always spoke well of them – and she had never heard him say that he had sold their village. The whites are numerous, and can take it from us if they choose, but she hoped they would not be so unfriendly. If they were, she had one favor to ask; she wished her people to be allowed to remain long enough to gather the provisions now growing in their fields; that she was a woman, and had worked hard to raise something to support her children! And, if we are driven from our village without being allowed to save our corn, many of our little children must perish with hunger!"

Accordingly, Mat-ta-tas' daughter was sent to the fort, accompanied by several of our young men. They were admitted. She went before the war chief, and told the story of the prophet! The war chief said that the president did not send him here to make treaties with the women, nor to hold council with them! That our young men must leave the fort, but she might remain if she wished![9]

All our plans were now defeated. We must cross the river, or return to our village and await the coming of the war chief with his soldiers. We determined on the latter; but finding that our agent, interpreter, trader, and Ke-o-kuck, (who were determined on breaking my ranks,) had seduced several of my warriors to cross the Mississippi, I sent a deputation to the agent, at the request of my band, pledging myself to leave the country in the fall, provided permission was given us to remain, and secure our crop of corn then growing – as we would be in a starving situation if we were driven off without means of subsistence.

The deputation returned with an answer from the war chief, "that no further time would be given than that specified, and if we were not then gone, he would remove us!"

I directed my village crier to proclaim, that my orders were, in the event of the war chief coming to our village to remove us, that not a gun should be fired nor any resistance offered. That if he determined to fight, for them to remain, quietly in their lodges, and let him *kill* them if he chose!

I felt conscious that this great war chief would not hurt our people – and my object was not *war*! Had it been, we could have attacked, and killed the war chief and his braves, when in council with us – as they were then

[9] The officer was making a lewd comment.

completely in our power. But his manly conduct and soldierly deportment, his mild, yet energetic manner, which proved his bravery, forbade it.

Some of our young men who had been sent out as *spies*, came in and reported, that they had discovered a large body of mounted men coming towards our village, who looked like a *war party*.[10] They arrived, and took a position below Rock river, for their place of encampment. The great war chief [General Gaines] entered Rock river in a steam-boat, with his soldiers and one big gun! They passed, and returned close by our village; but excited no alarm among my braves. No attention was paid to the boat by any of our people – even our little children, who were playing on the bank of the river, as usual, continued their amusement. The water being shallow, the boat got aground, which gave the whites some trouble. If they had asked for assistance, there was not a brave in my band, who would not willingly have aided them. Their people were permitted to pass and repass through our village, and were treated with friendship by our people.

The war chief appointed the next day to remove us! I would have remained and been taken prisoner by the *regulars*, but was afraid of the multitude of *pale faces*, who were on horse back, as they were under no restraint of their chiefs.[11]

We crossed the Mississippi during the night, and encamped some distance below Rock Island. The great war chief convened another council, for the purpose of making a treaty with us. In this treaty he agreed to give us corn in place of that we had left growing in our fields. I touched the goose quill to this treaty, and was determined to live in peace.

The corn that had been given us, was soon found to be inadequate to our wants ...

Source: Roger Nichols, ed., *Black Hawk's Autobiography* (Iowa State University Press, 1999), pp. 56–61.

Study: Kerry A. Trask, *Black Hawk: The Battle for the Heart of America* (Henry Holt, 2006).

Further exploration: We know what Black Hawk looked like because George Catlin (1796–1872) painted his portrait in 1832 (see fig. 6.6.1). The next year, Catlin began to display the painting in his traveling "Indian gallery." The painting was thus intended both to capture how Black Hawk wanted to be remembered and also what the American public might want to remember about him. Students who want to put the painting in context and then draw their own conclusions about it should begin with George Gurney and Therese Thau Heyman, eds., *George Catlin and His Indian Gallery* (Smithsonian American Art Museum, 2002).

[10] We are to understand that these were not soldiers, but armed citizens.

[11] Black Hawk had calculated that the US army ("the regulars") would take the group into custody with a minimum of bloodshed, but he had not foreseen the presence of the large body of armed volunteers. He feared – probably rightly – that they would be more willing to slaughter his people.

Figure 6.6.1 George Catlin, *Múk-a-tah-mish-o-káh-kaik, Black Hawk, Prominent Sac Chief* (1832)

7. William Apess's Condemnation of White America

In the early Republican era, most attention is generally given to the Indians on the frontiers of the ever expanding United States. However, Indians continued to live on the east coast, albeit in drastically reduced numbers and diminished circumstances. One of these, William Apess, became the first North American Indian to write a book. Apess, born in 1798, was of Pequot descent and grew up in Connecticut. His impoverished grandmother, in her desperation and unhappiness, nearly beat him to death at one point. He was then "bound out" to a white family as an indentured servant. (This was the equivalent of the foster care system in early America.) Later, he ran away and joined the army. He fought in the War of 1812, and after he was released in Canada, walked all the way home, passing right through Iroquoian (or Haudenosaunee) territory and seeing Indian communities intact for the first time. Back in Connecticut, he had a religious revival experience and spent the remaining years of his life working as a minister, a scholar of Native American history, and an activist on behalf of Indian people. One of his books, The Experiences of Five Christian

Indians *(1833) concludes with an essay entitled "An Indian's Looking-Glass for the White Man," which is an unqualified condemnation of the white world as he knew it. In 1837, when the book was reprinted, he removed that section, for reasons we will never know, and replaced it with a much briefer comment. Here is an excerpt from the original statement.*

Reader, I acknowledge that this is a confused world, and I am not seeking for office, but merely placing before you the black inconsistency that you place before me – which is ten times blacker than any skin that you will find in the universe. And now let me exhort you to do away that principle, as it appears ten times worse in the sight of God and candid men than skins of color – more disgraceful than all the skins that Jehovah ever made. If black or red skins or any other skin of color is disgraceful to God, it appears that he has disgraced himself a great deal – for he has made fifteen colored people to one white and placed them here upon this earth.

Now let me ask you, white man, if it is a disgrace to eat, drink, and sleep with the image of God, or sit, or walk, and talk with them. Or have you the folly to think that the white man, being one in fifteen or sixteen, are the only beloved images of God? Assemble all nations together in your imagination, and then let the whites be seated among them, and then let us look for the whites, and I doubt not it would be hard finding them; for to the rest of the nations, they are still but a handful. Now suppose these skins were put together, and each skin had its national crimes written upon it – which skin do you think would have the greatest? I will ask one question more. Can you charge the Indians with robbing a nation almost of their whole continent, and murdering their women and children, and then depriving the remainder of their lawful rights, that nature and God require them to have? And to cap the climax, rob another nation to till their grounds and welter out their days under the lash with hunger and fatigue under the scorching rays of a burning sun? I should look at all the skins, and I know that when I cast my eye upon the white skins, and if I saw those crimes written upon it, I should enter my protest against it immediately and cleave to that which is more honorable. And I can tell you that I am satisfied with the manner of my creation, fully – whether others are or not.

... Let me ask why the men of a different skin are so despised? Why are not they educated and placed in your pulpits? I ask if a marriage or a funeral ceremony or the ordinance of the Lord's house [for a man of color] would not be as acceptable in the sight of God as though he was white. And if so, why is it not to you? I ask again: Why is it not acceptable to have men to exercise their office in one place as well as in another? Perhaps you will say that if we admit you to all of these privileges you will want more. I expect that I can guess what that is – Why, say you, there would be intermarriages. How that would be I am not able to say – and if it should be, it would be nothing strange or new to me; for I can assure you that I know a great many that have intermarried, both of the whites and the Indians – and many are their sons and daughters and people, too, of the first respectability. And I could point to some in the famous city of Boston and elsewhere. You may look now at the disgraceful act in the statutes law passed by the legislature of Massachusetts, and behold the fifty-pound fine levied upon any clergyman or justice of the peace that dare to encourage the laws of God and nature by a legitimate union in holy wedlock between the Indians and whites. I would ask how this looks to your lawmakers. I would ask if this corresponds to your sayings – that you think as much of the Indians as you do of the whites. I do not wonder that you blush, many of you, while you read; for many have broken the ill-fated laws made by man to hedge up the laws of God and nature. I would ask if they who have made the law have not broken it – but there is no other state in New England that has this law but Massachusetts; and I think, as many of you do not, that you have done yourselves no credit.

But as I am not looking for a wife, having one of the finest cast ... you will see that it is not my object. And if I had none, I should not want anyone to take my right from me and choose a wife for me; for I think that I or any of my brethren have a right to choose a wife for themselves as well as the whites – and as the whites have taken the liberty to choose my brethren,[12] the Indians, hundreds and thousands of them, as partners in life, I believe the Indians have as much right to choose their partners among the whites if they wish. I would ask you if you can see anything inconsistent in your conduct and talk about the Indians. And if you do, I hope you will try to become more consistent. Now, if the Lord Jesus Christ, who is counted by all to be a Jew – and it is well known that the Jews are a colored people, especially those living in the East, where Christ was born – and if he should appear among us, would he not be shut out of doors by many, very quickly? And by those too who profess religion?

Source and study: Barry O'Connell, ed., *A Son of the Forest and Other Writings by William Apess, a Pequot* (University of Massachusetts Press, 1997), pp. 97–100.

Further exploration: All of Apess's writings are worth reading. He himself read everything he could find about King Philip's War and then gave a remarkable speech entitled "A Eulogy on King Philip" (reprinted in O'Connell, cited above). Students can look for the ways in which he understood the third and fourth documents of Chapter 4.

[12] Apess means Indian women. "Brethren" did not have a gender implication for him.

Questions for consideration

1. Based on what we know about the interactions between them, how do you think the Clatsops might have described Lewis and Clark? Will we ever be sure what they thought? What had they presumably learned from their neighbors' experiences with the Russians?
2. According to Tecumseh himself, what were the goals and methods of his generation's pan-Indianism?
3. Why would many Cherokees have believed it was important to have their own written language and newspaper?
4. What arguments were advanced in the 1820s to justify Indians being forced to leave their ancestral lands? What responses were offered by (a) Indians; (b) other whites?
5. In 1833, William Apess and Black Hawk both addressed white audiences in their written work. What did their public statements have in common? How did they differ?

Chapter 7 The Losing of the West

1. Charles Ohiyesa Eastman's Childhood Memories

Charles Eastman was born to the Dakota Sioux in Minnesota in about 1858. He was called Hakadah, meaning "the pitiful last one" because his mother died at his birth, but he later earned the name of Ohiyesa, "the winner." His father was involved in the Dakota uprising of 1862, and for years his family believed he had been hanged in retribution, as many participants were. But when Ohiyesa was about 15, his father suddenly reappeared, having spent the intervening years in prison. He had become convinced that if his people were to survive, they had to acculturate, and thus sent his son to a mission school in today's South Dakota. "Charles" was so successful as a student that he ended up traveling to other boarding schools, and eventually attended Dartmouth and then Boston University Medical School. He became the author of many books. People often asked him how he could move so easily from living a supposedly "primitive" lifestyle to meeting the demands of some of the finest American universities. In this excerpt from one of his works, he looks back from the vantage point of many years upon his experiences as a child in the Indian world and recalls the intellectual demands placed on native children.

It is commonly supposed that there is no systematic education of their children among the aborigines of this country. Nothing could be farther from the truth. All the customs of this primitive people were held to be divinely instituted, and those in connection with the training of children were scrupulously adhered to and transmitted from one generation to another.

The expectant parents conjointly bent all their efforts to the task of giving the new-comer the best they could gather from a long line of ancestors. A pregnant Indian woman would often choose one of the greatest characters of her family and tribe as a model for her child. This hero was daily called to mind. She would gather from tradition all of his noted deeds and daring exploits, rehearsing them to herself when alone. In order that the impression might be more distinct, she avoided company. She isolated herself as much as possible, and wandered in solitude, not thoughtlessly, but with an eye to the impress given by grand and beautiful scenery.

The Indians believed, also, that certain kinds of animals would confer peculiar gifts upon the unborn, while others would leave so strong an adverse impression that the child might become a monstrosity. A case of hare-lip was commonly attributed to the rabbit. It was said that a rabbit had charmed the mother and given to the babe its own features. Even the meat of certain animals was denied the pregnant woman, because it was supposed to influence the disposition or features of the child. Scarcely was the embryo warrior ushered into the world, when he was met by lullabies that speak of wonderful exploits in hunting and war. Those ideas which so fully occupied his mother's mind before his birth are now put into words by all about the child, who is as yet quite unresponsive to their appeals to his honor and ambition. He is called the future defender of his people, whose lives may depend upon his courage and skill. If the child is a girl, she is at once addressed as the future mother of a noble race.

In hunting songs, the leading animals are introduced; they come to the boy to offer their bodies for the sustenance of his tribe. The animals are regarded as his friends, and spoken of almost as tribes of people, or as his cousins, grandfathers and grandmothers. The songs of wooing, adapted as lullabies, were equally imaginative, and the suitors were often animals personified, while pretty maidens were represented by the mink and the doe.

Very early, the Indian boy assumed the task of preserving and transmitting the legends of his ancestors and his race. Almost every evening a myth, or a true story of some deed done in the past, was narrated by one of the parents or grandparents, while the boy listened with parted lips and glistening eyes. On the following evening, he was usually required to repeat it. If he was not an apt scholar, he struggled long with his task; but, as a rule, the Indian boy is a good listener and has a good memory, so that the stories were tolerably well mastered. The household became his audience, by which he was alternately criticized and applauded.

This sort of teaching at once enlightens the boy's mind and stimulates his ambition. His conception of his own future career becomes a vivid and irresistible force. Whatever there is for him to learn must be learned; whatever qualifications necessary to a truly great man he must seek at any expense of danger and hardship. Such was the feeling of the imaginative and brave young Indian. It became apparent to him in early life that he must accustom himself to rove alone and not to fear or dislike the impression of solitude.

It seems to be a popular idea that all the characteristic skill of the Indian is instinctive and hereditary. This is a mistake. All the stoicism and patience of the Indian are acquired traits, and continual practice alone makes him the master of the art of wood-craft. Physical training and dieting were not neglected. I remember that I was not allowed to have beef soup or any warm drink. The soup was for the old men. General rules of the young were never to take their food very hot, nor to drink much water.

My uncle, who educated me up to the age of fifteen years, was a strict disciplinarian and a good teacher. When I left the teepee in the morning, he would say: "Hakadah, look closely to everything you see"; and at evening, on my return, he used often to catechize me for an hour or so.

"On which side of the trees is the lighter-colored bark? On which side do they have most regular branches?"

It was his custom to let me name all the new birds I had seen during the day. I would name them according to the color or shape of the bill or their song or the appearance and locality of the nest – in fact, anything about the bird that impressed me as characteristic. I made many ridiculous errors, I must admit. He then usually informed me of the correct name. Occasionally I made a hit and this he would warmly commend.

He went much deeper into this science when I was a little older, that is, about the age of eight or nine years. He would say, for instance:

"How do you know that there are fish in yonder lake?"

"Because they jump out of the water for flies at mid-day."

He would smile at my prompt but superficial reply.

"What do you think of the little pebbles grouped together under the shallow water? And what made the pretty curved marks in the sandy bottom and the little sand-banks? Where do you find the fish-eating birds? Have the inlet and the outlet of a lake anything to do with the question?

He did not expect a correct reply at once to all the voluminous questions that he put to me on these occasions, but he meant to make me observant and a good student of nature …

Source: "An Indian Boy's Training," in Charles A. Eastman (Ohiyesa), *Indian Boyhood* (Little, Brown & Co., 1902), pp. 49–54.

Study: Eastman had a fascinating life. For a biography, see Raymond Wilson, *Ohiyesa: Charles Eastman, Santee Sioux* (University of Illinois Press, 1983).

Further exploration: Charles Eastman's books provide some of the richest material available on Native American life in his era. Students might also want to compare his work with that of Luther Standing Bear, a Lakota Sioux who wrote prolifically about his experiences.

2. Lone Dog's Winter Count, 1800–1870

Many indigenous people used pictographic records. The Plains Indians had a strong tradition in this regard. A man might tell his own life story, placing the work conspicuously on a shirt, blanket, or teepee, or he might work with others to tell the story of the band as a whole. The Sioux had a specialized tradition of what they called "winter counts," or what in English might be translated less literally as "year accounts," painted on deer or buffalo hides. Each year was represented by a small drawing of a noteworthy event, one that gave the year its name within a particular community. Often the tribal historian began the narrative before the moment of his birth. To gain the information he needed, he might consult older men's winter counts, or simply talk to elders and be guided by them. The recorder used red and black paint to create the images, often beginning in the center of the hide and spiraling outward. Periodically, the histories were brought out to the band's fire to inspire oral performances or be used for teaching the young.

The winter count on the cover of this book was made by a Yanktonai Sioux named Lone Dog. He began the story a number of years before he was born. It is probably coincidental that he began in the year equivalent to 1800 in the Western calendar, as other winter counts make no attempt to match the Western century. We have these images and their interpretation today because a colonel named Garrick Mallery, like many men of his generation, was interested in "salvaging" what he could of a disappearing culture, and was fascinated by Indian writing systems. In 1876 or 1877, Lieutenant Hugh Reed, knowing of his interest, brought him a drawing on paper that he had made of a hide shown to him by Basil Clement, who had been the interpreter at Fort Sully in Dakota territory in the mid-1870s. Clement said his hide was a copy of one made by a man named Lone Dog whom he had met shortly before near Fort Peck, Montana. Mallery published the images along with their translations in the bulletin of the US Geological and Geographical Survey in 1877, then continued to work on the project for 10 more years, publishing a more detailed version in the late 1880s. Mallery had in his possession only the copy on a piece of paper, of course. He produced the painting of the work we have today in order to convey what Lone Dog's winter count would have looked like in its original form. Later, though, in 1906, a buffalo hide bearing exactly the same images came into the possession of the Smithsonian Institution. It may well be Lone Dog's original work.[1]

---

[1] Interestingly, the museum received two other copies many years later, one on cowhide in 1952 and one on deerhide in 1960. Lone Dog's work was obviously considered of vital importance within his own community.

1800–1: Thirty Dakotas[2] *were killed by Crow Indians. (Thirty parallel black lines in three columns. Such black lines always signify the death of Dakotas killed by their enemies.)*

1801–2. Many died of smallpox. (Head and body of a man covered with red blotches.)

1802–3. A Dakota stole horses with shoes on, i.e., stole them either directly from the whites or from some other Indians who had before obtained them from whites. (Device is a horseshoe.)

1803–4. They stole some "curly horses" from the Crows. (A horse with black marks for tufts. The Crows are known to have been early in the possession of horses.)

1804–5. The Dakota had a calumet dance and then went to war. (The device is a long pipestem, ornamented with feathers and streamers.)

1805–6. The Crows killed eight Dakotas. (Again the short parallel black lines.)

1806–7. A Dakota killed an Arikara (Ree) as he was about to shoot an eagle. (The head and shoulders of a man with a red spot of blood on his neck, with a line drawn to a golden eagle.)

1807–8. Red Coat, a chief, was killed. (The red coat pierced by two arrows.)

[2] When Mallery wrote, all the Sioux were referred to as "Dakotas." Now we understand that only the eastern branches in today's Minnesota called themselves that. Lone Dog was a Yanktonai Sioux. In his work he referred not only to the Yantonai and Yankton bands (both middle region or Nakota Sioux), but also to six of the seven subgroups of the western or Lakota Sioux, with whom his people were obviously in close communication: the Two Kettles, Uncpapas, Blackfeet Lakota, Minneconjous, Sans Arcs, and Brulés. (The Oglala were the seventh group.)

1808–9. The Dakota who had killed the Ree was himself killed by the Rees. (He is represented running, and shot with two arrows.)

1809–10. A chief, Little Beaver, set fire to a trading store, and was killed. (The character simply designates his name totem.)

1810–11. Black-Stone made medicine. (A man figure, with the head of an albino buffalo held over his own.)

1811–12. The Dakota fought a battle with the Gros Ventres and killed a great many. (A circle inclosing three round objects with flat bases, resembling heads severed from trunks, which are too minute in this device for decision of objects represented; but they appear more distinctly in the record for 1864–5 as the heads of enemies slain in battle.)

1812–13. Wild horses were first run and caught by the Dakotas. (A lasso.)

1813–14. The whooping cough was very prevalent and fatal. (Sign is suggestive of a blast of air coughed out. Similar representations of this disease found in other winter counts.)

1814–15. A Dakota killed an Arapaho in his lodge. (A tomahawk or battle axe, the red being blood from the cleft skull.)

1815–16. The Sans Arcs made the first attempt at a dirt lodge. (This was at Peoria Bottom, Dakota.)

1816–17. "Buffalo belly was plenty." (A side of buffalo.)

1817–18. La Framboise, a Canadian, built a trading store with dry timber. (The dryness is shown by the dead tree.)

1818–19. The measles broke out and many died. (The head of this figure is clearly distinguished from that in 1801–2.)

1819–20. Another trading store was built, this time by Louis La Conte, at Fort Pierre, Dakota. (His timber, as one of the Indians consulted especially mentioned, was rotten, not dry.)

1820–1. The trader, La Conte, gave Two Arrow a war dress for his bravery. (The sign shows the two arrows as the warrior's name-totem.)

1821–2. The falling to earth of a very brilliant meteor.

1822–3. Another trading house was built, which was by a white man called Big-Leggings, and was at the mouth of the Little Missouri or Bad River.

1823–4. White soldiers made their first appearance in the region. (So said the [original] interpreter, Clement, but from the unanimous interpretation of others the event portrayed is the attack of the United States forces accompanied by Dakotas upon the palisaded Arikara villages.)

1824–5. Swan, chief of the Two-Kettle tribe, had all of his horses killed. (A horse pierced by a lance.)

1825–6. There was a remarkable flood in the Missouri river and a number of Indians were drowned. (The symbol may suggest heads appearing above a line of water, and this is more distinct in some other winter counts.)

1826–7. An Indian died of the dropsy. (So Clement said. The interpretations of other charts explained, however, that some Dakotas on the war path had nearly perished with hunger when they found and ate the rotting carcass of an old buffalo on which the wolves had been feeding. They were seized soon after with pains in the stomach, their abdomens swelled, and gas poured from the mouth. The disease is termed tympanites, the external appearance occasioned by it much resembling that of dropsy.)

1827–8. Dead-Arm was stabbed with a knife or dirk by a Mandan.

1828–9. A white man named Shadran built a dirt lodge. (In 1877 he was still living in the neighborhood.)

1829–30. A Yanktonai Dakota was killed by Bad-Arrow Indians. (Bad-Arrow Indians is a Dakota name for a certain band of Blackfeet Indians.)

1830–1. Bloody battle with the Crows, of whom it is said twenty-three were killed. (Nothing in the sign denotes number.)

1831–2. Le Beau, a white man, killed another named Kermel. (Le Beau was still alive in 1877.)

1832–3. Lone-Horn had his leg killed. (The single horn is on the figure. Not unlike the character for 1808–9, where running is depicted.)

1833–4. The stars fell. (Great meteoric shower observed all over the United States on the night of November 12.)

1834–5. The chief Medicine-Hide was killed. (It is distinguished from the character for 1830–1.)

1835–6. Lame-Deer shot a Crow Indian with an arrow; drew it out and shot him again with the same arrow. (Lame Deer was a distinguished chief among the hostiles in 1876.)

1836–7. Band's-Father, chief of the Two Kettles, died. (The device is nearly the same as that of 1816–17, denoting buffalo belly. Interpreter Fielder throws light on the subject by saying that this character was used to designate the year when The-Breast, father of The-Band, died. The character was the Buffalo Breast, a personal name.)

1837–8. A remarkably successful hunt, in which it is said 100 elk were killed.

1838–9. A dirt lodge was built for Iron Horn. (The other dirt lodge of 1815–16 has a mark of ownership, which this has not.)

1839–40. The Dakotas killed an entire village of Snake or Shoshoni Indians. (Tipi pierced by two arrows.)

1840–1. The Dakotas made peace with the Cheyennes. (The symbol of peace is the common one.)

1841–2. Feather-in-the-Ear stole 30 spotted ponies. (The spots are shown red, distinguishing them from the curly horses of 1803–4.)

1842–3. One-Feather raised a large war party against the Crows.

1843–4. The Sans Arcs made medicine to bring the buffalo. (In this instance, not the head of an albino buffalo.)

1844–5. The Minneconjous built a pine fort. (A pine tree connected with a tipi.)

1845–6. Plenty of buffalo meat. (Represented as hung upon poles and trees, with the sign for dry.)

1846–7. Broken-Leg died. (Compare 1832–3.)

1847–8. Two-Man was killed.

1848–9. Humpback was killed. (He was a distinguished chief of the Minneconjous.)

1849–50. The Crows stole a large drove of horses (it is said eight hundred) from the Brulés. (A camp or corral from which a number of horse tracks are departing.)

1850–1. A buffalo cow was killed in that year and an old woman found in her belly. [The questioner pressed for more information but could glean nothing clearly, except that the matter was connected with their religion.]

1851–2. Peace with the Crows. (Exchanging pipes for a peace smoke.)

1852–3. The Nez Percés came to Lone-Horn's lodge at midnight. (Touch-the-Clouds, a Minneconjou, son of Lone-Horn, when this cart was shown to him by the present writer, designated this character as being particularly known to him from the fact of its being his father's lodge. He remembered all about it from talk in his family.)

1853–4. Spanish blankets were first brought to the country.

1854–5. Brave Bear was killed. Gen. Harney made peace with a number of the tribes or bands of the Dakotas. (Executive document No. 94, 34th Congress, first session, Senate, contains the minutes of a council with delegations from nine of the bands of the Sioux – viz. the Two Kettle band, Lower Yankton, Uncpapas, Blackfeet Sioux, Minneconjous, Sans Arcs, Yantonnais [two bands], Brulés.)

1855–6. General Harney, called Putinska ("white beard" or "white mustache") made peace with a number of the tribes or bands of the Dakotas.

1856–7. Four-Horn was made a calumet or medicine man. (Four-Horn was one of the subchiefs of the Uncpapas.)

1857–8. The Dakotas killed a Crow squaw.

1858–9. Lone-Horn made buffalo medicine.

1859–60. Big-Crow, a chief, was killed by the Crows.

1860–1. The Chief called "The elk made you understand the voice while he was walking" made buffalo medicine.

1861–2. Buffalo were so plentiful that their tracks came close to the tipis. (The cloven-hoof mark is cleverly distinguished from the tracks of horses in 1849–50).

1862–3. Red-Feather, a Minneconjou, was killed.

1863–4. Eight Dakotas were killed. (Again the short, parallel black lines.)

1864–5. The Dakotas killed four Crows. (Four of the same rounded objects, like severed heads, shown in 1825–6, but these are bloody.)

1865–6. Many horses died for want of grass.

1866–7. Swan, father of Swan, chief of the Minneconjous in 1877, died. (His totem may be recognized as a swan swimming on the water.)

1867–8. Many flags were given by the Peace Commission. (Generals Sherman, Terry, and others met at Fort Leavenworth in August of 1867, and then between August 30 and September 13 held councils with the various bands of the Dakota Indians at Forts Sully and Thompson, and at the Yankton, Ponka and Santee reservations. Resulted in the Dakota Treaty of 1868.)

1868–9. Texas cattle were brought into the country.

1869–70. An eclipse of the sun. (This was August 7, 1869).

1870–1. The Uncpapas had a battle with the Crows. [Mallery notes from other records that 29 were killed, matching the total number of figures represented here. Crows typically lived within wooden enclosures, though in this case they were attacked by the Sioux at a small trading post established for them on the Upper Missouri River.]

Source: Garrick Mallery, "Picture-Writing of the American Indians," *Tenth Annual Report of the Bureau of American Ethnology, 1888–89* (US Government Printing Office, 1893), pp. 266–87. I have abridged Mallery's commentaries in several cases. When I depart from his wording I use brackets rather than parentheses.

Study and further exploration: The Smithsonian has an extraordinary collection of winter counts, and the curators have made images of these available internationally through a website: http://wintercounts.si.edu.

3. Sarah Winnemucca's Choices

As the Plains Indians faced the incoming US troops, they each had to learn to cope with a rapidly changing situation. Some fought until their people were nearly destroyed; others, bent on survival, chose to accommodate the strangers.

Sarah Winnemucca, who was born about 1844, was the daughter of a chief among the northern Paiutes of the Great Basin, in what is now Nevada. Between 1850 and 1870, she saw her people lose their way of life. She herself was sent to California for a Western education by her father, and she came home convinced that fighting the whites was a mistake that would only lead to the deaths of all her people. In the 1870s, when the embittered Bannocks and the Paiutes of the Malheur reservation rose in revolt, she was horrified, convinced that her father and many of her relatives were only going to get themselves killed. Thus she helped lead the army to the rebels' encampment, in exchange for being allowed to lead the members of her own band out.

Later, she became a vocal advocate on behalf of her people, touring, speaking, and writing. Indeed, she became the first Native American woman to publish a book. In this excerpt about her earlier involvement in the Bannock War, there is clear evidence that she took pride in her indigenous heritage and in the decisions of those who chose to fight, though she did not want her people to die. As the piece opens, she, along with two male scouts, is near Juniper Lake, seeking the rebel camp, when she spots what she believes is a familiar figure and hails him.

It was Lee Winnemucca, my brother, who had called out. "Oh, sister, have you brought us some good news? Have you come for us? Oh, dear sister, here I am standing and talking to you, knowing the great dangers you are in by coming here, and these men, too. The Bannocks are out in the mountains, looking out. Take off your hat and your dress and unbraid your hair, and put this blanket round you, so if they should come down they would not know who it is. Here is some paint. Paint your face quick. Here, men, hide your guns and take off your clothes and make yourselves look as well as you can."

All this was done as quickly as possible, and we were all dressed like the hostile Bannocks. I asked, –

"Where is our father?"

"We are all up over that mountain. We are but six miles from here."

"I must go to him. I have a message for him and for all our people, too."

"Oh, no, dear sister, you will be killed if you go there, for our brother Natchez has made his escape three days ago. They were going to kill him because he had saved the lives of three white men. Oh, dear sister, let me pray you not to go, for they will surely kill you, for they have said they will kill every one that comes with messages from the white people, for Indians who come with messages are no friends of ours, they say every night."

"But, dear brother, they will not know me."

"Yes, Oytes will [remember you], for he is their chief now, since Buffalo Horn is killed."

"Dear brother, I am sorry to tell you that I must go to my father, for I have come with a message from General O. O. Howard. I must save my father and his people if I lose my life in trying to do it, and my father's too. That is all right. I have come for you all. Now let us go."

The mountain we had to go over was very rocky and steep, almost perpendicular. Sometimes it was very hard for us to climb up on our hands and knees. But we got up at last, and looked down into the hostile encampment. Oh, such a sight my eyes met! It was a beautiful sight. About three hundred and twenty-seven lodges, and about four hundred and fifty warriors were down Little Valley catching horses, and some more were killing beef. The place looked as if it was all alive with hostile Bannocks. I began to feel a little afraid.

Source: Sarah Winnemucca Hopkins, *Life among the Paiutes: Their Wrongs and Claims* (G. P. Putnam's Sons, 1883), pp. 157–9.

Study: Many assertions have been made about this controversial figure. A good start would be Gae Whitney Canfield, *Sarah Winnemucca of the Northern Paiutes* (University of Oklahoma Press, 1983) and Sally Zanjani, *Sarah Winnemucca* (University of Nebraska Press, 2001).

4. The Views of George Armstrong Custer

George Armstrong Custer graduated last in his class at West Point in 1861, not long after the opening salvos of the Civil War. Due to the need for officers, he rose quickly through the ranks and, thanks to his charismatic personality, he soon gained a national reputation. After the war, he was named Lieutenant Colonel of the Seventh Cavalry and became a professional Indian fighter in the west. In 1874, he published My Life on the Plains, *in which he recounted in detail his participation in the Indian wars, complete with exciting battles, chase scenes, and rescues of young women. In the introduction, he shared his views of Native Americans with the reading public, believing that it was important for US citizens to face the idea that they should simply let the Indians die out. Two years later, he himself would be killed at the Battle of the Little Big Horn.*

If the character given to the Indian by [James Fenimore] Cooper and other novelists, as well as by well-meaning but mistaken philanthropists of a later day, were the true one; if the Indian were the innocent, simple-minded being he is represented, more the creature of romance than reality, imbued only with a deep veneration for the works of nature, freed from the passions and vices which must accompany a savage nature; if, in other words, he possessed all the virtues which his admirers and works of fiction ascribe to him, and were free from all the vices which those best qualified to judge assign to him, he would be just the character to complete the picture which is presented by the country embracing the Wichita mountains [in Kansas]. Cooper, to whose writings more than to those of any other author are the people speaking the English language indebted for a false and ill-judged estimate of the Indian character, might well have laid the scenes of his fictitious stories in this beautiful and romantic country.

It is to be regretted that the character of the Indian as described in Cooper's interesting novels is not the true one. But as, in emerging from childhood into the years of a maturer age, we are often compelled to cast aside many of our earlier illusions and replace them by beliefs less inviting but more real, so we, as a people, with opportunities enlarged and facilities for obtaining knowledge increased, have been forced by a multiplicity of causes to study and endeavor to comprehend thoroughly the character of the red man. So intimately has he become associated with the Government as ward of the nation, and so prominent a place among the questions of national policy does the much mooted "Indian question" occupy, that it behooves us no longer to study this problem from works of fiction, but to deal with it as it exists in reality. Stripped of the beautiful romance with which we have been so long willing to envelop him, transferred from the inviting pages of the novelist to the localities where we are compelled to meet with him, in his native village, on the war path, and when raiding upon our frontier settlements and lines of travel, the Indian forfeits his claim to the appellation of the "*noble* red man." We see him as he is, and, so far as all knowledge goes, as he ever has been, a *savage* in every sense of the word; not worse, perhaps, than his white brother would be similarly born and bred, but one whose cruel and ferocious nature far exceeds that of any wild beast of the desert. That this is true no one who has been brought into intimate contact with the wild tribes will deny . . .

To those who advocate the application of the laws of civilization to the Indian, it might be a profitable study to investigate the effect which such application produces upon the strength of the tribe as expressed in numbers. Looking at him as the fearless hunter, the matchless horseman and warrior of the Plains, where Nature placed him, and contrasting him with the reservation Indian, who is supposed to be reveling in the delightful comforts and luxuries of an enlightened condition, but who in reality is groveling in beggary, bereft of many of the qualities which in his wild state tended to render him noble, and heir to a combination of vices partly his own, partly bequeathed to him from the pale-face, one is forced, even against desire, to conclude that there is unending antagonism between the Indian nature and that with which his well-meaning white brother would endow him. Nature intended him for a savage state; every instinct, every impulse of his soul inclines him to it. The white race might fall into a barbarous state, and afterwards, subjected to the influence of civilization, be reclaimed and prosper. Not so the Indian. He cannot be himself and be civilized. He fades away and dies. Cultivation such as the white man would give him deprives him of his identity. Education, strange as it may appear, seems to weaken rather than strengthen his intellect. Where do we find any specimens of educated Indian eloquence comparing with that of such native, untutored orators as Tecumseh, Osceola, Red Jacket, and Logan?

Source: Gen. G. A. Custer, *My Life on the Plains, or, Personal Experiences with Indians* (New York: Sheldon & Co., 1874), pp. 11–19.

Study and further exploration: Dozens of books have been written on Custer, beginning in his own time and continuing through to ours. An interesting project would be to compare the treatment he has received in different time periods or by different segments of society.

5. Black Elk's Memories of the Battle of the Little Big Horn

In 1874, Custer led an expedition into the sacred Black Hills of South Dakota and confirmed reports that there was gold present in the region. The Lakota Sioux had in 1868 signed a treaty guaranteeing that they could keep that land, but now the US government told them they would have to give it up. The army issued orders that the people must all come to reside on reservations. In 1876, Custer led an attack on a large gathering of many bands in the valley of the Little Big Horn. He was certain that he could disperse them, but he and his men were annihilated. Of course, the army soon sent more troops, and by the end of the decade, the Sioux were defeated.

A young Oglala boy named Black Elk witnessed the famous battle. He grew up to be a medicine man, and in the late 1880s, seeking both knowledge and money, he accompanied Buffalo Bill's Wild West show to the east coast and to Europe for three years. In 1930, when he was an old man, a poet named John Neihardt came to talk to him, to record his story and his religious insights. Black Elk's son, Benjamin, translated. Surviving notes indicate that Neihardt changed and arranged what he heard, seeking to create the sort of "inspirational" figure that many whites in the twentieth century wanted to believe in. There is, however, clearly much of Black Elk in the narrative; it remains an invaluable text. Here Black Elk remembers the battle that no one who was there could ever forget.

My father woke me at daybreak and told me to go with him to take our horses out to graze, and when we were out there he said: "We must have a long rope on one of them, so that it will be easy to catch; then we can get the others. If anything happens, you must bring the horses back as fast as you can, and keep your eyes on the camp."

Several of us boys watched our horses together until the sun was straight above and it was getting very hot. Then we thought we would go swimming, and my cousin said he would stay with our horses till we got back. When I was greasing myself, I did not feel well; I felt queer. It seemed that something terrible was going to happen. But I went with the boys anyway. Many people were in the water now and many of the women were out west of the village digging turnips. We had been in the water quite a while when my cousin came down there with the horses to give them a drink, for it was very hot now.

Just then we heard the crier shouting in the Hunkpapa camp, which was not very far from us, "The chargers are coming! They are charging! The chargers are coming!" Then the crier of the Oglalas shouted the same words; and we could hear the cry going from camp to camp northward clear to the Santees and Yanktonais.

Everybody was running now to catch the horses. We were lucky to have ours right there just at that time. My older brother had a sorrel, and he rode away fast toward the Hunkpapas. I had a buckskin. My father came running and said: "Your brother has gone to the Hunkpapas without his gun. Catch him and give it to him. Then come right back to me." He had my six-shooter too – the one my aunt gave me. I took the guns, jumped on my pony and caught my brother. I could see a big dust rising just beyond the Hunkpapa camp and all the Hunkpapas were running around and yelling, and many were running wet from the river. Then out of the dusk came the soldiers on their big horses. They looked big and strong and tall and they were all shooting. My brother took his gun and yelled for me to go back. There was brushy timber just on the other side of the Hunkpapas, and some warriors were gathering there. He made for that place, and I followed him. By now women and children were running in a crowd downstream. I looked back and saw them all running and scattering up a hillside down yonder.

When we got into the timber, a good many Hunkpapas were there already and the soldiers were shooting above us so that leaves were falling from the trees where the bullets struck. By now I could not see what was happening in the village below. It was all dust and cries and thunder; for the women and children were running there, and the warriors were coming on their ponies.

Among us there in the brush and out in the Hunkpapa camp a cry went up: "Take courage! Don't be a woman! The helpless are out of breath!" I think this was when Gall stopped the Hunkpapas, who had been running away, and turned them back.

I stayed there in the woods a little while and thought of my vision. It made me feel stronger, and it seemed that my people were all thunder-beings and that the soldiers would be rubbed out.

Then another great cry went up out in the dust: "Crazy Horse is coming! Crazy Horse is coming!" Off toward the west and north they were yelling, "Hoka hey!" like big wind roaring, and making the tremolo; and you could hear eagle bone whistles screaming.

The valley went darker with dusk and smoke, and there were only shadows and a big noise of many cries and hoofs and guns. On the left of where I was I could hear the shod hoofs of the soldiers' horses going back into the brush and there was shooting everywhere. Then the hoofs came out of the brush, and I came out and was in among men and horses weaving in and out and going up-stream, and everybody was yelling, "Hurry! Hurry!" The soldiers were running upstream and we were all mixed there in the twilight and the great noise. I did not see much; but once I saw a Lakota charge at a soldier who stayed behind and fought and was a very brave man. The Lakota took the soldier's horse by the bridle, but the soldier killed him with a six-shooter. I was small and could not crowd in to where the soldiers were, so I did not kill anybody. There were so many ahead of me, and it was all dark and mixed up.

Soon the soldiers were all crowded into the river, and many Lakota too; and I was in the water awhile. Men and horses were all mixed up and fighting in the water, and it was like hail falling in the river. Then we were out of the river, and people were stripping dead soldiers and putting the clothes on themselves. There was a soldier on the ground and he was still kicking. A Lakota rode up and said to me: "Boy, get off and scalp him." I got off and started to do it. He had short hair and my knife was not very sharp. He ground his teeth. Then I shot him in the forehead and got his scalp.

Many of our warriors were following the soldiers up a hill on the other side of the river. Everybody else was turning back down stream, and on a hill away down yonder above the Santee camp there was a big dust, and our warriors whirling around in and out of it just like swallows, and many guns were going off.

I thought I would show my mother my scalp, so I rode over toward the hill where there was a crowd of women and children. On the way down there I saw a very pretty young woman among a band of warriors about to go up to the battle on the hill, and she was singing like this:

> Brothers, now your friends have come!
> Be brave! Be brave!
> Would you see me taken captive?

. . . When I got to the women on the hill they were all singing and making the tremolo to cheer the men fighting across the river in the dust on the hill. My mother gave a big tremolo just for me when she saw my first scalp.

I stayed there awhile with my mother and watched the big dust whirling on the hill across the river, and horses were coming out of it with empty saddles.

*

That evening everybody got excited and began shouting, "The soldiers are coming!" I looked, and there they were riding abreast right toward us. But it was some of our own men dressed in the soldiers' clothes. They were doing this for fun.

The scouts reported that the soldiers had not followed us and that everything was safe now. All over the camp there were big fires and kill dances all night long.

I will sing you some of the kill-songs that our people made up and sang that night. Some of them went like this:

> Long Hair[3] has never returned,
> So his woman is crying, crying.
> Looking over here, she cries.
>
> Long Hair, guns I had none.
> You brought me many. I thank you!
> You make me laugh!
>
> Long Hair, horses I had none!
> You brought me many. I thank you!
> You make me laugh!

[3] This was the Lakota name for Custer.

Long Hair, where he lies nobody knows
Crying, they seek him.
He lies over here.

Let go your holy irons[4]
You are not men enough to do any harm.
Let go your holy irons!

After awhile I got so tired dancing that I went to sleep on the ground right where I was.

My cousin, Black Wasichu, died that night.[5]

Source: John Neihardt, ed., *Black Elk Speaks: Being the Life Story of a Holy Man of the Oglala Sioux* (University of Nebraska Press, 2000 [1932]), pp. 82–6 and 98–9.

Study and further exploration: Black Elk's story became a major religious text of the twentieth century, beginning in the 1960s. The debate on the degree of Neihardt's manipulation has been widespread. On that subject, students might consult the appendices by Lori Utrecht found in the 2000 edition cited above: she includes a particular segment on the peace pipe as it was found in Neihardt's original notes, and as it appeared in the finished work. Students may also look at the full version of Neihardt's notes as published in Raymond J. DeMallie, ed., *The Sixth Grandfather: Black Elk's Teachings Given to John C. Neihardt* (University of Nebraska Press, 1984).

6. Elaine Goodale's Observations of the Ghost Dance

In 1886, a 23-year-old white woman from Massachusetts named Elaine Goodale traveled to the Great Sioux Reservation in the Dakota Territory to teach in a small village school. She worked there for three years, and became so good at the language that, in 1889, the commissioner of Indian Affairs appointed her supervisor of education in the Dakotas, a position that allowed her to travel and work with local people in the development of their schools. In 1890 she met Charles Eastman (Ohiyesa), a Sioux who had attended school in the east and returned to his people's reservation to work as a medical doctor. (See sections 1 and 7) She married him a year later. They had six children together and became known for their writings about Indian reform.

In the 1930s, Elaine Goodale Eastman wrote her own memoirs, mostly concerning the years she spent on the Great Sioux Reservation. In the late 1880s the millenarian "ghost dance movement" swept through the reservation, engendering fear in many white officials and causing them to prepare for an "uprising" on the part of the Indians.

---

[4] That is, guns.

[5] In an earlier section, Black Elk has told us that he was wounded in the battle.

While all this was going on, I set out matter-of-factly with my Sioux couple [as my guides] and camp outfit on a tour of inspection among the scattered schools. No courage was required for I had no thought of danger and regarded the scare-mongers with contempt. I visited the homes as usual and talked freely with everyone I met. I was received with the familiar kindness and treated to pounded meat with cherries and other native delicacies.

There was no secrecy about the dance which had caused such frantic alarm. It was held in the Open, with neither fire nor light, after the participants had fasted for a day or two and passed through the purifying ordeal of the sweat-lodge. Anyone might look on, and on a bright November night I joined a crowd of spectators near Porcupine Tail Butte – the only person who was not a Sioux.

Under the soft flow of the hunter's moon perhaps a hundred men, women and children, with clasped hands and fingers interlocked, swung in a great circle about their "sacred tree," chanting together the monotonous Ghost Dance songs. The hypnotic repetition of the words: "Once more we shall hunt the buffalo – Our Father has said it!" alternated with short invocations by prophet or priest and occasional intervals of wailing by the women – that musical heart-piercing sound which, once heard, is never forgotten. No one with imagination could fail to see in the rite a genuine religious ceremony, a faith which, illusory as it was, deserved to be treated with respect.

"You have your churches; why can we not have ours?" was the natural reaction of the people.

In the course of an hour or two, one of the worshipers would break abruptly from the ring, rush wildly about, and fall in a trance or faint, lying for some time motionless. One old woman fell so near me that I could have touched her. Presently she stirred, got to her feet unaided, and addressed the gathering in a strong voice:

"My children, I have seen those dear ones we lost long ago!"

"Ah-h-h! He-ye-ye!" responded the people.

"They are living in a most beautiful country covered with buffalo!"

"He-ye-ye! Ate heye lo!" (Our Father has said it.)

"Their tipis are of skins. They are feasting and playing. They are perfectly happy!" (After each statement the people intone their deep-voiced response.)

"Here everything looks hateful to me – how can I bear it!"

The congregation responds with groans and cries. Then the priest repeats that the Messiah will appear "with the new grass" in the spring and the vision will come true for all believers.

After listening to this strange litany for half the night, I lay down in my tent quite worn out with sympathetic excitement. The spell, or incantation, or rite continued with increasing fervor until dawn.

Source: Kay Graber, *Sister to the Sioux: The Memoirs of Elaine Goodale Eastman, 1885–1891* (University of Nebraska Press, 1985), pp. 148–9.

Study: There is an extensive literature on the significance of the ghost dance. Most recent works are Gregory Smoak, *Ghost Dances and Identity: Prophetic Religion and American Indian Ethnogenesis in the Nineteenth Century* (University of California Press, 2006) and Jeffrey Ostler, *The Plains Sioux and U.S. Colonialism from Lewis and Clark to Wounded Knee* (Cambridge University Press, 2004).

Further exploration: Many white men married (or at least had relationships with) native women. It rarely happened in reverse. However, a few other leading Native American figures in the nineteenth century were married to white women, and some of their letters survive. See, for example, Theresa Strouth Gaul, *To Marry an Indian: The Marriage of Harriett Gold and Elias Boudinot in Letters, 1823–1839* (University of North Carolina Press, 2005).

7. Charles Ohiyesa Eastman's Visit to Wounded Knee

Charles Ohiyesa Eastman, the Dakota Sioux who had gone to medical school in Boston and returned to work on the Pine Ridge Reservation, was there on December 29, 1890, when the Seventh Cavalry (the unit that had previously been destroyed at the Little Big Horn) headed out to Wounded Knee Creek, 18 miles away. The military men were jumpy because of the recent commotion around the ghost dance, and those back at the reservation offices thought they could hear the report of guns. Messengers soon returned to say that there had been some sort of engagement, and Big Foot's band of Minneconjou had been annihilated. It later was revealed that they were unarmed when they were killed.

At dusk, the Seventh Cavalry returned with their twenty-five dead and I believe thirty-four wounded, most of them by their own comrades, who had encircled the Indians, while few of the latter had guns. A majority of the thirty or more Indian wounded [whom they brought back] were women and children, including babies in arms. As there were not tents enough for all, Mr. Cook offered us the mission chapel, in which the Christmas tree still stood, for a temporary hospital. We tore out the pews and covered the [cold] floor with hay and quilts. There we laid the poor creatures side by side in rows, and the night was devoted to caring for them as best we could. Many were frightfully torn by pieces of shells, and the suffering was terrible. General Brooke placed me in charge and I had to do nearly all the work, for although the army surgeons were more than ready to help as soon as their own men had been cared for, the tortured Indians would scarcely allow a man in uniform to touch them. Mrs. Cook, Miss Goodale, and several of Mr. Cook's Indian helpers acted as volunteer nurses. In spite of all our efforts, we lost the greater part of them, but a few recovered, including several children who had lost all their relatives and who were adopted into kind Christian families.

On the day following the Wounded Knee massacre there was a blizzard, in the midst of which I was ordered out with several Indian police, to look for a policeman who was reported to have been wounded and left some two miles from the agency. We did not find him. This was the only time during the whole affair that I carried a weapon; a friend lent me a revolver which I put in my overcoat pocket, and it was lost on the ride. On the third day it cleared, and the ground was covered with an inch or two of fresh snow. We had feared that some of the Indian wounded might have been left on the field, and a number of us volunteered to go and see. I was placed in charge of the expedition of about a hundred civilians, ten or fifteen of whom were white men. We were supplied with wagons in which to convey any whom we might find still alive. Of course a photographer and several reporters were of the party.

Fully three miles from the scene of the massacre we found the body of a woman completely covered with a blanket of snow, and from this point on we found them scattered along as they had been relentlessly hunted down and slaughtered while fleeing for their lives. Some of our people discovered relatives or friends among the dead, and there was much wailing and mourning. When we reached the spot where the Indian camp had stood, among the fragments of burned tents and other belongings we saw the frozen bodies lying close together or piled one upon another. I counted eighty bodies of men who had been in the council and who were almost as helpless as the women and babes when the deadly fire began, for nearly all their guns had been taken from them. A reckless and desperate young Indian fired the first shot when the search for weapons was well under way, and immediately the troops opened fire from all sides, killing not only unarmed men, women, and children, but their own comrades who stood opposite them, for the camp was entirely surrounded.

It took all of my nerve to keep my composure in the face of this spectacle, and of the excitement and grief of my Indian companions, nearly every one of whom was crying aloud or singing his death song. The white men became very nervous, but I set them to examining and uncovering everybody to see if one were living. Although they had been lying untended in the snow and cold for two days and nights, a number had survived. Among them I found a baby of about a year old warmly wrapped and entirely unhurt. I brought her in, and she was afterward adopted and educated by an army officer. One man who was severely wounded begged me to fill his pipe. When we brought him into the chapel he was welcomed by his wife and daughters with cries of joy, but he died a day or two later.

Under a wagon I discovered an old woman, totally blind and entirely helpless. A few had managed to crawl away to some place of shelter and we found in a log store near by several who were badly hurt and others who had died after reaching there. After we had dispatched several wagon loads to the agency, we observed groups of warriors watching us from adjacent buttes; probably friends of the victims who had come there for the same purpose as ourselves. A majority of our party, fearing an attack, insisted that some one ride back to the agency for an escort of soldiers, and as mine was the best horse, it fell to me to go. I covered the eighteen miles in quick time and was not interfered with in any way, although if the Indians had meant mischief they could easily have picked me off from any of the ravines and gulches.

All this was a severe ordeal for one who had so lately put all his faith in the Christian love and lofty ideals of the white man. Yet I passed no hasty judgment, and was thankful that I might be of some service and relieve even a small part of the suffering.

Source: Charles A. Eastman (Ohiyesa), *From the Deep Woods to Civilization: Chapters in the Autobiography of an Indian* (University of Nebraska Press, 1977 [1916]), pp. 109–14.

Study: The killings at Wounded Knee constitute the culminating chapter of the classic work by Dee Brown, *Bury My Heart at Wounded Knee* (Holt, Rinehart & Winston, 1970).

Further exploration: There are other published primary accounts of the massacre at Wounded Knee written by Indian survivors and military men. See William S. E. Coleman, ed., *The Voices of Wounded Knee* (University of Nebraska Press, 2000). Students may want to compare the events with those that unfolded 400 years earlier at the first massacre of natives by Europeans on the American continent, which occurred at the feast of Toxcatl while Hernando Cortés's men were visiting the Aztec capital. See document 2.1 and James Lockhart, ed., *We People Here: Nahuatl Accounts of the Conquest of Mexico* (University of California Press, 1993).

8. Geronimo's Story of His Life

Region by region, the American West passed into the hands of white settlers. Group after group, the indigenous were confined to ever shrinking reservations. The Apache were the last to be permanently reduced to reservation living. The Warm Springs band led by a man named Victorio was not defeated until 1880. The US Army spent six more years chasing a small band of Chiricahua Apache led by the famous Geronimo and Naiche back and forth across the Mexican border. In the end, Geronimo did not surrender but was brought in through false promises. He and his people were sent to Florida, where they sickened and died of malaria. Finally, after significant popular protest, they were taken to Alabama, and then, in 1894, brought to the Kiowa and Comanche reservation in today's Oklahoma. There Geronimo was to die in 1909, but before he passed away, he agreed to work with S. M. Barrett, the area's superintendent of schools, on his autobiography. In 1913, after his death, Geronimo's people were allowed to return to the southwest. Many of them went to live on the reservation of the Mescalero Apache in New Mexico.

Dedicatory

Because he has given me permission to tell my story; because he has read the story and knows I try to speak the truth; because I believe that he is fair-minded and will cause people to receive justice in the future; and because he is chief of a great people, I dedicate this story of my life to Theodore Roosevelt, President of the United States.

GERONIMO

Introductory, by S. M. Barrett

I first met Geronimo in the summer of 1904, when I acted for him as interpreter of English into Spanish, and vice versa, in selling a war bonnet. After that he always had a pleasant word for me when we met, but never entered into a general conversation with me until he learned that I had once been wounded by a Mexican. As soon as he was told of this, he came to see me and expressed freely his opinion of the average Mexican, and his aversion to all Mexicans in general.

I invited him to visit me again, which he did, and upon his invitation, I visited him at his tepee in the Fort Sill Military reservation.

In the summer of 1905 Dr. J. M. Greenwood, superintendent of schools at Kansas City, Missouri, visited me, and I took him to see the chief. Geronimo was quite formal and reserved until Dr. Greenwood said, "I am a friend of General Howard, whom I have heard speak of you." "Come," said Geronimo, and led the way to a shade, had seats brought for us, put on his war bonnet, and serve watermelon à l'Apache (cut in big chunks), while he talked freely and cheerfully. When we left he gave us a pressing invitation to visit him again.

In a few days the old chief came to se me and asked about "my father." I said "you mean the old gentleman from Kansas City – he has returned to his home." "He is your father?" said Geronimo. "No," I said, "my father died twenty-five years ago, Dr. Greenwood is only my friend." After a moment's silence the old Indian spoke again, this time in a tone of voice intended to carry conviction, or at least to allow no further discussion. "Your natural father is dead, this man has been your friend and adviser from youth. By adoption he is your father. Tell him he is welcome to come to my home at any time." It was of no use to explain any more, for the old man had determined not to understand my relation to Dr. Greenwood except in accordance with Indian customs, and I let the matter drop.

In the latter part of that summer I asked the old chief to allow me to publish some of the things he had told me, but he objected, saying, however, that if I would pay him, and if the officers in charge did not object, he would tell me the whole story of his life. I immediately called at the fort (Fort Sill) and asked the officer in charge, Lieutenant Purington, for permission to write the life of Geronimo. I was promptly informed that the privilege would not be granted. Lieutenant Purington explained to me the many depredations committed by Geronimo and his warriors, and the enormous cost of subduing the Apaches, adding that the old Apache deserved to be hanged rather than spoiled by so much attention from civilians. A suggestion from me that our government had paid many solders and officers to go to Arizona and kill Geronimo and the Apaches, and that they did not seem to know how to do it, did not prove very gratifying to the pride of the regular army officer, and I decided to seek elsewhere for permission. Accordingly I wrote to President Roosevelt that here was an old Indian who had been held a prisoner of war for [almost] twenty years and had never been given a chance to tell his side of the story, and asked that Geronimo be granted permission to tell for publication, in his own way, the story of his life, and that he be guaranteed that the publication of his story would not affect unfavorably the Apache prisoners of war. By return mail I received word that the authority had been granted. In a few days I received word from Fort Sill that the President had ordered the officer in charge to grant permission as requested ...

Early in October I secured the services of an educated Indian, Asa Deklugie, son of Whoa, chief of the Nedni Apaches, as interpreter, and the work of compiling the book began.

Geronimo refused to talk when a stenographer was present, or to wait for corrections or questions when telling the story. Each day he had in mind what he would tell and told it in a very clear, brief manner. He might prefer to talk at his own tepee, at Asa Deklugie's house, in some mountain dell, or as he rode in a swinging gallop across the prairie; wherever his fancy led him, there he told whatever he wished to tell and no more. On the day that he first gave any portion of his autobiography he would not be questioned about any details, nor would he add another word, but simply said, "Write what I have spoken," and left us to remember and write the story without one bit of assistance. He would agree, however, to come on another day to my study, or any place designated by me, and listen to the reproduction (in Apache) of what had been told, and at such times would answer all questions or add information wherever he could be convinced that it was necessary.

He soon became so tired of book making that he would have abandoned the task but for the fact that he had agreed to tell the complete story. When he once gives his word, nothing will turn him from fulfilling his promise. A very striking illustration of this was furnished by him early in January, 1906. He had agreed to come to my study on a certain date, but at the appointed hour the interpreter came alone, and said that Geronimo was very sick with cold and fever. He had come to tell me that we must appoint another date, as he feared the old warrior had an attack of pneumonia. It was a cold day and the interpreter drew a chair up to the grate to warm himself after the exposure of the long ride. Just as he was seating himself he looked out of the window, then rose quickly and without speaking pointed to a rapidly moving object coming our way. In a moment I recognized the old chief riding furiously (evidently trying to arrive as soon as the interpreter did), his horse flecked with foam and reeling from exhaustion. Dismounting he came in and said in a hoarse whisper, "I promised to come. I am here."

I explained to him that I had not expected him to come on such a stormy day, and that in his physical condition he must not try to work. He stood for some time, and then without speaking left the room, remounted his tired pony, and with bowed head faced ten long mile of cold north wind – he had kept his promise.

When he had finished his story I submitted the manuscript to Major Charles W. Taylor, Eighteenth Cavalry, commandant, Fort Sill, Oklahoma, who gave me some valuable suggestions as to additional related information which I asked Geronimo to give. In most cases the old chief gave the desired information, but in some instances, he refused, stating his reasons for doing so …

The objection [was] raised to the mention on pages 73 and 74 of the manuscript of an attack upon Indians in a tent at Apache Pass or Bowie, by U.S. soldiers. The statement of Geronimo is, however, substantially confirmed by L.C. Hughes, editor of *The Star*, Tucson, Arizona.

On pages 90 and 91 of the manuscript, Geronimo criticized General Crook. This criticism is simply Geronimo's private opinion of General Crook. We deem it a personal matter and leave it without comment, as it in no way concerns the history of the Apaches …

Chapter XVII: The Final Struggle

… Soon General Miles was made commander of all the western posts, and troops trailed us continually. They were led by Captain Lawton, who had good scouts. The Mexican soldiers[6] also became more active and more

[6] Barrett's note: "Governor Torres of Sonora had agreed to cooperate with our [US] troops in exterminating or capturing the tribe."

numerous. We had skirmishes almost every day, and so we finally decided to break up into small bands. With six men and four women I made for the range of mountains near Hot Springs, New Mexico. We passed many cattle ranches, but had no trouble with the cowboys. We killed cattle to eat whenever we were in need of food, but we frequently suffered greatly for water. At one time we had no water for two days and nights and our horses almost died from thirst. We ranged in the mountains of New Mexico for some time, then thinking that perhaps the troops had left Mexico, we returned. On our return through Old Mexico we attacked every Mexican found, even if for no other reason than to kill. We believed they had asked the United States troops to come down to Mexico to fight us.

South of Casa Grande, near a place called by the Indians Gosoda, there was a road leading out from the town. There was much freighting carried on by the Mexicans over this road. Where the road ran through a mountain pass we stayed in hiding, and whenever Mexican freighters passed we killed them, took what supplies we wanted, and destroyed the remainder. We were reckless of our lives, because we felt that every man's hand was against us. If we returned to the reservation we would be put in prison and killed; if we stayed in Mexico they would continue to send solders to fight us; so we gave no quarter to anyone and asked no favors.

Figure 7.8.1 "How the Book was Made"

Figure 7.8.2 "Dressed as in Days of Old"

Figure 7.8.3 "Last of the Bedonkohe Apache Tribe: Tuklonnen, Nadeste, Nah-ta-neal, Porica (White Horse)"

Figure 7.8.4 "Apache Princess: Daughter of Naiche, chief of the Chiricahua Apaches"

Source: S. M. Barrett, ed., *Geronimo's Story of His Life* (Garrett Press, 1969 [1906]), pp. iii–xxvi and 140–1. Figures 7.8.1–7.8.4 (above) are from this book, pages vii, 8, 18, 38

Study: There are numerous biographies of Geronimo. An interesting one is Peter Aleshire, *The Fox and the Whirlwind: General Geroge Crook and Geronimo: A Paired Biography* (John Wiley, 2000).

Further exploration: There are some published primary sources which were produced by US military men. See, for example, Louis Kraft, ed., *Lieutenant Charles Gatewood and His Apache Wars Memoir* (University of Nebraska Press, 2005). An anthropologist named Eve Ball lived among the Apache in the mid twentieth century and recorded some of their stories, but her methods were idiosyncratic and it is often difficult to tell which words were hers and which theirs. A responsible sifting of the evidence is Sherry Robinson, *Apache Voices: Their Stories of Survival as Told to Eve Ball* (University of New Mexico Press, 2000).

Questions for consideration

1. How did young people on the Great Plains learn about their history and culture, and come to embrace what was expected of them?
2. What kind of events were considered most memorable to the keepers of the winter counts? What can we learn about their mental framework at that time?
3. Confronted with the US Cavalry, the Indians of the west made different choices. Do the narratives of Sarah Winnemucca and Black Elk make you think that people often felt torn, or that different types of people simply had dramatically different reactions to the situation?
4. It has become popular in recent years to recast George Armstrong Custer as one who sympathized with Indians, as he was critical of the reservation system and did not believe it would ever be effective. What is left out of this account of his views? Why do you think it is comforting to people today to quote selectively from his works?
5. Why did Charles Eastman (Ohiyesa) not express his pain and anger about what he saw at Wounded Knee more directly?
6. Why do you think Geronimo was willing to participate in the proposed autobiography project? Was he being used? Is there another way to look at the matter?

Chapter 8 Surviving Assimilation and the National Imagination

1. The 1887 Statement of the Commissioner of Indian Affairs

When the United States came into being, Native American issues were handled by the War Department. It was not until 1849 that the "Indian Office" was moved to the Department of the Interior. From the 1870s onward, with the tribes of the Great Plains defeated and nearly all Indians living on reservations, the Bureau of Indian Affairs formed an extensive bureaucracy. Every year, the Commissioner produced an annual report outlining new policies and publishing data that had been collected from the various reservations. Below is an excerpt from Commissioner J. D. C. Atkins' report for 1887.

1887 was an important year in the development of US government policy regarding Indians. In that year Congress passed the Dawes Act, according to which individual Indians were to receive allotments of land, so as to break up the tribal territory. At the same time, efforts to remove native children from their homes and cultures were stepped up. Many white people assumed that if Indians could be remolded to fit the wider American culture, they would be more likely to survive.

Longer and closer consideration of the subject has only deepened my conviction that it is a matter not only of importance, but of necessity that the Indians acquire the English language as rapidly as possible. The Government has entered upon the great work of educating and citizenizing the Indians and establishing them upon homesteads. The adults are expected to assume the role of citizens, and of course the rising generation will be expected and required more nearly to fill the measure of citizenship, and the main purpose of educating them is to enable them to read, write, and speak the English language and to transact business with English-speaking people. When they take upon themselves the responsibilities and privileges of citizenship their vernacular will be of no advantage. Only through the medium of the English tongue can they acquire a knowledge of the Constitution of the country and their rights and duties thereunder.

Every nation is jealous of its own language, and no nation ought to be more so than ours, which approaches nearer than any other nationality to the perfect protection of its people. True Americans all feel that the Constitution laws, and institutions of the United States, in their adaptation to the wants and requirements of man, are superior to those of any other country; and they should understand that by the spread of the English language will these laws and institutions be more firmly established and widely disseminated. Nothing so surely and perfectly stamps upon an individual a national characteristic as language. So manifest and important is this that nations the world over, in both ancient and modern times, have ever imposed the strictest requirements upon their public schools as to the teaching of the national tongue. Only English has been allowed to be taught in the public schools in the territory acquired by this country from Spain, Mexico, and Russia, although the native populations spoke another tongue. All are familiar with the recent prohibitory order of the German Empire forbidding the teaching of the French language in either public or private schools in Alsace and Lorraine. Although the population is almost universally opposed to German rule, they are firmly held to German political allegiance by the military hand of the Iron Chancellor. If the Indians were in Germany or France or any other civilized country, they should be instructed in the language there used. As they are in an English-speaking country, they must be taught the language which they must use in transacting business with the people of this country. No unity or community of feeling can be established among different peoples unless they are brought to speak the same language, and thus become imbued with like ideas of duty.

Deeming it for the very best interest of the Indian, both as an individual and as an embryo citizen, to have this policy strictly enforced among the various schools on Indian reservation, orders have been issued accordingly to Indian agents, and the texts of the orders and of some explanations made thereof are given below:

December 14, 1886

In all schools conducted by missionary organizations it is required that all instructions shall be given in the English language.

February 2, 1887

In reply I have to advise you that the rule applies to all schools on Indian reservations, whether they be Government or mission schools. The instruction of the Indians in the vernacular is not only of no use to them, but is detrimental to the cause of their education and civilization, and no school will be permitted on the reservation in which the English language is not exclusively taught.

July 16, 1887

Your attention is called to the regulation of this office which forbids instruction in schools in any Indian language. This rule applies to all schools on an Indian reservation, whether Government or mission schools. The education of Indians in the vernacular is not only of no use to them, but is detrimental to their education and civilization.

You are instructed to see that this rule is rigidly enforced in all schools upon the reservation under your charge.

No mission school will be allowed upon the reservation which does not comply with the regulation.

... I have given the text of these orders in detail because various misrepresentations and complaints in regard to them have been made, and various misunderstandings seem to have arisen. They do not, as has been urged, touch the question of the preaching of the Gospel in the churches nor in any wise hamper or hinder the efforts of missionaries to bring the various tribes to a knowledge of the Christian religion. Preaching of the Gospel to Indians in the vernacular is, of course, not prohibited. In fact, the question of the effect of this policy upon any missionary body was not considered. All the office insists upon is that in the schools established for the rising generation of Indians shall be taught the language of the Republic of which they are to become citizens.

It is believed that if any Indian vernacular is allowed to be taught by the missionaries in the schools on Indian reservations, it will prejudice the youthful pupil as well as his untutored and uncivilized or semi-civilized parent against the English language, and, to some extent at least, against Government schools in which the English language exclusively has always been taught. To teach Indian school children their native tongue is practically to exclude English, and to prevent them from acquiring it. This language, which is good enough for a white man and a black man, ought to be good enough for the red man. It is also believed that teaching an Indian youth in his own barbarous dialect is a positive detriment to him. The first step to be taken toward civilization, toward teaching the Indians the mischief and folly of continuing their barbarous practices, is to teach them the English language ...

Source: Annual Report of the Commissioner of Indian Affairs, September 21, 1887. House Executive Document no. 1, 50th Congress, 1st session, serial 2542, pp. 19–21.

Study: There are several excellent studies of the effects of US-imposed education on native students and the ways in which they responded. See K. Tsianina Lowawaima,

They Called It Prairie Light: The Story of Chilocco Indian School (University of Nebraska Press, 1994) and Amanda Cobb, *Listening to Our Grandmothers' Stories: The Bloomfield Academy for Chickasaw Females, 1852–1949* (University of Nebraska Press, 2000).

Further exploration: Libraries that serve as depositories of US government documents house the annual reports of the commissioners.

2. Francis La Flesche's Memories of Boarding School

One young clerk working in the office of the Commissioner of Indian Affairs in the 1880s (see section 1 above) was not comfortable with what he heard there. Francis La Flesche was an Omaha Indian. His grandfather had been a French trader, and his father was therefore somewhat acquainted with white culture and decided to send his young son to a Presbyterian boarding school. As an adult living and working in Washington, DC, the former boarding school scholar decided to go to law school. He also worked with anthropologist Alice C. Fletcher, who had long been his mentor, in hopes of preserving knowledge of his people's culture. In 1910, he went to work for the Bureau of American Ethnology. He had become, in fact if not in name, an anthropologist in his own right. In a book he published in 1900, he attempted to convey to educated, policy-making Americans what he believed they needed to know about Indian children, writing in as accessible a style as possible.

Preface

As the object of this book is to reveal the true nature and character of the Indian boy, I have chosen to write the story of my school-fellows rather than that of my other ... friends who knew only the aboriginal life. I have made this choice not because the influences of the school alter the qualities of the boys, but that they might appear under conditions and in an attire familiar to the reader. The paint, feathers, robes, and other articles that make up the dress of the Indian, are marks of savagery to the European, and he who wears them, however appropriate or significant they might be to himself, finds it difficult to lay claim to a share in common human nature. So while the school uniform did not change those who wore it, in this instance, it may help these little Indians to be judged, as are other boys, by what they say and do.

It is not my purpose to give a continued story with a hero in the following pages, but, in a series of sketches, to present the companions of my own young days to the children of the race that has become possessed of the land of my fathers ...

All the boys in our school were given English names, because their Indian names were difficult for the teachers to pronounce. Besides, the aboriginal names were considered by the missionaries as heathenish, and therefore should be obliterated. No less heathenish in their origins were the English substitutes, but the loss of their original meaning and significance through long usage had rendered them fit to continue as appellations for civilized folk. And so, in the place of Tae-noo'-ga-wa-zhe, came Philip Sheridan; in that of Wa-pah'-des, Ulysses S. Grant, that of Koo'-we'he'ge'ra, Alexander, and so on ... The names thus acquired by the boys are used in these sketches in preference to their own, for the reason that Indian words are not only difficult to pronounce, but are apt to sound all alike to one not familiar with the language, and the boys who figure in these pages might lose their identity and fail to stand out clearly in the mind of the reader were he obliged to continually struggle with their Omaha names ...

The misconception of Indian life and character so common among the white people has been largely due to an ignorance of the Indian's language, of his mode of thought, his beliefs, his ideals, and his native institutions. Every aspect of the Indian and his manner of life has always been strange to the white man, and this strangeness has been magnified by the mists of prejudice and the conflict of interests between the two races. While these in time may disappear, no native American can ever cease to regret that the utterances of his father have been constantly belittled when put into English, that their thoughts have frequently been travestied and their native dignity obscured. The average interpreter has generally picked up his knowledge of English in a random fashion, for very few have ever had the advantage of a thorough education, and all have had to deal with the difficulties that attend the translator. The beauty and picturesqueness, and euphonious playfulness, or the gravity of diction which I have heard among my own people, and other tribes as well, are all but impossible to be given literally in English ...

Chapter 11: A New Study

It was a hot September afternoon; our gingham handkerchiefs, which matched our shirts, were wet with mopping our faces. We all felt cross; Gray-beard was cross, and everything we did went wrong.

Warren, who had been sent to the spring for a pail of cold water, leaned over his desk to Brush, and whispered loud enough for the boys around us to hear, "A big black carriage came up to the gate just now, and the Agent and three other big fat men got out. The super'tendent shook hands with them, and they went to his room."

While Gray-beard was shaking a boy to make him read correctly, the news of the black carriage and the fat men went from boy to boy. The girls were dying to know what word it was the boys were passing around; but the aisle that separated them from us was too wide to whisper across. Warren's girl made signs to him which he at first did not understand; when he caught her meaning, he tore a fly-leaf out of his book, wrote on it, rolled it into a ball and threw it to the girl, who deftly caught it; these two were adepts at such transmission of messages. The girl unfolded the paper, read it, and passed it on; then the girls felt better and resumed their work.

The class in mental arithmetic took the floor. Not one of the boys knew his lesson. As the recitation went on, Gray-beard's face darkened and his forehead wrinkled; he came to a timid youngster with a hard question. I knew there was going to be trouble for the little chap; so, to save him pain and distress, I thought of a plan by which to distract Gray-beard's attention. I reached under my desk and took hold of a thread which I carefully drew until my thumb and finger touched the stiff paper to which it was attached, then, as the boy stammered out the wrong answer and Gray-beard made an impatient movement toward him, I gave the thread a gentle pull, "Biz-z-z-z!" it went.

"Who's making that noise?" asked Gray-beard, turning toward our end of the school-room.

I loosened the pressure, and the noise ceased. When Gray-beard returned to the boy, I again pulled the thread, "Biz-z-z-z-!" Something was wrong this time; the buzzing did not cease, it became louder and angrier.

"Who's doing that?" exclaimed Gray-beard.

Every boy and girl looked up to him as though to say, "I did not do it." The buzzing went on; I alone kept my eyes on my book, and so aroused suspicion. I did not dare put my hand under the desk again to stop the buzzing, for I had lost the thread. Gray-beard came towards me and asked, "What have you there?" I did not answer.

"Stand up and let me see!" he exclaimed. Before I could give him any warning, he put his hand in the desk and felt about; he sprang back with a cry, "Ah! I'm bitten! Is it a snake?"

"No, it isn't," I answered; and, peering carefully into the desk, I drew out the buzzing thing and showed it to him; it was only a wasp fastened by its slender waist to a sheet of paper.

Although he felt relieved of his fright, the pain of the sting was arousing his anger, and I saw that there was trouble coming to me: but at that moment the door opened and in walked the superintendent and the four fat men. Gray-beard went forward and was introduced to them. There was a scramble by three of the large boys to get chairs from the dining-room for the visitors. When the gentlemen had made a quiet survey of our faces, they sat down and questioned Gray-beard about the branches taught at the school, and the progress made by the pupils. In the meantime I had released my prisoner; it went buzzing around the room, and then maneuvered over the bald head of one of the visitors, who beat the air with his hands to ward it off.

"Frank, catch that wasp," said Gray-beard.

I caught the troublesome creature in my hat and turned it out of doors.

When the questioning of the visitors was over, Gray-beard turned to us and said, "Now, children, pay strict attention; these gentlemen want to see what you have learned. I will put some questions to you."

We became so silent that we could hear a pin drop. The visitors smiled upon us pleasantly, as though to encourage us.

"Who discovered America?" asked the Gray-beard. Dozens of hands went up. "Abraham, you may answer."

An expression of amusement spread over the faces of the scholars as the great awkward boy stood up. Gray-beard must have been bewildered by the sting of the wasp and the sudden appearance of visitors, else he would not have made such a blunder; for he knew very well what every boy and girl of the school could do; however there was no help for it now; Abraham Lincoln, standing with his hands in his pockets had the floor; he put his weight on one foot and then on the other, the very picture of embarrassment; he cleared his throat, looked helplessly at me, and then at Brush, – "Come," said Gray-beard, "we are waiting."

"George Washington!" answered Abraham.

A titter ran around among the pupils. Gray-beard's face turned red, then white, as he said, "Abraham, take your seat. Brush, can you tell us who discovered America?"

"Columbus," promptly answered the boy. Then a series of questions were asked, which the children answered voluntarily, and did credit to their teacher. The visitors nodded approvingly to each other. When the examination was over, the Agent arose and, addressing the school, said:

"You have acquitted yourselves well in this sudden and unexpected test; I will now ask you to spell for me. Here is a book," said he, turning the leaves of a pretty gilt edged volume, "which I will give to the scholar who can spell best."

Taking a spelling book, he gave out the words himself. We all stood up, and those who misspelled a word sat down. One by one the pupils dropped to their seats, until only Brush, a big girl, and I remained on the floor; finally I was sent down, and the girl and Brush went on; they were now in the midst of the hard words. At last Brush failed; the girl also misspelled the word, but as the prize book could not be divided, it was given to her.

"Are the children taught music?" asked one of the strangers.

"No, replied the superintendent; "but they can sing nearly all of the Sunday-school hymns."

"They should be taught music as well as reading and spelling," remarked the gentlemen, then, addressing the children, he asked:

"Have your people music, and do they sing?"

"They do," answered one of the large boys.

"I wish you would sing an Indian song for me," continued the man. "I never heard one."

There was some hesitancy, but suddenly a loud clear voice close to me broke into a Victory song; before a bar was sung another voice took up the song from the beginning, as is the custom among the Indians, then the whole school fell in, and we made the room ring. We understood the song, and knew the emotion of which it was the expression. We felt, as we sang, the patriotic thrill of a victorious people who had vanquished their enemies; but the men shook their heads, and one of them said, "That's savage, that's savage! They must be taught music."

Source: Francis La Flesche, *The Middle Five: Indian Schoolboys of the Omaha Tribe* (University of Nebraska Press, 1963 [1900]), pp. xv–xix, 96–100.

Study and further exploration: See section 1 above. In addition, Luther Standing Bear, Charles Ohiyesa Eastman, and others wrote compellingly on their experiences in boarding schools. Their work could be meaningfully compared with Francis La Flesche's.

3. A Navajo Girl's Letters Home from Boarding School

Dating from colonial times to the 1960s, there are surviving letters written home by native children in boarding schools. The three letters below were written by a young Navajo girl named Alice Becenti between 1914 and 1916, at the height of the Progressive era. She had been sent to the Sherman Institute in Riverside, California. She did not write directly to her parents, who most probably could not read, but to Samuel Stacher, the head of the Crowpoint Indian Agency in New Mexico. He may have been instrumental in sending young Alice to school, as she seems to have assumed he would feel some responsibility for her and would communicate with her parents, and she was clearly frustrated by his infrequent correspondence. As we read Alice's letters written over the course of two years, we watch her struggle to learn English and to put her deepest feelings into foreign words for a foreign man to read.

August 24, 1914

Dear Friend Mr. Stacher,

This morning I am going todays a few lines to let you know how I am getting along here at this place. Well, I am trying to make myself happy all time. But I can not do. I always have to be sick. I have been very sick again. I am here at the hospital now, in bed. I haven't been here for a long time.

Last time I had to stay here for a month. Most of the time I stay at the hospital I can get along fine because I am sick. I can eat nothing.

I eat but it comes right out. Can['t] stay. I am very weak so no use to eat again after this: last year I was sick all summer too. This year again. Hat's why they wont let me go out working because I was weak to work that's what they told me once. Last year they were going to send me home but they didn't. Because I did want to go home that time. I don't know where Grace Padilla[1] is. She was here with me last week. She came to see me. Well how are all my folks getting along now. Well, you told me why don't I ask Mr. Consor to go out working. Because they told me that I was to weak to go out working and it to hot for me too; that's what they told me once. Ever since I been here I never did feel well. I always sick.

Well, Mr. Stacher I want to go home. I am sure Mr. Consor will let me go because he let the boys and girls go home when they sick like me. I don't want to stay here. I want to go home and get well. Will you think about that Mr. Stacher and tell my folks about it too. I am sure they have money enough to take me home.

Doctor thought I have T.B. Just getting last year. I don't know now. If they not going to sent for me they must sent me some more money. I got to get me show and dress. When I get well again. How is my dear mother now. She used to get sick all time to. I wonder how she is now.

Say where is E.B. and D.B. are they working over there yet or not. Also I got faint last night. I didn't know what I was doing all night. Before that I got like that too that time I was down the Farm.

This will be all so I must close now. Hope to hear from you soon if you please.

To Mr. Stacher
From Alice Becenti
Give my best love to Mrs. Stacher.
Also to Earl B.

*

November 3, 1915

Dear Friends:

Mr. Stacher and the family

Mr. Stacher, I received you letter alright but the package you spoke of hasn't reach me yet.

I have no ideal what has delay on the way I am also still looking every day.

Well Mr. Stacher, if you only knew how tickle I was when I got your letter saying enclosing a letter with Navajo bread.

[1] Grace was another girl from Crowpoint Agency.

I was so tickle to death, I couldn't help but read my letter up to my room mate. Now I am quite disappointed.

The girls always ask me if my bread has come yet.

Indeed I get often cheap.

Oh well, I supposed it was sended or it's lost.

Tell my mother or brother, I'm much rather have them send my Navajo blankets that I wonder about two month ago, that to have them take trouble sending bread.

Indeed that was very nice of you to think or taking lot of trouble sending what I never expected.

But I haven't get.

But I wishe you could please kindly see about my blankets, see it they are planning to sended.

Excuse me for bothering you Mr. Stacher, as you know very well, I have no one to depended on.

I am always glad to hear everything in its perfectly condition at home, its surely dose make me feel or look more brighter with my school work.

About a hundred or more of the children have had the measles, but most are well and back to their school.

But it has not reach us Grace and I. I hope it would.

Last Saturday night we had a nice masqueraded part, everyone seem to enjoyed very much, some of the girls and boys dressed up in odd fashion.

Will close with many regards to you all.

Your friend,

Alice Becenti

Write soon.

But please send telegraph that's the quickest way I can hear about my people.

*

May 1916

Dear Mr. Stacher,

This afternoon I am going to write a few lines to you to let you know how I am getting along at Sherman. I am getting along very fine indeed with all the school children but now there are only few children here. Because some of them are gone out working. Tomorrow some girls are going home. I would like to know how my mother getting along. I am very sorry to hear that my mother sick and beside that my brother died. Which my brother is that? But I hope my mother will be better soon. Supt. is not here and I not tell him if I could go and see my mother. Well Mr. Stacher I wish you could tell her to not to worry about. We having to died someday. I guess that's what made her sick. Dear mother don't worry.

This will be all.

Be sure and tell me weather its so or not. I am just sick about it.

From Alice Becenti

Why don't they tell me along ago when he was sick

P.S. Please Mr. Stacher; if you will send for me as soon as possible for its quite a long while for me to sit around with tease and worrying. Especially to think that my mother is sick and worrying. I am sure it wouldn't do me any good for me to sit around crying day after day, to waite for 20 days to be up. I don't see while I can't go as some children are already going home from east. Mr. Conser is not here just now, but please Mr. Stacher, I am asking this with my tears. For you to sent a word or telegraph to Mr. Conser as soon as you get this letter.

Source: Alice Becenti's letters can be found in the National Archives, Laguna Niguel, and are printed in Peter Iverson, ed., *"For Our Navajo People": Diné Letters Speeches and Petitions, 1900–1960* (University of New Mexico Press, 2002), pp. 82–5.

Further exploration: Students might compare the numerous letters included in Iverson (cited above) with others written 150 years earlier by the first generation of Indian students to be taken from their homes, those who attended Eleazar Wheelock's "Indian Charity School." That institution was founded in Connecticut in the 1750s and was then moved to New Hampshire in 1769 and became Dartmouth College. See James Dow McCallum, ed., *The Letters of Eleazar Wheelock's Indians* (Dartmouth College Publications, 1932).

4. William Stoddard's *The Talking Leaves*

In this era, Native Americans no longer appeared fearsome to the dominant white culture. Instead, in the popular imagination, Indians became "fascinating" and "charming" relics of a vanishing age. Demeaning images of them appeared on such items as toys and cigar boxes. "Wild West" shows became a standard feature of American life. "Buffalo Bill" Cody's show toured in Europe as well. Even Sitting Bull was persuaded to go on tour for a brief period after his people were forced to enter reservations and faced dire poverty.

Between the 1880s and the 1930s, hundreds of popular stories and novels were also written about "life among the Indians" as it had supposedly been before their ultimate defeat. These works were almost all by white authors, written with a white audience in mind, and often centered on a white protagonist. Many were intended for young people and became part of the rising generation's earliest impressions of Native American people.

William Stoddard (1835–1925) was Abraham Lincoln's secretary in the White House. He also had an abiding interest in writing "historical romance" and produced many such works. The Talking Leaves *was first published in 1882. It was reprinted several times; this selection comes from the 1910 edition. The main character, "Rita," captured by the Apache as a girl, was raised by a chief, and became the adoptive sister of Ni-ha-be, the chief's daughter. In the last few pages, Rita's father, Murray, finds her and she returns to her former life.*

Ni-ha-be had heard and understood, and a scared look arose in her face. "Rita! Rita! You are going away? You will not be an Apache girl anymore?"

"Oh, Ni-ha-be, come with me!"

Their arms were around each other, and they were both weeping, but Ni-ha-be's mind was made up instantly.

"No. You are born white. You will go with your father. I am an Apache, and I will go with my father.

Many Bears was listening. "Send-Warning hear what young squaw say? All Apaches say good. She will stay with her own people."

Ni-ha-be consented, nevertheless, to remain with Rita at the post headquarters as long as her friends were camped close by.

Murray and Steve were anxious to begin their return to civilization, but it would be several days before a "train" would go with an escort, and they did not care to run any further risks. So the "farewell" was spread over sufficient time to make all sorts of explanations and promises, and Rita's mind became so full of dreams of her new life that she could easily give up the old one.

Ni-ha-be had never seen so much of the pale-faces before, and Rita tried again and again to persuade her to change her mind, but, on the very last morning of all, she resolutely responded, "No, Rita, you are all pale-face. All over. Head and heart both belong with white friends. Feel happy. Ni-ha-be only little Indian girl here. Out there, on plains, among mountains, Ni-ha-be is the daughter of a great chief. She is an Apache."

No doubt she was right, but she and Rita had a good long cry over it then, and probably more than one afterward. . . . Out from the fates of the fort that morning wheeled the cavalry escort of the waiting "train" of supply wagons and traders' "outfits," and behind the cavalry rode a little group of three. The ladies of the garrison, with the major and the rest, had said their last farewells at the gates, and the homeward journey had begun.

"Steve," said Murray, "are you a Lipan or an Apache today?"

"Seems to me that is all ever so long ago. I am white again."

"So am I. At one time I had little hope that I ever should be. I never would if I had not found Rita. Oh, my daughter!"

"Father, father, see – there she is! Oh, Ni-ha-be!"

A swift and beautiful mustang was bounding toward them across the plain from a sort of cloud of wild-looking figures at a little distance, and on its back was a form they all knew well. Nearer it came and nearer.

"She wants to say good-bye again."

Nearer still, so near that they could almost look into her dark, streaming eyes, and Rita held out her arms beseechingly; but at that moment the mustang was suddenly reined in and wheeled to the right-about, while Ni-ha-be clasped both hands upon her face.

"Ni-ha-be! Oh, Ni-ha-be!"

But she was gone like the wind, and did not come again.

"There, Rita," said her father. "It is all for the best. All your Indian life is gone, like mine and Steve's. We have something better before us now."

The end.

Source: William O. Stoddard, *The Talking Leaves: An Indian Story* (Grosset & Dunlap, 1910), pp. 248–50.

Study: There are numerous studies of the ways in which Native Americans have been constructed in the popular imagination, ranging from Benjamin Keen, *The Aztec Image in Western Thought* (Rutgers University Press, 1971) to the more recent work by Alan Trachtenberg, *Shades of Hiawatha: Staging Indians, Making Americans, 1880–1930* (Hill & Wang, 2004).

Further exploration: A search through any used book store is virtually guaranteed to turn up several books much like *The Talking Leaves*. Read whatever you can find, and try to imagine that is all you know about Native Americans. Consider the effects of educated people's being steeped in such literature.

5. The Arguments of *The Quarterly Journal*

By the early part of the twentieth century, many Indians believed that their people were facing cultural and psychological destruction. The loss of tribal lands, the boarding school experiences, and the condescension of nearly all white Americans threatened to eliminate people who defined themselves as Indians or who understood what it meant to be Indian. A number of educated Native Americans formed the Society of American Indians; they worked together to publish The Quarterly Journal *in Washington, DC. In its pages were printed searing indictments of the world they knew.*

These two selections were both published in 1914, one year after the founding of the journal. The author of the first was Carlos Montezuma. He was born a Yavapai but was taken prisoner by the Pima when he was 6 years old. Eventually, he was sold to an itinerant photographer named Carlos Gentile who treated him as a foster son and gave him the romantic Aztec name. Montezuma became a medical doctor. Later, he sought and found his birth family. The author of the second piece, Chauncey Yellow Robe, was a Sioux whose great-uncle was Sitting Bull. He was sent to the famous Carlisle

Indian school in Pennsylvania when he was a boy, but then returned to South Dakota and became an officer of the Indian boarding school in Rapid City.

"What Indians Must Do" by Carlos Montezuma

We must free ourselves. Our people's heritage is freedom. Freedom reigned in their whole make-up. They harmonized with nature and lived accordingly. Preaching freedom to our people on reservations does not make them free any more than you can, by preaching, free those prisoners who are in the penitentiary. Reservations are prisons where our people are kept to live and die, where equal possibilities, equal education and equal responsibilities are unknown . . .

We must do away with the Indian Bureau. The reservation system has debarred us as a race from acquiring that knowledge to appreciate our property. The government after teaching us how to live without work has come to the conclusion that "the Indians are not commercialists" and, therefore, "we (his guardian) will remove them as we think best and use them as long as our administration lasts and make friends." The Indian Department has drifted into commercialism at the expense of our poor benighted people. So they go on and say, "Let us not allot those Indians on that sweet flowing water because there are others who will profit by damming it up and selling it out to the newcomers; that the Indians do not use or develop their lands; five acres of irrigated land is all that one Indian can manage, but in order to be generous, we will give him ten acres and close up the books and call it square; that their vast forest does them no good, before the Indian can open his eyes let us transfer it to the Forestry Reserve Department. Never mind, let the Indian scratch for his wood to cook with and to warm himself in the years to come; that the Indians have no use for rivers, therefore, we will go into damming business and build them on their lands without their consent. Pay? No! Why should we?" They give us "C" class water instead of "A" class. They have got us! Why? Because we do not know the difference.

"In this valley the Indians have too much land. We will move them from where they have lived for centuries (by Executive order in behalf of the coming settlers). Even if he had cultivated and claims more than that, we will allot that Indian only ten acres. If he rebels and makes trouble, we will put him in jail until he is ready to behave himself." This poor Indian may try to get an Indian friend to help him out of his predicament. But right there the Indian helper is balked by the Indian Department and is told he is not wanted on the reservation. When an Indian collects money from among his tribe to defray expenses to Washington and back in order to carry their complaints, and to be heard and considered in their rights the superintendent with the aid of the Indian policeman takes this Indian, takes the money away from him and gives back the money to those who contributed, put[s] him in jail and brands him as a grafter ...

The sooner the Government abolishes the Indian Bureau, the better it will be for we Indians in every way. The system that has kept alive the Indian Bureau has been instrumental in dominating over our race for fifty years. In that time the Indian's welfare has grown to be secondary and the Indian Bureau the whole thing, and therefore a necessary political appendage of the government. It sends out exaggerated and wonderful reports to the public in order to suck the blood of our race, so that it may have perpetual life to sap your life, my life and our children's future prospects. There are many good things to say about the Indian Department. It started out right with our people. It fed them, clothed them and protected them from going outside of the reservations. It was truly a place of refuge. Then they were dominated by agents; now they are called superintendents. On the reservation our people did not act without the consent of the Superintendent, and *they did not dare to think*, for that would be to rival, the Superintendent. Yesterday, today, our people are in the same benighted condition. As Indians they are considered non-entities. They are not anything to themselves and not anything to the world ...

We must be independent. When with my people for a vacation in Arizona I must live outdoors; I must sleep on the ground; I must cook in the fire on the ground; I must sit on the ground, I must eat nature's food and I must be satisfied with inconveniences that I do not enjoy at my Chicago home. Yet those blood relations of mine are independent, happy, because they were born and brought up in that environment, while as a greenhorn I find myself dependent and helpless in such simple life. In order for we Indians to be independent in the whirl of this other life, we must get into it and used to it and live up to its requirements and take our chances with the rest of our fellow creatures. Being caged up and not permitted to develop our faculties has made us a dependent race. We are looked upon as hopeless to save and hopeless to do anything for ourselves. The only Christian way, then, is to leave us alone and let us die in that condition. The conclusion is true that we will die that way if we do not hurry and get out of it and hustle for our salvation. Did you ever notice how other races hustle and bustle in order to achieve independence?[2] Reservation Indians must do the same as the rest of the wide world.

[2] Most probably he is referring to African Americans, who were extremely active on their own behalf during the Progressive Era.

As a full-blooded Apache Indian[3] I have nothing more to say. Figure out your responsibility and the responsibility of every Indian that hears my voice.

*

"The Menace of the Wild West Show" by Chauncey Yellow Robe

... It is now more than four centuries since Columbus came to our shores and claimed the country and gave us the name of Indians, and at the same time inaugurated the first Indian show by importing some of the Indians across the water for exhibition before the Spanish throne, and to-day the practice continues to exist in the wild-west Indian shows.

Some time ago, Judge [Cato] Sells, the United States Commissioner of Indian Affairs, said: "Let us save the American Indian from the curse of whiskey." I believe these words hold the key to the Indian problem of to-day, but how can we save the American Indian if the Indian Bureau is permitting the special privileges in favor of the wild-west Indian shows, moving-picture concerns, and fair associations for commercializing the Indian? This is the greatest hindrance, injustice, and detriment to the present progress of the American Indians toward civilization ...

In some of the celebrations, conventions, and county fairs in Rapid City and other reservation border towns, in order to make the attraction a success, they think they cannot do without wild-west Indian shows, consequently certain citizens have the Indian show craze ... We can see from this state of affairs that the white man is persistently perpetuating the [false idea of] tribal habits and customs. We see that the showman is manufacturing the Indian plays intended to amuse and instruct young children and is teaching them that the Indian is only a savage being. We hear now and then of a boy or girl who is hurt or killed by playing savage. These are the direct consequences of the wild-west Indian shows and moving pictures that depict lawlessness and hatred.

[3] Montezuma was Yavapai, but he usually described himself as Apache in public statements. The Apache were the best-known tribe of the southwest and were associated in the popular imagination with Geronimo. The Yavapai, on the other hand, were entirely unknown to most. Claiming his connection to them would not identify him in the minds of his readers. He insisted on being "full-blooded" because white commentators of the era frequently asserted that educated and articulate Indians were "half-breeds" who inherited their talents from their white ancestors.

Before closing the history of the nineteenth century an awful crime was committed in this great Christian nation. ... A band of Sioux Indians, including women and children, unarmed, were massacred. The wounded were left on the field to die without care at Wounded Knee by the United States troops just because they had founded a new religion called "The Indian Messiah." This was a cowardly and criminal act without diplomacy. Twenty-three years afterward, on the same field of Wounded Knee, the tragedy was reproduced for "historical preservation" in moving picture films and called "The Last Great Battle of the Sioux." The whole production of the field was misrepresented and yet approved by the Government. This is a disgrace and injustice to the Indian race.

I am not speaking here from selfish and sensitive motives, but from my own point of view, for cleaner civilization, education, and citizenship for my race ...

Source: *Quarterly Journal* 2 (1914), pp. 224–5 and 294–9, reprinted in Frederick E. Hoxie, ed., *Talking Back to Civilization: Indian Voices from the Progressive Era* (Bedford/St. Martin's, 2001).

Study: Frederick E. Hoxie, *A Final Promise: The Campaign to Assimilate the Indians, 1880–1920* (University of Nebraska Press, 1984).

Further exploration: Students would do well to read other selections from *The Quarterly Journal* as published in *Talking Back to Civilization* (cited above) or in the original. There are, in addition, other published collections of material from this era, such as Daniel F. Littlefield, ed., *Native American Writing in the Southeast, 1875–1935* (University Press of Mississippi, 1995). Researching Carlos Montezuma in particular is possible because a collection of his papers is readily available on microfilm: John Larner, Jr., ed., *The Papers of Carlos Montezuma, M.D.* (Scholarly Resources, 1983). Montezuma was for a time engaged to a Yankton Sioux woman named Zitkala Ša, an extremely talented writer in her own right. Several of her works are in print, among them *American Indian Stories* and *Itkomi and the Ducks* (University of Nebraska Press, 1985 and 2004 respectively).

Questions for consideration

1 How does Francis la Flesche subtly argue that the educational policies of the Commissioner of Indian Affairs are misguided? Do the letters of Alice Becenti uphold or refute his views?
2 If native children were unlikely to read such stories as *The Talking Leaves*, how were they nevertheless affected by them?
3 Why do you think Carlos Montezuma and Chauncey Yellow Robe, who were themselves well educated and financially successful, evinced such anger and frustration?

Chapter 9 Mid-Twentieth-Century Changes

1. The Arts and Crafts Act of 1935

The New Deal that followed the onset of the Great Depression brought numerous changes to Indian life. In 1933, Franklin Delano Roosevelt appointed John Collier as the new Commissioner of Indian Affairs. He was well versed in the arguments made by Native American Progressives in the preceding 20 years and chose to pursue the policies of ending allotment, encouraging Indian children to attend local day schools rather than boarding schools, and generally supporting tribal self-rule. The Indian Reorganization Act (IRA) of 1934 became something of a lightning rod, as many Indians, having learned to distrust the federal government, were certain that change would bode ill for them. There were specific factors that alienated them: the IRA, for example, depended on the principle of majority rule, but most tribes were accustomed to operating by consensus.

Collier also desired to promote knowledge of indigenous culture, and even hoped that doing so might actually lead to lucrative employment for Indians, as their artwork could be sold to tourists. The Arts and Crafts Act carefully tried to prevent non-tribal people from being the ones to make money by selling purportedly "Indian" artwork. The Indians of the southwest were encouraged to sell their traditional textiles and pottery. Those of the northeast were to produce more of the intricate beadwork they had been making since the first colonists gave them beads that they could use in their embroidered articles more easily than the dyed porcupine quills they had been accustomed to using. In some cases, tribes had lost all knowledge of their traditional arts and crafts. Specialists were brought to the Pamunkey reservation in Virginia, for example, to re-teach the people pottery making and to design a series of pictoglyphs to use as decorations. The pot shown in fig. 9.1.3 purports to tell the "traditional" story of a young "Indian maiden" named Pocahontas saving the life of a white man.

Be it enacted ... that a Board is hereby created in the Department of the Interior to be known as "Indian Arts and Crafts Board," and hereinafter referred to as the Board. The Board shall be composed of five commissioners, who shall be appointed by the Secretary of the Interior as soon as possible after the passage of this Act and shall continue in office, two for a term of two years, one for a term of three years, and two for a term of four years from the date of their appointment, the term of each to be designated by the Secretary of the Interior...

The commissioners shall serve without compensation: *Provided*, That each Commissioner shall be reimbursed for all actual expenses, including travel expenses, subsistence and office overhead, which the Board shall certify to have been incurred as properly incidental to the performance of is duties as a member of the Board.

SEC 2. It shall be the function and the duty of the board to promote the economic welfare of the Indian tribes and the Indian wards of the Government through the development of Indian arts and crafts and the expansion of the market for the products of Indian art and craftsmanship. In the execution of this function the Board shall have the following powers: (a) To undertake market research to determine the best opportunity for the sale of various products; (b) to engage in technical research and give technical advice and assistance; (c) to engage in experimentation directly or through selected agencies; (d) to correlate and encourage the activities of the various governmental and private agencies in the field; (e) to offer assistance in the management of operating groups for the furtherance of specific projects; (f) to make recommendations to appropriate agencies for loans in furtherance of the production and sale of Indian products; (g) to create Government trade marks of genuineness and quality for Indian products and the products of particular tribes or groups; to establish standards and regulations for the use of such trade marks; to license corporations, associations, or individuals to use them; and to charge a fee for their use; to register them in the United States Patent Office without charge; (h) to employ executive officers, including a general manager, and such other permanent and temporary personnel as may be found necessary, and prescribe the authorities, duties, responsibilities, and tenure and fix the compensation of such officers and other employees ...; (i) as a Government agency to negotiate and execute in its own name contracts with operating groups to supply management, personnel and supervision at cost, and to negotiate and execute in its own name such other contracts and to carry on such other business as may be necessary for the accomplishment of the duties and purposes of the Board: *Provided*, That nothing in the foregoing enumeration of powers shall be construed to authorize the Board to borrow or lend money or to deal in Indian goods ...

SEC 5. Any person who shall counterfeit or colorably[1] imitate any Government trade mark used or devised by the Board as provided in section 2 of this Act, or shall, except as authorized by the Board, affix any such government trade mark, or shall knowingly, willfully, and corruptly affix any reproduction, counterfeit copy or colorable imitation thereof upon any products, Indian or otherwise, or to any labels, signs, prints, packages, wrappers, or receptacles intended to be used upon or in connection with the sale of such products, or any person who shall knowingly make any false statement for the purpose of obtaining the use of any such Government trade mark, shall be guilty of a misdemeanor, and upon conviction thereof shall be enjoined from further carrying on the act or acts complained of and shall be subject to a fine not exceeding $2,000, or imprisonment not exceeding six months, or both such fine and imprisonment …

Sources: US Statutes at Large, 49: 891–3; figures 9.1.1–9.1.3 courtesy the author.

Figure 9.1.1 Doll purchased by tourists in the southwest in the 1930s. Photo by Danny Zeledon

[1] *Colorable* in this context means seemingly valid or genuine, plausible.

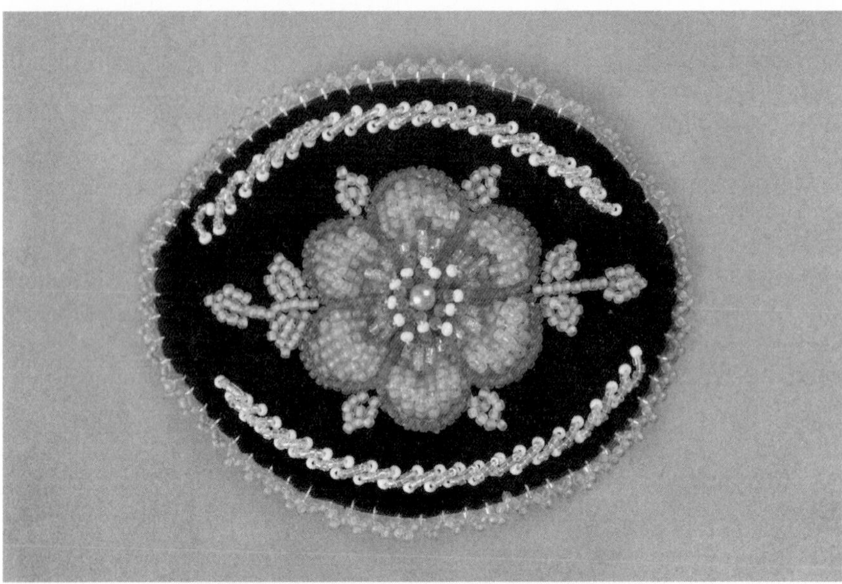

Figure 9.1.2 Hair barrette from the Oneida reservation (New York) in nineteenth-century style, made late twentieth century. Photo by Danny Zeledon

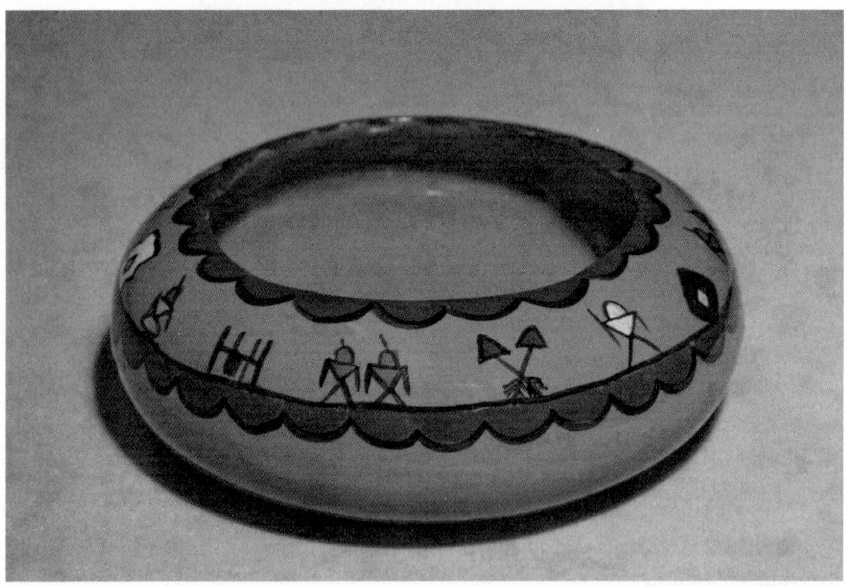

Figure 9.1.3 Pot from the Pamunkey reservation (Virginia) with pictographs designed in the 1930s, made late twentieth century. Photo by Danny Zeledon

2. The Navajo Contribution to the War Effort

Native Americans fought in all US wars, including not only the Revolution and War of 1812, but also the Civil War and World War I. Their contributions to World War II have received more attention, however, because in that conflict they played a crucial role. In the Pacific theater, the armed forces found that the Japanese could intercept almost any message. Many of them spoke English, and so they could even impersonate American officers and send wrong information by radio and field telephone. The problem was solved only when Navajos were recruited as Marines and assigned the task of developing and using a special code. They themselves came up with the idea of spelling many words, using animal names to convey letters. (A was wol-la-chee, *meaning "ant"; B was* shush, *meaning "bear"; C was* moasi, *meaning "cat", etc.) They also developed expressive ways of translating into their own language certain high-frequency military terms that they did not want to have to spell out on every occasion. In the midst of battles they were able to talk to each other by field telephone and radio, conveying essential information with the kind of clarifying give-and-take that only a genuine conversation can provide. Several white men tried to learn to use the code to join the war effort, but none of them were ever able to pass the test and go to the field. The Navajo were required to refrain from discussing their contribution for 25 years, until 1969. Since then, the former Marines have spoken openly about their pride in their contribution to the war effort.*

Sample vocabulary lists

Airplanes

Dive bomber	*gini*	chicken hawk
Torpedo plane	*tas-chizzie*	swallow
Observation plane	*ne-as-jah*	owl
Fighter plane	*da-he-tih-hi*	hummingbird
Bomber	*jay-sho*	buzzard
Patrol plane	*ga-gih*	crow
Transport plane	*atsah*	eagle

General vocabulary

Action	*ah-ha-tinh*	action
Advance	*nas-say*	ahead
Airdrome	*nilchi-began*	air house

Alert	*ha-ih-des-ee*	watchful
Allies	*nih-hi-cho*	friends
Along	*wol-la-chee-snez*	long ant
Amphibious	*chal*	frog
Army	*lei-cha-ih-yil-knee-hi*	dog faces

Sample messages relayed on Iwo Jima, at Motoyama

Than-zie a-kha: Hash-kay-gi-na-tah
Bi-tsan-dehn: Ah-jad D-ah taa n-kih tsotsid Tabaha
Dibeh ah-jah a-chin be ah-deel-tahi deh-nah-as tso-si d-ah tlo-chin klesh dzeh tse-nihl ah-jad ta-atah tsa-ond naz-pas-tkin-tsah-jeha gah-ghil-keid-klesh do lin-daa-tsaa hastaa n-kih shush

To: Commanding Officer
From: LT 327 Regiment
Send demolition team to seal all caves and surrounding ridges and Hill 362B.

D-ah a-woh: ashdla be-al-doh-tso-lani
Bi-tsan-dehn: Ah-jad D-ah taa n-kih tsotsid Tabaha
Jo-kayed-goh be-al-doh-tso-lani besh-be-wa-chind n-kih a-la-ih tseebii shush ah-di jad-ho-loni us-dzoh taa ashdla d-ah a-kha shi-da gah d-ah tlo-chin ba-ah-hot-gli cha-gee al-tah-je-jay ne-ahs-jah tsah lin-daa-tsaa taa hastaa n-kih shush

To: 5th Artillery Battalion
From: LT 327 Regiment
Request artillery barrage 218B at K minus (−) 35 to K hour to support the attack on Hill 362B.

Source and study: Sally McClain, *Navajo Weapon* (Rio Nuevo, 1994). The appendices in this book contain numerous important memos related to the project, as well as the complete dictionary developed by the "code talkers," as they styled themselves.

Further exploration: Some people have argued that life on the reservation destroyed the warrior pride that had sustained native men for many generations. Others, however, argue that knowledge of the warrior heritage remained very much alive and would manifest itself when the opportunity arose. See, for example, L. James Dempsey, *Blackfoot War Art: Pictographs of the Reservation Period, 1880–2000* (University of Oklahoma Press, 2007).

3. The Musings of an Iroquois High Steel Man

Over the course of the twentieth century, many Native Americans moved to cities in search of work. Indeed, in the 1950s, it became official government policy to encourage relocation from reservations to urban areas: one-way bus tickets were available free for the asking. But the migration had begun before those years. One particular group of Indians had met with remarkable success in the industrial world: Iroquois men had been involved in the construction of steel bridges since the nineteenth century, and in the twentieth century they began to build skyscrapers, including such famous edifices as Rockefeller Center.

In the 1940s, the writer Joseph Mitchell interviewed some of the "high steel men" living in Brooklyn and working in Manhattan, and in 1949 he published an article about them in The New Yorker. *In the following passage he quotes 54-year-old Orvis Diabo, or O-ron-ia-ke-te ("He who carries the sky"). It is clear that Mitchell made some changes to what the man actually said: no one presents topics in such an organized way in the normal flow of speech, for example. And Mitchell himself said that in reality he spoke to Mr. Diabo and took notes on what he said on several different occasions, not just one. But it also seems likely that Mitchell was true to the spirit of the musings. Mr. Diabo was living in Brooklyn and his wife had gone back to the Caughnawaga (Kahnawake) reservation (see section 4.2) and was insisting that he join her there. He felt torn, and aired feelings that other sources indicate were shared by many urban Indians in the twentieth century.*

I heated a million rivets. When they talk about the men that built this country, one of the men they mean is me. I enjoy New York. The people are as high-strung as rats and the air is too gritty, but I enjoy it. . . . [Today] I feel very low in my mind. I've got to go back to the reservation. I've run out of excuses and I can't put it off much longer. I got a letter from my wife today and she's disgusted with me. "I'm sick and tired of begging you to come home," she said. "You can sit in Brooklyn until your tail takes root." The trouble is, I don't want to go. That is, I do and I don't. I'll try to explain what I mean. An Indian high-steel man, when he first leaves the reservation [in Canada] to work in the States, the homesickness just about kills him. The first few years, he goes back as often as he can. Every time he finishes a job, unless he's thousands of miles away, he goes back. If he's working in New York, he drives up weekends, and it's a twelve-hour drive. After a while, he gets married and brings his wife down and starts a family, and he doesn't go back so often. Oh, he mostly takes the wife and children up for the summer, but he doesn't stay with them. After three or four days, the reservation gets on his nerves and he highballs it back to the States. He gets used to the States. The years go by. He gets to be my age, maybe a little older, maybe a little younger, and one fine morning he comes to the conclusion he's a little too damned stiff in the joints to be walking a naked beam five hundred feet in the air. Either that, or some foreman notices he hasn't got a sure step any longer and takes him aside and tells him a few home truths. He gives up high-steel work and he packs his belongings and he takes his money out of the bank or the postal savings, what little he's been able to squirrel away, and he goes back to the reservation for good. And it's hard on him. He's used to danger, and reservation life is very slow; the biggest thing that ever happens is a funeral. He's used to jumping around from job to job, and reservation life boxes him in. He's used to having a drink, and it's against the law to traffic in liquor on the reservation; he has to buy a bottle in some French-Canadian town across the river and smuggle it in like a high-school boy, and that annoys the hell out of him.

There's not much he can do to occupy the time. He can sit on the high way and watch the cars go by, or he can sit on the riverbank and fish for eels and watch the boats go by, or he can weed the garden, or he can go to church, or he can congregate in the grocery store with the other old retired high-steel men and play cards and talk. That is, if he can stand it. You'd think those old men would talk about the cities they worked in, the sprees they went on, the girls that follow construction all over the country that they knew, the skyscrapers and bridges they put up – only they don't. After they been sitting around the reservation for five years, six years, seven years, they seem to turn against their high-steel days. Some of them, they get to be as Indian as all hell; they won't even speak English any more; they make out they can't understand it. And some of them, they get to be soreheads, the kind of old men that can chew nails and spit rust. When they do talk, they talk gloomy. They like to talk about family fights. There's families on the reservation that got on the outs with each other generations ago and they're still on the outs; maybe it started with a land dispute, maybe it started with a mixed-marriage dispute, maybe it started when some woman accused another woman of meeting her husband in the bushes in the graveyard. Even down here in Brooklyn, there's certain Indians that won't work in gangs with certain other Indians because of bad blood between their families; their wives, when they meet on Atlantic Avenue, they look right through each other. The old men like to bring up such matters and refresh their recollections on some of the details. Also, they like to talk about religion. A miraculous cure they heard about, something the priest said – they'll harp on it for weeks. They're all amateur priests, or preachers. They've all got some religious notion lurking around in their minds.

And they like to talk about reservation matters. The last time I was home, I sat down with the bunch in a store and I tried to tell them about something I'd been studying up on that interested me very much . . . They were too busy discussing the matter of street names for Caughnawaga village. The electric light company that supplies the village had been trying and trying to get the Indians to name the streets and lanes. The meter-readers are always getting balled up, and the company had offered to put up street signs and house numbers free of charge. The old men didn't want street names; they were raising holy hell about it. It wouldn't be Indian. And they were discussing the pros and cons of a water-works system. They're eternally discussing that. Some want a waterworks, but the majority don't. The majority of them, they'd a whole lot rather get behind a poor old horse that his next step might be his last and cart their water up from the river by the barrel. It's more Indian. Sometimes, the way an Indian reasons, there's no rhyme or reason to it. Electric lights are all right and the biggest second-hand car they can find, and radios that the only time they turn them off is when they're changing the tubes, and seventy-five-dollar baby carriages, and four-hundred-dollar coffins, but street names and tap water – oh, Jesus, no! That's going entirely too damned far.

On the other hand, there's things I look forward to. I look forward to eating real Indian grub again. Such as *o-nen-sto*, corn soup. That's the Mohawk national dish. Some of the women make it down here in Brooklyn, but they use Quaker corn meal. The good old women up on the reservation, they make it the hard way, the way the Mohawks were making it five hundred years ago. They shell some corn, and they put it in a pot with a handful of maple ashes and boil it. The lye in the ashes skins the hulls off the kernels, and the kernels swell up into big fat pearls. Then they wash off the lye. Then they put in some red kidney beans. Then they put in a pig's head; in the old days, it was a bear's head. Then they cook it until it's as thick as mud. And when it's cooking, it smells so good. If you were breathing your last, if you had the rattle in your throat, and the wind blew you a faint suggestion of a smell of it, you'd rise and walk ...

And another thing I look forward to, if I can manage it – I want to attend a longhouse festival.[2] If I have to join to do so, I'll join. One night, the last time I was home, the longhousers were having a festival. I decided I'd go up to the Catholic graveyard that's right below the longhouse and hide in the bushes and listen to the music. So I snuck up there and waded through the thistles and the twitch grass and the Queen Anne's lace, and I sat down on a flat stone on the grave of an uncle of mine, Miles Diabo, who was a warwhooper with the Miller Brothers 101 Ranch Wild West Show and died with the pneumonia in Wheeling, West Virginia, in 1916. Uncle Miles was one of the last of the Caughnawaga circus Indians. My mother is in that graveyard, and my father, old Nazareth Diabo that I hardly even

[2] After the American Revolution, a prophet named Handsome Lake propounded a traditionalist religion with some Christian additions. Ever since then, traditional spirituality in the form of the Longhouse religion has survived within the Iroquoian community.

knew. They called him Nazzry. He was a pioneer high-steel Indian. He was away from home the majority of the time, and he was killed in the disaster – when the Quebec Bridge went down. There's hundreds of high-steel men buried in there. The ones that were killed on the job, they don't have stones; their graves are marked with lengths of steel girders made into crosses. There's a forest of girder crosses in there. So I was sitting on Uncle Miles's stone, thinking of the way things go in life, and suddenly the people in the longhouse began to sing and dance and drum on their drums. They were singing Mohawk chants that came down from the old, old red-Indian times. I could hear men's voices and women's voices and children's voices. The Mohawk language, when it's sung, it's beautiful to hear. Oh, it takes your breath away. A feeling ran through me that made me tremble. I had to take a deep breath to quiet my heart, it was beating so fast. I felt very sad; at the same time, I felt very peaceful. I thought I was all alone in the graveyard, and then who loomed up out of the dark and sat down beside me but an old high-steelman I had been talking with in a store that afternoon, one of the soreheads, an old man that fights every improvement that's suggested on the reservation, whatever it is, on the grounds it isn't Indian – this isn't Indian, that isn't Indian. So he said to me, "You're not alone up here. Look over there." I looked where he pointed, and I saw a white shirt in among the bushes. And he said, "Look over there," and I saw a cigarette gleaming in the dark. "The bushes are full of Catholics and Protestants," he said. "Every night there's a longhouse festival, they creep up here and listen to the singing. It draws them like flies." So I said, "The longhouse music is beautiful to hear, isn't it," And he remarked it ought to be, it was the old Indian music. So I said the longhouse religion appealed to me. "One of these days," I said, "I might possibly join." I asked him how he felt about it. He said he was a Catholic and it was out of the question. "If I was to join the longhouse," he said, "I'd be excommunicated, and I couldn't be buried in holy ground, and I'd burn in Hell." I said to him, "Hell isn't Indian." It was the wrong thing to say. He didn't reply to me. He sat there awhile – I guess he was thinking it over – and then he got up and walked away."

Source: Joseph Mitchell, "The Mohawks in High Steel," foreword to Edmund Wilson, *Apologies to the Iroquois* (Farrar, Straus & Cudahy, 1959), pp. 27–36. The essay was reprinted from the 1949 *New Yorker* article.

Study: David Blanchard, "High Steel! The Kahnawake Mohawk and the High Construction Trade," *Journal of Ethnic Studies* 11 (Summer 1983): 32–60; Laurence M. Hauptman, *The Iroquois Struggle for Survival: World War II to Red Power* (Syracuse University Press, 1976).

Further exploration: A Penobscot woman named Molly Dellis Nelson or "Molly Spotted Elk" worked as a performer in Paris in the 1930s and left as the Nazis invaded France. She did not write extensively about feelings of being torn between her two lives, yet she made it clear that she was. See Bunny McBride, *Molly Spotted Elk: A Penobscot in Paris* (University of Oklahoma Press, 1995).

4. The Menominee Struggle against Termination

After World War II, John Collier's policies of strengthening tribal identity and encouraging self-rule were reversed. He resigned, and the policy of dismantling tribal entities took root. Relocation to cities was encouraged, and in 1954 Congress signed into law a bill to begin legal "termination" of tribal units, leaving the people simply as citizens of the state and nation. The process was to be gradual: certain tribes were named as being ready for such a change; others were deemed still unready. The Menominees of Wisconsin were considered ready because their land contained valuable timber and sawmills, so it was thought that they would not be thrown into poverty. However, by the 1960s, economic conditions on the former reservation had deteriorated considerably. The people had no history of any governmental structure other than the tribe and reservation. When these were suddenly removed, numerous problems ensued. They did not even have a school district, for example. The people began to organize in protest. A young Menominee social worker named Ada Deer took a leading role, working with many others. Thirteen people worked as a collective to write a book about their concerns. They wove their writings together seamlessly in traditional tribal style, without attributing individual authorship to individual sections. Here is one segment of the resulting book, Freedom with Reservation: The Menominee Struggle to Save Their Land and People. *The activists were eventually successful: in 1973 Menominee tribal status was restored.*

Some may say I am too adamant in my feelings toward the education system to which the Menominee children are exposed. However, I did not develop these feelings or opinions overnight. As a child, I too had been exposed to a destructive educational system. In 1968, when I moved back to Menominee County to take a teaching position in a primary school, my feelings about the education of Menominee youth were to become intensified. On the surface, life in the County did not appear to have changed much since termination. But I hadn't been teaching long before a seething anger developed, an anger which came to a head while I was working with a group of Upward Bound Students. I had been hired to teach a course which they had requested in Indian history or culture. The first questions of these children stunned me. "Who are we?" "We are told we are no longer Indians. We know we are not white, so who are we?" To add fuel to the fire, these children were born right after the tribal rolls had been closed, and the last Menominee to be registered would taunt them about not being Indian.

When I realized the harm that had been done to these children and to future generations, I wanted to lash out at all the great leaders who had imposed this chaotic mess of termination. But rage would not help these children. Instead, I contained my anger and tried to help set in motion the process to undo this damage ...

Many bureaucrats and, sad to say, some Menominee feel that we are not yet ready to assume control over the education of our children. But one could easily ask if even the most uneducated Indian could create a worse mess than has been forced on us by the various school systems over the past one hundred years. Until the Menominee rid themselves of their feelings of incompetence and gain control of their children's education, that education will continue to be an unpleasant, frightening and painful experience for Menominee children.

When talking to various people, both white and non-white, about the possibility of a separate Menominee school district, I invariably heard similar remarks. "The Menominee children must learn to get along with others, and the sooner the better"; or "It is the supreme law of the land that schools must be integrated"; or the tremendous cost is mentioned, so Menominee children must be bussed into Shawano. However, there are two elementary schools in Menominee County and no Shawano County children are bussed into Menominee County! This learning to get along with others is very obviously a one way street. The implication is that there is something wrong with Menominee children and in order to get rid of this something, they must be exposed to white children.

Source: Deborah Shames, coordinating ed., *Freedom with Reservation: The Menominee Struggle to Save Their Land and People* (National Committee to Save the Menominee People and Forests, 1972), pp. 63–5.

Study: Donald Fixico, *Termination and Relocation: Federal Indian Policy, 1945–1960* (University of New Mexico Press, 1986).

Further Exploration: Kenneth R. Philip, ed., *Indian Self-Rule: First-Hand Accounts of Indian–White Relations from Roosevelt to Reagan* (Howe Bros., 1986) centers around the issue of Termination. It contains many interesting and important statements by Native Americans involved with the struggle, including Ada Deer.

Questions for consideration

1 Was it right or wrong to attempt in the 1930s to create artistic "traditions" in areas where native community memory of the arts had been destroyed?
2 Was it positive or negative for the Navajo "code talkers" that most of them had spent time in English-speaking schools? How did a traditional tribal ethos play into their new role?
3 Why would an urban Indian feel torn between returning to a reservation and making a city "home"?
4 Would Indians also feel torn about the termination of tribal status?
5 Why do questions about the twentieth century revolve around ambiguity more than those of the previous chapters?

Chapter 10 The Upheavals of the 1960s and 1970s

1. The 1961 Declaration of Indian Purpose

By the early 1960s, anger among Native Americans had reached a critical point, just as it had among other minority communities. In June of 1961, a week-long conference was held in Chicago which was attended by over 400 people from 65 tribes. Together, the attendees prepared a statement and sent it to President John F. Kennedy. Soon after, many of the same people would come together to form the National Indian Youth Council. Then other coalitions formed and, by the mid 1960s, the "Red Power" movement was in existence. Here is the Declaration of Indian Purpose sent to the President.

In order to give due recognition to certain basic philosophies by which Indian people and all other people endeavor to live, We, the Indian people, must be governed by high principles and laws in a democratic manner, with a right to choose our own way of life. Since our Indian culture is slowly being absorbed by the American society, we believe we have the responsibility of preserving our precious heritage; recognizing that certain changes are inevitable. We believe that the Indians should provide the adjustment and thus freely advance with dignity to a better life educationally, economically, and spiritually.

*

We believe in the inherent right of all people to retain spiritual and cultural values, and that the free exercise of these values is necessary to the normal development of any people. Indians exercised this inherent right to live their own lives for thousands of years before the white man came and took their lands. It is a more complex world in which Indians live today, but the Indian people who first settled the New World and built the great civilizations which only now are being dug out of the past, long ago demonstrated that they could master complexity.

We believe that the history and development of America show that the Indian has been subjected to duress, undue influence, unwarranted pressures, and policies which have produced uncertainty, frustration, and despair. Only when the public understands these conditions and is moved to take action toward the formulation and adoption of sound and consistent policies and programs will these destroying factors be removed and the Indian resume his normal growth and make his maximum contribution to modern society.

We believe in the future of a greater America, an America which we were the first to love, where life, liberty and the pursuit of happiness will be a reality. In such a future, with Indians and all other Americans cooperating, a cultural climate will be created in which the Indian people will grow and develop as members of a free society . . .

It has long been recognized that one Commissioner cannot give the personal attention to all tribal matters which they deserve. He cannot meet all callers to his office, make necessary visits to the field, and give full attention to the review of tribal programs and supporting budget requests. In view of these conditions, we most urgently recommend that the present organization of the Bureau of Indian Affairs be reviewed and that certain principles be considered no matter what the organizational change might be.

The basic principle involves the desire on the part of Indians to participate in developing their own programs with help and guidance as needed and requested, from a local decentralized technical and administrative staff, preferably located conveniently to the people it serves. . . . The Indians as responsible individual citizens, as responsible tribal representatives, and as responsible Tribal Councils want to participate, want to contribute to their own personal and tribal improvements and want to cooperate with their Government on how best to solve the many problems in a businesslike, efficient, and economical manner as rapidly as possible . . .

We believe that where programs have failed in the past, the reasons were lack of Indian understanding, planning, participation, and approval.

A plan of development should be prepared by each Indian group, whose land or other assets are held in trust, whether such lands or assets are fully defined or not; such plans to be designed to bring about maximum utilization of physical resources by the dependent population and the development of that population to its full potential; such plans to be prepared by the Indians of the respective groups, with authority to call upon the agencies of the federal government for technical assistance, and the ultimate purpose of such planning to be the growth and development of the resources and the people;

That requests for annual appropriations of funds be based on the requirements for carrying into effect these individual development plans, including credit needs and capital investment, and the annual operation budget for the Bureau of Indian Affairs to include sufficient funds to cover the costs of preparing plans and estimates similar in operation to a Point IV Plan.

Source: *American Indian Chicago Conference Proceedings*, University of Chicago, June 13–20, 1961, reprinted in Alvin M. Josephy, Jr., Joane Nagel, and Troy Johnson, eds., *Red Power: The American Indians' Fight for Freedom*, 2nd edn. (University of Nebraska Press, 1999 [1971]).

Study: George P. Castile, *To Show Heart: Native American Self-Determination and Federal Indian Policy, 1960–1975* (University of Arizona Press, 1998).

2. The Alcatraz Proclamation

By the late 1960s, Indians in various parts of the United States were involved in political actions aimed at drawing attention to the situation of their people. The most famous example was the take-over of Alcatraz Island in San Francisco Bay, which had once housed a prison but was now empty. On November 20, 1969, early in the morning, 89 California college students who came from a number of different ethnic groups and styled themselves "Indians of All Tribes" used small boats to get to the island. It was the start of a 19-month occupation. The young people issued numerous statements to the press. The first was the Alcatraz Proclamation – which was actually released before the occupation began in order to guarantee press coverage of the events and drum up support. It was laced with sarcasm, but behind it stood serious intent.

To the Great White Father and All His People:

We, the native Americans, re-claim the land known as Alcatraz Island in the name of all American Indians *by right of discovery*. We wish to be fair and honorable in our dealings with the Caucasian inhabitants of this land, and hereby offer the following treaty: We will purchase said Alcatraz Island for 24 dollars ($24) in glass beads and red cloth, a precedent set by the white man's purchase of a similar island about 300 years ago. We know that $24 in trade goods for these sixteen acres is more than was paid when Manhattan Island was sold, but we offer that land values have risen over the years. Our offer of $1.24 per acre is greater than the 47 cents per acre the white men are now paying the California Indians for their land. We will give to the inhabitants of this land a portion of that land for their own, to be held in trust by the American Indian Government – for as long as the sun shall rise and the rivers go down to the sea – to be administered by the Bureau of Caucasian Affairs (BC). We will further guide the inhabitants in the proper way of living. We will offer them our religion, our education, our life-ways, in order to help them achieve our level of civilization and thus raise them and all their white brothers up from their savage and unhappy state. We offer this treaty in good faith and wish to be fair and honorable in our dealings with the white men.

We feel that this so-called Alcatraz Island is more than suitable as an Indian reservation, as determined by the white man's own standards. By this we mean that this place resembles most Indian reservations, in that:

1. It is isolated from modern facilities, and without adequate means of transportation.
2. It has no fresh running water.
3. The sanitation facilities are inadequate.
4. There are no oil or mineral rights.
5. There is no industry and so unemployment is very great.
6. There are no health care facilities.
7. The soil is rocky and non-productive and the land does not support game.
8. There are no educational facilities.
9. The population has always been held as prisoners and kept dependent upon others.

Further, it would be fitting and symbolic that ships from all over the world, entering the Golden Gate would first see Indian land, and thus be reminded of the true history of this nation. This tiny island would be a symbol of the great lands once ruled by free and noble Indians.

Use to be made of Alcatraz Island

What use will be made of this land?

Since the San Francisco Indian Center burned down, there is no place for Indians to assemble and carry on our tribal life here in the white man's city. Therefore, we plan to develop on this island several Indian institutes:

1. A Center for Native American Studies will be developed which will train our young people in the best of our native cultural arts and sciences ... Attached to this center will be traveling universities, managed by Indians, which will go to the Indian Reservations in order to learn the traditional values from the people, which are now absent in the Caucasion higher education system.

2. An American Indian Spiritual Center will be developed which will practice ancient tribal religious ceremonies and medicine. Our cultural arts will be featured and our young people trained in music, dance, and medicine.
3. An Indian Center of Ecology will be built which will train and support our young people in scientific research and practice in order to restore our lands and waters to their pure and natural state ...
4. A great Indian training school will be developed to teach our peoples how to make a living in the world, improve our standards of living, and end hunger and unemployment among all our peoples. This training school will include a center for Indian arts and crafts, and an Indian restaurant serving native foods and training Indians in culinary arts ...
5. Some of the present buildings will be taken over to develop an American Indian museum, which will depict our native foods and other cultural contributions we have given to the world. Another part of the museum will present some of the things the white man has given to the Indians in return for the land and life he took: disease, alcohol, poverty and cultural decimation (as symbolized by old tin cans, barbed wire, rubber tires, plastic containers, etc.). Part of the museum will remain a dungeon, to symbolize both those Indian captives who were incarcerated for challenging white authority, and those who were imprisoned on reservations ...

In the name of all Indians, therefore, we reclaim this island for Indian nations, for all these reasons. We feel this claim is just and proper, and that this land should rightfully be granted to us for as long as the rivers shall run and the sun shall shine.

Signed,

INDIANS OF ALL TRIBES
November 1969
San Francisco, California

Source and study: "The Alcatraz Proclamation," reprinted in Troy R. Johnson, *The Occupation of Alcatraz Island: Indian Self-Determination and the Rise of Indian Activism* (University of Illinois Press, 1996), pp. 53–5, and in Alvin Josephy, Jr., Joane Nagel, and Troy Johnson, *Red Power: The American Indians' Fight for Freedom*, 2nd edn. (University of Nebraska Press, 1999 [1971]), pp. 40–3.

3. Vine Deloria's *Custer Died for Your Sins*

While some Indians made public and flamboyant gestures, others began to write for a wide audience, likewise with the goal of drawing attention to the injustice of the natives' situation. Vine Deloria, Jr., who came from a prominent Lakota Sioux family and was himself trained as a minister and lawyer, became a pioneer in the field of Native American Studies. He became famous with the publication of his first book, Custer Died for Your Sins: An Indian Manifesto *in 1969. In the opening pages, he used humor to make his point, as many other natives had done before him.*

Indians are like the weather. Everyone knows all about the weather, but none can change it. When storms are predicted, the sun shines. When picnic weather is announced, the rain begins. Likewise, if you count on the unpredictability of Indian people, you will never be sorry.

One of the finest things about being an Indian is that people are always interested in you and your "plight." Other groups have difficulties, predicaments, quandaries, problems, or troubles. Traditionally we Indians have had a "plight."

Our foremost plight is our transparency. People can tell just by looking at us what we want, and what should be done to help us, how we feel, and what a "real" Indian is really like. Indian life, as it relates to the real world, is a continuous attempt not to disappoint people who know us. Unfulfilled expectations cause grief and we have already had our share.

Because people can see right through us, it becomes impossible to tell truth from fiction or fact from mythology. Experts paint us as they would like us to be. Often we paint ourselves as we wish we were or as we might have been.

The more we try to be ourselves the more we are forced to defend what we have never been. The American public feels most comfortable with the mythical Indians of stereotype-land who were always THERE. These Indians are fierce, they wear feathers and grunt. Most of us don't fit this idealized figure since we grunt only when over eating, which is seldom.

To be an Indian in modern American society is in a very real sense to be unreal and ahistorical. In this book we will discuss the other side – the unrealities that face *us* as Indian people. It is this unreal feeling that has been welling up inside us and threatens to make this decade the most decisive in history for Indian people. In so many ways, Indian people are re-examining themselves in an effort to redefine a new social structure for their people. Tribes are reordering their priorities to account for the obvious discrepancies between their goals and the goals whites have defined for them.

Indian reactions are sudden and surprising. One day at a conference we were singing "My Country 'Tis of Thee" and we came across the part that goes:

Land where our fathers died
Land of the Pilgrims' pride ...

Some of us broke out laughing when we realized that our fathers undoubtedly died trying to keep those Pilgrims from stealing our land. In fact, many of our fathers died because the Pilgrims killed them as witches. We didn't feel much kinship with those Pilgrims, regardless of who they did in.

We often hear "give it back to the Indians" when a gadget fails to work. It's a terrible thing for a people to realize that a society has set aside all nonworking gadgets for their exclusive use.

During my three years as Executive Director of the National Congress of American Indians it was a rare day when some white didn't visit my office and proudly proclaim that she or she was of Indian descent.

Cherokee was the most popular tribe of their choice and many people placed the Cherokees anywhere from Maine to Washington State. Mohawk, Sioux, and Chippewa were next in popularity. Occasionally I would be told about some mythical tribe from lower Pennsylvania, Virginia, or Massachusetts which had spawned the white standing before me.

At times I became quite defensive about being a Sioux when these white people had a pedigree that was so much more respectable than mine. But eventually I came to understand their need to identify as partially Indian and did not resent them. I would confirm their wildest stories about their Indian ancestry and would add a few tales of my own hoping that they would be able to accept themselves someday and leave us alone.

Whites claiming Indian blood generally tend to reinforce mythical beliefs about Indians. All but one person I met who claimed Indian blood claimed it on their grandmother's side. I once did a projection backward and discovered that evidently most tribes were entirely female for the first three hundred years of white occupation. No one, it seemed, wanted to claim a male Indian as a forebear.

It doesn't take much insight into racial attitudes to understand the real meaning of the Indian-grandmother complex that plagues certain whites. A male ancestor has too much of the aura of the savage warrior, the unknown primitive, the instinctive animal, to make him a respectable member of the family tree. But a young Indian princess? Ah, there was royalty for the taking. Somehow the white was linked with a noble house of gentility and culture if his grandmother was an Indian princess who ran away with an intrepid pioneer. And royalty has always been an unconscious but all-consuming goal of the European immigrant.

The early colonists, accustomed to life under benevolent despots, projected their understanding of the European political structure onto the Indian tribe in trying to explain its political and social structure. European royal houses were closed to ex-convicts and indentured servants, so the colonists made all Indian maidens princesses, then proceeded to climb a social ladder of their own creation. Within the next generation, if the trend continues, a large portion of the American population will eventually be related to Powhattan ...

Those whites who dare not claim Indian blood have an asset of their own. They *understand* Indians.

Understanding Indians is not an esoteric art. All it takes is a trip through Arizona or New Mexico, watching a documentary on TV, having known *one* in the service, or having read a popular book on *them*.

There appears to be some secret osmosis about Indian people by which they can magically and instantaneously communicate complete knowledge about themselves to these interested whites. Rarely is physical contact required. Anyone and everyone who knows an Indian or who is *interested*, immediately and thoroughly understands them.

You can verify this great truth at your next party. Mention Indians and you will find a person who saw some in a gas station in Utah, or who attended the Gallup ceremonial celebration, or whose Uncle Jim hired one to cut logs in Oregon, or whose church had a missionary come to speak last Sunday on the plight of Indians and the mission of the church.

There is no subject on earth so easily understood as that of the American Indian. Each summer, work camps disgorge teenagers on various reservations. Within one month's time the youngsters acquire a knowledge of Indians that would astound a college professor.

Early knowledge about Indians is a historical tradition. After Columbus "discovered" America he brought back news of a great new world which he assumed to be Indian, and therefore, filled with Indians. Almost at once European folklore devised a complete explanation of the new land and its inhabitants which featured the Fountain of Youth, the Seven Cities of Gold, and other exotic attractions. The absence of elephants apparently did not tip off the explorers that they weren't in India. By the time they realized their mistake, instant knowledge of Indians was a cherished tradition.

Source: Vine Deloria, Jr., *Custer Died for Your Sins: An Indian Manifesto* (Macmillan, 1969), pp. 1–6.

Further exploration: Deloria was probably the leading Native American intellectual of the second half of the twentieth century. He was the author of numerous important books which are available in most libraries.

4. The Thoughts of Mary Crow Dog

In February of 1973, some Sioux Indians occupied the site of Wounded Knee Creek, where hundreds of their people had been killed a few days after Christmas in 1890, and declared an independent Oglala Sioux nation. Members of the American Indian Movement (AIM) had recently met with a positive reception among many young people on the Lakota reservations and had led several protests, culminating in the decision to go to Wounded Knee. The federal government sent troops to surround the area. The siege lasted 71 days. Two Indians were killed and several others wounded. When the participants agreed to end the occupation and return to their homes, it was on condition that the government investigate their grievances.

One young woman named Mary Brave Bird gave birth to a baby during the siege. Afterwards, she married Leonard Crow Dog, a noted spiritual leader who had also been present at the occupation. Years later, she looked back on her experiences, explaining at the same time why she thought so many young Indians turned to alcohol and why a social movement like AIM seemed so full of promise.

I am Mary Brave Bird. After I had my baby during the siege of Wounded Knee they gave me a special name – Ohitika Win, Brave Woman, and fastened an eagle plume in my hair, singing brave-heart songs for me. I am a woman of the Red nation, a Sioux woman. That is not easy.

I had my first baby during a firefight, with the bullets crashing through one wall and coming out through the other. When my newborn son was only a day old and the marshals really opened up upon us I wrapped him up in a blanket and ran for it. We had to hit the dirt a couple of times, I shielding the baby with my body, praying, "It's all right if I die, but please let him live."

When I came out of Wounded Knee I was not even healed up, but they put me in jail at Pine Ridge and took my baby away. I could not nurse. My breasts swelled up and grew hard as rocks, hurting badly. In 1975 the feds put the muzzles of their M-16s against my head, threatening to blow me away. It's hard being an Indian woman.

My best friend was Annie Mae Aquash, a young, strong-hearted woman from the Micmac Tribe with beautiful children. It is not always wise for an Indian woman to come on too strong. Annie Mae was found dead in the snow at the bottom of a ravine on the Pine Ridge Reservation. The police said that she had died of exposure, but there was a .38-caliber slug in her head. The FBI cut off her hands and sent them to Washington for fingerprint identification, hands that had helped my baby come into the world.

My sister-in-law, Delphine, a good woman who had lived a hard life, was also found dead in the snow, the tears frozen on her face. A drunken man had beaten her, breaking one of her arms and legs leaving her helpless in a blizzard to die.

My sister Barbara went to the government hospital in Rosebud to have her baby and when she came out of anesthesia found that she had been sterilized against her will. The baby lived only for two hours, and she had wanted so much to have children. No, it isn't easy.

When I was a small girl at the St. Francis Boarding School, the Catholic sisters would take a buggy whip to us for what they called "disobedience." At age ten I could drink and hold a pint of whiskey. At age twelve the nuns beat me for "being too free with my body." All I had been doing was holding hands with a boy. At age fifteen I was raped. If you plan to be born, make sure you are born white and male.

It is not the big, dramatic things so much that get us down, but just being Indian, trying to hang on to our way of life, language, and values while being surrounded by an alien, more powerful culture. It is being an *iyeska*, a half-blood, being looked down upon by whites and full-bloods alike. It is being a backwoods girl living in a city having to rip off stores in order to survive. Most of all it is being a woman. Among Plains tribes, some men think that all a woman is good for is to crawl into the sack with them and mind the children. It compensates for what white society has done to them. They were famous warriors and hunters once, but the buffalo is gone and there is not much rep in putting a can of spam or an occasional rabbit on the table.

As for being warriors, the only way some men can count coup nowadays is knocking out another skin's teeth during a barroom fight. In the old days a man made a name for himself by being generous and wise, but now he has nothing to be generous with, no jobs, no money; and as far as our traditional wisdom is concerned, our men are being told by the white missionaries, teachers and employers that it is a merely savage superstition they should get rid of if they want to make it in this world. Men are forced to live away from their children, so that the family can get ADC – Aid to Dependent Children. So some warriors come home drunk and beat on their old ladies in order to work off their frustration. I know where they are coming from. I feel sorry for them, but I feel even sorrier for their women.

To start from the beginning, I am a Sioux from the Rosebud Reservation in South Dakota. I belong to the "Burned Thigh," the Brulé Tribe, the Sicangu in our language . . . I wish I could tell about the big deeds of some ancestors of mine who fought at the Little Big Horn, or the Rosebud counting coup during the Grattan or Fetterman battle, but little is known of my family's history before 1880. I hope that some of my great-grandfathers counted coup on Custer's men, I like to imagine it, but I just do not know. Our Rosebud people did not play a big part in the battles against generals Cook or Custer. This was due to the policy of Spotted Tail, the all-powerful chief at the time. Spotted Tail had earned his eagle feathers as a warrior, but had been taken East as a prisoner and put in jail. Coming back years later, he said that he had seen the cities of the whites and that a single one of them contained more people than could be found in all the Plains tribes put together, and that every one of the wasičuns'[1] factories could turn out more rifles and bullets in one day than were owned by all the Indians in the country. It was useless, he said, to try to resist the wasičuns. During the critical year of 1876 he had his Indian police keep most of the young men on the reservation, preventing them from joining Sitting Bull, Gall, and Crazy Horse. Some of the young bucks, a few Brave Birds among them managed to sneak out trying to get to Montana, but nothing much is known. After having been forced into reservations, it was not thought wise to recall such things …

Our land itself is a legend, especially the area around Grass Mountain where I am living now. The fight for our land is at the core of our existence, as it has been for the last two hundred years. Once the land is gone, then we are gone too. The Sioux used to keep winter counts, picture writings on buffalo skin, which told our people's story from year to year. Well, the whole country is one vast winter count. You can't walk a mile without coming to some family's sacred vision hill, to an ancient Sun Dance circle, an old battle ground, a place where something worth remembering happened. Mostly a death, a proud death or a drunken death. We are a great people for dying. "It's a good day to die!" that's our old battle cry. But the land with its tar paper shacks and outdoor privies, not one of them straight, but all leaning this way or that way, is also a land to live on, a land for good times and telling jokes and talking of great deeds done in the past. But you can't live forever off the deeds of Sitting Bull or Crazy Hose. You can't wear their eagle feathers, freeload off their legends. You have to make your own legends now. It isn't easy.

Source: Mary Crow Dog with Richard Erdoes, *Lakota Woman* (Harper Collins, 1990), pp. 3–11.

Study: Paul Chaat Smith and Robert Allen Warrior, *Like a Hurricane: The Indian Movement from Alcatraz to Wounded Knee* (New Press, 1996). Another way to approach this text is as an example of modern native women's writing. See Inés Hernandez-Avila, ed., *Reading Native American Women: Critical/Creative Representations* (Altamira, 2005).

Further exploration: Mary Crow Dog's book is a rich source on a variety of subjects. It is worth reading more than once, asking yourself different questions each time. Russell Means was a leader at Wounded Knee, and he, too, has written of his experiences. See Russel Means with Marvin J. Wolf, *Where White Men Fear to Tread: The Autobiography of Russell Means* (St. Martin's, 1995).

[1] This is the term for "whites" in Lakota.

5. A Reporter's Comments on the Deaths at Pine Ridge

After the siege at Wounded Knee ended, many of the participants, including Mary Crow Dog, found themselves suddenly facing unrelated charges. It felt to them as though they were being punished in an indirect way, and indeed, declassified FBI documents do provide some evidence that they were being targeted for a form of harassment. There were numerous mysterious deaths at the Pine Ridge reservation over the next three years, some of them mentioned by Mary Crow Dog. Many residents believed that a certain circle of Indians working for Richard ("Dickie") Wilson, the tribal chair, were operating in league with the FBI with the intention of intimidating the people of the reservation. In a 1975 shoot-out, two FBI agents were killed. AIM activist Leonard Peltier is still imprisoned for the crime, though many see the evidence against him as uncertain at best. In 2000, a reporter who lived on the reservation in this difficult period shared his perceptions of the situation at a Congressional briefing concerning the Leonard Peltier case.

KEVIN MCKIERNAN: Good Afternoon. I am a journalist. I was inside Wounded Knee during the 1973 71-day occupation ... it was a long time ago, but it seems like yesterday in many respects. In those days, the Pine Ridge Reservation was a place of great violence with little or no law enforcement. If you wanted as a reporter to gather information about the American Indian Movement (AIM) or the Lakota Traditional, there was a price to pay. I was one of a number of journalists personally threatened and even assaulted physically by vigilantes associated with Wilson's tribal government: my pickup truck on one occasion was hit by a bullet and another time the breaks [*sic*] on my car were cut.

At that time most of the traditional people on Pine Ridge believed that the FBI targeted the AIM Indians – as they were called – and overlooked crimes committed by Wilson and his followers. George O'Clock, the special agent in charge of the Rapid City office, once told me some years later, that the FBI got its SWAT team from Pine Ridge – that during this period from 1973 to 1976, the FBI used Pine Ridge as a SWAT training ground for as many as 2,600 FBI agents. That's a period of only three years and that's when most of the abuses took place.

There is strong evidence of a relationship between the GOONs and the FBI; US Federal Judge Fred Nichols once told me that the FBI and the GOONs worked together because both were against the American Indian Movement. In another interview, then Senator James Abourzek told me the FBI chose sides in the Pine Ridge conflict, failed to investigate an epidemic of Indian killings, and engaged in the selective prosecution of AIM members.

In the 1970's I myself saw an illegal GOON roadblock on the Pine Ridge Reservation and I filmed the armed vigilantes taking property from AIM attorneys at gunpoint. At other times I saw the FBI pass easily through these roadblocks making small talk with the armed men, shaking hands, and then going on their way. And once I was with federal agents in a government van which drove off the road, into a ditch, and around such a GOON roadblock. No attempt was made to confront or question the armed vigilantes.

In 1976 I investigated the murder of Byron DeSersa, an unarmed resident who was ambushed and killed on a highway near the town of Wanblee. The survivors of that incident said that several vehicles associated with Wilson's GOONs had driven by their car and then opened fire on the DeSersa car. The survivors in the car identified the vehicles only less than an hour after the incident and gave the license numbers to the FBI in Wanblee. Although the killers had gathered to drink, celebrate, party, and discharge weapons in the direction of houses owned by AIM sympathizers in Wanblee, FBI agents in town refused to approach the house. Instead of making arrests, they allowed the party to continue all weekend and permitted the Wilson caravan the next day to leave town. Despite the many vehicles involved, only one Wilson man was eventually charged, and he served only two-to-three years on a reduced manslaughter charge.

I investigated other assaults as well, including the GOON caravan that attacked AIM lawyers and destroyed an airplane they had rented and flown to Pine Ridge. They had come there to gather evidence in several legal cases ... The GOONs sliced open the top of one lawyer's car, beating the occupants and cutting a paralegal with a knife. Wilson himself commanded that operation and later he told me that he considered it a "justifiable stomping." He was indicted on a misdemeanor by the judge and then acquitted by an all-white jury.

Years later I interviewed the commander of the GOON squad Duane Brewer who was also involved in that attack. He was well known on the reservation. In fact, he was a member of the tribal police. On camera, he told me that the FBI had provided him with intelligence on the activities of AIM members and that FBI agents had supplied him with armor-piercing bullets to use against the American Indian Movement. That is my statement.

Source: Congressional Briefing for Leonard Peltier, Washington, DC, May 17, 2000.

Further exploration: Some of the recently declassified documents concerning the Peltier case are available on the Internet. After reading all that you can find, what conclusions do you draw about the situation? You can also read the comments of Leonard Peltier in his book *Prison Writings: My Life is My Sundance* (St. Martin's, 1999). Three interesting films that deal with the events of the 1970s are *Lakota Woman*, *Incident at Oglala: The Leonard Peltier Story*, and *Thunderheart*.

Questions for consideration

1 How did Indian activists' tone change between 1961 and 1969?
2 Where did the depth of feeling that is obviously present on the Lakota Sioux reservations in the 1970s come from?
3 How does the activism of the 1960s and 1970s make you feel when you read about it? Inspired? Confused? Alienated? If you were of a race different from your own, what do you imagine your reaction would be?

Chapter 11 The End of the Twentieth Century: A New Era?

1. The Origins of the Native American Graves Protection and Repatriation Act (NAGPRA)

Over the course of the last generation, numerous elements of Native American life have changed. In the 1980s, the general anger of the 70s gave way to specific and concerted movements for change. For many years, for example, the treatment of Native American dead had pained many people: that so many skeletons, even from the relatively recent past, were exhumed and stored in museums for study seemed to those who perceived themselves as a conquered people to add insult to injury. In 1990, pressure brought to bear on this issue yielded the Native American Graves and Repatriation Act (NAGPRA), providing for the return of skeletons kept by museums to descendant communities for reburial, and instituting certain controls at archaeological digs. Delving into the materials that surrounded activists in the 1970s and 1980s helps to illuminate the reasons for the growing anger on this issue. The following archaeological report on a Virginia site was available for sale for many years, complete with 30 images of skeletons curled in their graves, eye sockets staring out at the reader. The site dated from the period immediately preceding the establishment of the Jamestown colony. If the remains had been of Jamestown settlers, they would most likely have been treated differently. It was particularly infuriating to some Virginia Indians that the text was in some ways reminiscent of the words of Robert Beverly, a seventeenth-century colonist who described looting Indian graves while native people were powerless to do anything about it: "As I was ranging the Woods, with some other Friends, we fell upon their Quioccosan *(which is their House of Religious Worship) at a time, when the whole Town were gathered together in another place, to consult about the bounds of the Land given them by the English. Thus finding ourselves masters of so fair an opportunity... we resolved to make use of it, and to examine their* Quioccasan, *the inside of which, they never suffer any* English *Man to see. ... We found some vast Bones, which we judg'd to be the Bones of Men, particularly we measur'd one Thigh-bone, and found it two foot nine inches long ..."*[1] *Here is a segment of the text of the modern archaeological report on an Indian village's burial ground.*

Burial 1. A female, 50–55 years old, tightly flexed, lying on the left side with the cranium toward the east, and accompanied by 7400 marginella and 52 columella shell beads. The columella were at the neck, while the marginella were beneath and covering the body, indicating that they had been sewed to a garment or shroud.

Burial 2. An infant lying face downward with the left arm tightly flexed and the right one extended along the right side. The position suggests that the body had slumped and rotated slightly before the pit was filled. No burial offerings were present.

Burial 3. A young adult female lying on the right side in a tightly flexed position with the cranium toward the southeast. The arms were tightly flexed with the hands under the right side of the face. No burial offerings were present.

Burial 4. A male 55–60 years of age, tightly flexed, lying on the back with the head toward the south. The arms were extended with the wrists crossing over the lower abdominal region. Burial offerings consisted of 2 turtle carapace containers, 1 elk tooth, 1 eagle talon, 1 amethyst crystal, 1 natural stone pendant, 1 chert end scraper, 1 small tube made from turkey bone, 1 large mussel shell, 1 large bone tube made from human humerus, and two bone awls, one made from turkey tibiotarsal, and the other from deer cannon bone. These objects suggest that the individual was a shaman.

Burial 5. An infant loosely flexed and lying on the back with the head toward the southeast. A shell gorget lay on the chest.

Burial 6. A young adolescent, tightly flexed with the head toward the southeast and lying on the right side. Five large stones had been placed over the burial. The cranium had been destroyed by a recent rodent burrow. Burial offerings consisted of 4 bone beads and 6 columella shell beads near the neck.

[1] Robert Beverly, *The History and Present State of Virginia*, ed. Louis B. Wright (University of North Carolina Press, 1947 [1705]), pp. 195–6.

Burial 7. A male 22 years of age, tightly flexed and lying on the right side with the head toward the northeast. The arms were tightly flexed with the hands clasped in front of the mandible.

Burial 8. A male, 50 years of age, tightly flexed and lying on the right side with the head toward the northeast. Burial offerings consisted of 15 columella and 126 disc shell beads near the neck.

Burial 9. A female, 50–55 years old, tightly flexed with the head toward the southeast. No burial offerings were present.

Burial 10. A male, 50 years of age, tightly flexed and lying on the right side with the head toward the northeast. Burial offerings were 56 marginella shell beads at the neck. Evidence of an arrow injury is indicated by a flint projectile point embedded in the left sixth rib. The bone had healed and partly obliterated the projectile point.

Burial 11. A male, 18 years of age, tightly flexed and lying on the right side with the head toward the southeast. Burial offerings consisted of 300 marginella, 39 shell disc, and 20 columella shell beads located near the neck.

Burial 12. An infant 6 months old loosely flexed and lying on the back with the arms extended along the side and the head toward the southeast. With this burial were 959 marginella shell beads which lay under and over the body...

Burial 26. A child 7 years of age, loosely flexed, lying on the left side, with the cranium toward the northeast. There were 15 columella shell and one bone bead near the neck region.

Burial 27. A badly disturbed burial of a child, 9 years of age, lying on the left side with the head toward the northeast. No burial offerings were present.

Burial 28. An infant lying in an extended position with the head toward the southeast. The condition of the bones was poor, and no burial offerings were present.

Burial 29. A fully flexed female, 22 years of age, lying face downward with the arms flexed and the head toward the northeast. A single turkey bone bead was near the neck.

Burial 30. A male, 50 years of age, fully flexed, lying on the right side with the arms folded across the lower chest, and the head toward the south. No burial offerings were present.

Burial 31. A female 25 years of age with the bones disarranged. It was initially believed that this was a disturbed burial, but the absence of any intrusive pit or animal burrow suggested that this had been a re-burial.[2] No burial offerings were present.

[2] This would indicate that for some reason the woman had been moved from where she had died and initially been buried, and brought home to the village for reburial.

Source and study: Joseph L. Benthall, *Archaeological Investigation of the Shannon Site, Montgomery County, Virginia* (Virginia State Library, 1969), pp. 44–52.

Further exploration: Intense debate has continued since the passage of NAGPRA in 1990. Many archaeologists have been concerned about their ability to study the past, and thus to gain knowledge that would ultimately be of interest to Native Americans themselves. Many Native Americans, on the other hand, have been hurt by the lack of respect for their wishes, for their need to be the final arbiters over the fate of the bones of their ancestors. Today, archaeologists are making a more concerted effort to involve all sectors of the community in their work. For four works which vary markedly in their tone, see Tamara Bray, ed., *The Future of the Past: Archaeologists, Native Americans, and Repatriation* (Garland, 2001); Kathleen Fine-Dare, *Grave Injustice: The American Indian Repatriation Movement and NAGPRA* (University of Nebraska Press, 2002); Barbara Alice Mann, *Native Americans, Archaeologists, and the Mounds* (Peter Lang, 2003); David Hurst Thomas, *Skull Wars: Kennewick Man, Archaeology, and the Battle for Native American Identity* (Basic Books, 2000).

2. Growing Pan-Indian Activism and the Native Press

At the same time as the movement for spiritual and cultural self-determination was under way (see section 1 above), many Native Americans became involved in pan-Indian activism, that is, efforts to defend the rights of natives elsewhere in the hemisphere. During the 1970s and 1980s, the US State Department backed military dictatorships in Latin America that displayed zero tolerance for movements on behalf of workers, peasants, or indigenous peoples. In Guatemala, approximately a quarter of a million Mayan Indians were murdered, among them many descendants of the creators of the glyphs at Piedras Negras (see Chapter 1). A number of Mohawk activists (of the Haudenosaunee or Iroquois League) had already been down to Guatemala on intercultural exchange visits. When the worst of the atrocities began in 1982 and 1983, their newspaper, Akwesasne Notes, *was among the first to publish news of what was occurring. These early harbingers of the tidings eventually encouraged journalists at more mainstream papers to cover the story. Once the world's attention was focused on the issue, the military government's activities began to be curbed. Meanwhile, staff members of* Akwesasne Notes, *who could no longer travel to Guatemala without risking death themselves, worked to help Mayan refugees who had made it into the United States. They asked their readers for help. Their circulation at that time was in the tens of thousands.*

Corn-Maya: Orientation for Mayan Refugees

In our [previous] issue we carried a ... report on the situation of several hundred Guatemalan Indian refugees who were threatened with deportation in Southern Florida. Part of a much larger migration (more than a million internal and external refugees), the K'anjobal Indian families who ended up in southern Florida were direct victims of a brutal anti-civilian and anti-Indian war being waged by the Guatemalan government and military against its own people. In the previous report, we recorded and printed several long oral testimonies by the Guatemalan refugees, detailing many instances of repression in their home country, including several large scale massacres. The following is an updated report on the fate of the K'anjobal families in southern Florida. It is also about their attempt to survive the pitfalls of migration by organizing a cooperative – a worthwhile project which promises to be a model for other peoples in similar situations. We are thankful to Dr. Shelton H. Davis of Anthropology Resource Center for much of the information contained in it.

Indiantown, Florida – Mr. Jeronimo Camposeco, a K'anjobal speaker and Mayan Indian who accompanied the originial I.P.N. team last March, returned to Florida in May to continue to assist the K'anjobal refugees. Since then, he has collaborated with attorneys in submitting political asylum applications for the Kanjobal people here. The earliest applications were for the eight people detained in January at Krome Detention Center in Miami. Since then, applications for another 120 people have been submitted. Almost every week, another Kanjobal person or group of persons seeks the assistance of Jeronimo and the attorneys. To support these applications, attorneys have compiled a document of several hundred pages describing the campaign of terror that the Guatemalan army has unleashed against the Indian population. Hundreds of hours of work have gone into this documentation process. This legal assistance is only a first step in helping the Kanjobal people to find a decent home here in the United States. The people here are farmworkers, and they face misery, despair, and poverty. For the Kanjobal women and children, the situation is particularly sad: they stay in shacks or roachridden houses during the day, while the men work long hours for low wages in the flower gardens and citrus fields. The personal and family tensions created by being an immigrant, as well as a farmworker, are enormous. The problems go even deeper for the Kanjobal people, who enter the migrant-and farm-labor stream as traditional Indians with a culture radically different from that of other rural poor people in the United States.

In response to this situation, we are looking for ways to assist the Kanjobal people to maintain their sense of cultural integrity during their stay in the United States. One of the ideas we have been discussing is the establishment of a small production cooperative that will provide income to the Kanjobal community when there is no farmwork available. We are not sure of the exact type of production we would like to promote: for example, piecework for the textile industry, making of traditional craft items, or maguey production as in the cooperative that the people have in Guatemala.

We believe, however, that the establishment of a cooperative is essential to keep these people together and to ensure that they are not totally at the mercy of the exploitative farm labor system.

On August 7, about 50 Kanjobal people discussed the cooperative idea at the fiesta at the Holy Cross Church in Indiantown. A six-person committee was created, made up of two people from each of the migrant communities. As political violence in Guatemala continues to force thousands of Mayan Indians to flee their villages, it is clear that the refugee services being developed by the Corn-Mayan Project will become increasingly important. The Anthropology Resource Center is committed to assisting Jeronimo and his collaborators in raising funds for this project. They are also willing to provide the project with administrative, research and other support services which may be needed to make this project a success. As a 501(c)(3) organization, ARC can accept public donations and grants to the CORN-MAYAN Project. There are several current needs of the Corn-Maya Project. These include: (1) Funds for Jeronimo Camposeco to continue as project coordinator. Grants from individuals and the Presbyterian Church's Office of World Service and World Hunger enabled Jeronimo to receive a monthly salary, automobile expenses, and maintenance funds during the last spring and summer. These funds are now exhausted, and we are seeking interim funds until the project can stabilize itself financially. (2) Technical assistance to plan the production cooperative. We need some individual or organization with management and business experience to do a planning study of various types of productive enterprises. The Kanjobal community contains people who are experts in craftswork, commerce and textile production, as well as agriculture and farm labor; they also have experience with cooperatives. What they need is managerial assistance and advice before entering into the economic venture. Persons interested in assisting the Corn-Maya Project should contact Shelton Davis, at ARC 37 Temple Place, No. 521, Boston, Mass. 02111. Phone: 617 426-9286. Or, Jeronimo Camposeco at P.O. Box 613, Indiantown, FL 33456.

A Call for Help: To All Native North Americans Nations: A Report on the Forced Migration of Mayan Peoples: Kanjobal Refugees in Southern Florida

Many Mayan people, victims of the brutal war being waged against them in their homelands, are migrating north. They are fleeing for their lives and seeking refuge and sanctuary. After nearly three years of a near-complete news blackout, the largely-uninformed North American news media is reporting regularly on these events. The following is a report on one case, already pending before U.S. Immigration and Naturalization

Service (I.N.S.) Court. It is the story of one family's flight from terror, from massacres, rape, torture. The NOTES obtained this report from a documentation team of Indigenous Peoples' Network (I.P.N.), to whom we are thankful. I.P.N. is a Native Peoples' news service currently in formation.

In Southern Florida, there are at present approximately 250 Kanjobal Indians from Guatemala. They represent several inter-related families from the San Miguel Acatan area of the Department of Huehuetenango and are people who migrated from their homelands as a result of the all-pervasive state of violence and war which dominates the region. These 250 people are part of a larger pattern of migration involving hundreds of thousands of internal and external refugees from the Guatemalan highlands, where the majority of the population is Mayan Indians. They represent particularly large migrations from the Kanjobal, Mam, Jacalteco, Quiche, Kakchiquel and Kekchi Nations of the Guatemalan countryside. Many of the Guatemalan Indians have settled in refugee camps on the Mexican side of the border, an 800 mile long frontier. Others, having lost their villages to the torch and endured massacres, torture and death threats, have settled in more or less permanent camps around the larger cities of Guatemala, particularly around the capital, Guatemala City. It is estimated that just from the Kanjobal Nation, with a total population of 30,000 people, some 3,000 refugees have made their way to United States jurisdiction.

The approximately 250 Kanjobals in Southern Florida are presently working and residing at or near agricultural migrant labor camps, having been incorporated into the North American migrant stream along with United States–Mexico border. One group of some 50 people are residing and working in the vicinity of Indiantown Florida. The rest are to be found in one of three camps in the area of the towns of Immokalee and Fort Myers. United States Immigration and Naturalization Service (INS) officials have made two raids against the Kanjobal group at the Indiantown site, resulting in the detention of seven people (six men, one woman) on January 25th and one man on March 9, 1983. Four women and eight children were also held briefly and released during the second INS raid. The eight detainees are currently going through deportation proceedings, and are scheduled for a deportation hearing within the month. There is good reason to believe that these eight K'anjobal people will face torture and execution, if deported back to Guatemala. In their case, as in many others, deportation very realistically equals death.

Resolutions of support by North American Indian peoples, organizations, groups and law offices would be most appreciated. There is a most pressing need to let the United States State Department know of the Native People's concern for our Southern relatives, of their right to seek asylum and sanctuary from repression and death, and of North American Native Peoples' right to call for and extend such sanctuary. Many peoples of the world come to North America seeking sanctuary from violent conflicts. In many cases, they are extended political asylum and/or extended voluntary deportation status by the United States and Canada. Will these same governments now be allowed to close their arms and refuse a people native to this continent the right to seek shelter from genocide?

Source: *Akwesasne Notes* 15/1 (February 1983): 5; 15/2 (Spring 1983): 4.

Study: There is to date no study of this aspect of native North American activism. There are, however, significant studies of the experiences of the Mayas. Start with Greg Grandin, *The Last Colonial Massacre: Latin America in the Cold War* (University of Chicago Press, 2004) and *The Blood of Guatemala: A History of Race and Nation* (Duke University Press, 2000).

Further exploration: A complete list of grassroots publications produced by the native community and their years of publication is available at the website of the American Native Press Archives, based at the University of Arkansas (www.anpa.ualr.edu). The full text of a number of these papers is available through the Ethnic Newswatch database, to which most research libraries subscribe.

3. Louise Erdrich's "Dear John Wayne"

In the late twentieth century many Native Americans began to participate in an artistic florescence, or perhaps one should say renaissance, in that indigenous artists have perhaps not been so free to express themselves since before the conquest. Native American poets, novelists, screenwriters, artists, and singers have recently appeared on the national stage.

One of the best-known writers is Louise Erdrich. She was born in Minnesota in 1954 to a German-American father and an Anishinabe mother. She grew up in North Dakota and then attended Dartmouth. Her first novel, Love Medicine *(1984), told the story of several families living on a North Dakota Anishinabe reservation. It won several awards, and since then Erdrich has written prolifically on many subjects. The poem below speaks of what the popular stereotypes of Indians do to the young people who must bear their burden even as they are trying desperately to laugh them off. Their knowledge of history is with them all the time.*

Dear John Wayne

August and the drive-in picture is packed.
We lounge on the hood of the Pontiac

Surrounded by the slow-burning spirals they sell
At the window, to vanquish the hordes of mosquitoes.
Nothing works. They break through the smoke screen for blood.

Always the lookout spots the Indians first,
Spread north to south, barring progress.
The Sioux or some other Plains bunch
In spectacular columns, ICBM missiles,
Feathers bristling in the meaningful sunset.

The drum breaks. There will be no parlance.
Only the arrows whining, a death-cloud of nerves
Swarming down on the settlers
Who die beautifully tumbling like dust weeds
Into the history that brought us all here
Together: this wide screen beneath the sign of the bear.

The sky fills, acres of blue squint and eye
That the crowd cheers. His face moves over us,
A thick cloud of vengeance, pitted
Like the land that was once flesh. Each rut,
Each scar makes a promise: *It is*
Not over, this fight, not as long as you resist.
Everything we see belongs to us.

A few laughing Indians fall over the hood
Slipping in the hot spilled butter.
The eye sees a lot, John, but the heart is so blind.
Death makes us owners of nothing.
He smiles, a horizon of teeth
The credits reel over, and then the white fields
Again blowing in the true-to-life dark.

The dark films over everything.
We get into the car
Scratching our mosquito bites, speechless and small
As people are when the movie is done.
We are back in our skins.

How can we help but keep hearing his voice,
The flip side of the sound track, still playing:
Come on, boys, we got them
Where we want them, drunk, running.
They'll give us what we want, what we need.
Even his disease was the idea of taking everything.
Those cells, burning, doubling, splitting out of their skins.

Source: Louise Erdrich, "Dear John Wayne," in *Jacklight* (Henry Holt, 1984), pp. 12–13.

Further exploration: The work of many Native American writers is now in print. One of the younger generation is Sherman Alexie, whose best-known book *The Lone Ranger and Tonto Fistfight in Heaven* (Atlantic Monthly Press, 1993) inspired the film *Smoke Signals*.

4. President Clinton's 1994 Conference with Native Leaders

> *... By the 1990s, many agreed that a new era had come. New laws were made to encourage tribal self-rule. On April 29, 1994, President Bill Clinton invited the leaders of the 547 federally recognized tribes to the White House, and 322 came to hear what he had to say and make their own demands. Clinton was the first Democrat to hold office since 1980 and his liberal agenda included promises of progress to Native Americans. During the succeeding years of his presidency, he signed into law the American Indian Religious Freedom Act (1994), the American Indian Trust Management Reform Act (1994), the Tribal Self-Government Act (1994), and the Native American Housing Assistance and Self-Determination Act (1996), and he also encouraged a new Strategic Plan for the Bureau of Indian Affairs (1997).*

I say to the leaders of the first Americans, the American Indian and Alaska natives, welcome to the White House. Welcome home.

So much of who we are today comes from who you have been for a long time. Long before others came to these shores there were powerful and sophisticated cultures and societies here: yours. Because of your ancestors, democracy existed here long before the Constitution was drafted and ratified ...

I believe in your rich heritage and in our common heritage. What you have done to retain your identity, your dignity, and your faith in the face of often immeasurable obstacles is profoundly moving, an example of the enduring strength of the human spirit.

We desperately need this lesson now. We must keep faith with you and with that spirit and with the common heritage so many of us cherish. That is what you came to talk to me about and what I would like to respond to today.

In every relationship between our people, our first principle must be to respect your right to remain who you are and to live the way you wish to live. And I believe the best way to do that is to acknowledge the unique government-to-government relationship we have enjoyed over time. Today I reaffirm our commitment to self-determination for tribal governments. I pledge to fulfill the trust obligations of the Federal Government. I vow to honor and respect tribal sovereignty based upon our unique historic relationship. And I pledge to continue my efforts to protect your right to fully exercise your faith as you wish.

Let me speak for a moment about religious freedom, something precious to you, something deeply enshrined in our Constitution. For many of you, traditional religions and ceremonies are the essence of your culture and your very existence. Last year, I was pleased to sign a law that restored certain constitutional protections for those who want to express their faith in this country.

No agenda for religious freedom will be complete until traditional native American religious practices have received all the protections they deserve. Legislation is needed to protect native American religious practices threatened by Federal action.[3] The native American free exercise of religion act is long overdue. And I will continue to work closely with you and members of Congress to make sure the law is constitutional and strong. I want it passed so that I can invite you back here and sign it into law in your presence.

And to make certain that you can obtain the ritual symbols of your religious faith, in a moment I will sign a directive to every executive department and agency of Government, not just the Department of Interior, instructing them to cooperate with tribal governments to accommodate wherever possible the need for eagle feathers in the practice of native American religions.

This then is our first principle: respecting your values, your religions, your identity, and your sovereignty. This brings us to the second principle that should guide our relationship: We must dramatically improve the Federal Government's relationships with the tribes and become full partners with the tribal nations.

I don't want there to be any mistake about our commitment to a stronger partnership between our people. Therefore, in a moment I will also sign an historic Government directive that requires every executive department and agency of the Government to take two simple steps: first, to remove all barriers that prevent them from working directly with tribal governments, and second, to make certain that if they take action affecting tribal trust resources, they consult with tribal governments prior to that decision. It is the entire government, not simply the Department of the Interior, that has a trust responsibility with tribal governments. And it is time the entire Government recognized and honored that responsibility . . .

All governments must work better. We must simply be more responsive to the people we serve and to each other. It's the only way we'll be able to

[3] These would include, for example, the use of certain drugs and of eagle feathers in religious ceremonies.

do good things with the resources we have. I know that you agree with that. More and more of you are moving to assume fuller control of your governments. Many are moving aggressively to take responsibility for operating your own programs. Each year the Bureau of Indian Affairs is providing more technical services and fewer direct services.

One avenue for greater tribal control is through self-governance contracts. There are about 30 self-compacting tribes today. We're working with Congress to raise that number by 20 tribes every year. We'd like self-governance to become a permanent program. But we must ensure services will still be provided to the smaller tribes that do not choose to participate.

What is the goal of a better and more equal partnership, and more empowered tribes and more efficient government? Ultimately it must be to improve the living conditions of those whom we serve. And that must be our third and final principle.

Together we must position American Indians and Alaska Natives to compete economically as we move toward the 21st century ...

We must do more to create jobs, raise incomes, and develop capital for new businesses. I know there are more success stories in Indian country every year but not nearly enough as the people who bore witness to your conditions here today so eloquently said. Strengthening tribal economies will require new thinking and the courage to change. It will require investing in the health, the education, and the skills of American Indians and Alaska Natives, as we must do for all Americans ...

Our goal is clear: to work with you to enhance economic development in every tribe ... This great, historic meeting today must be the beginning of our new partnership, not the end of it.

I'd like to make a point about economic development that has to do with gaming ... My goal is this: I want the tribes to continue to benefit from gaming, and I want current disputes over the 1988 gaming regulatory act to be worked out. I strongly support the process now underway to achieve that goal. But just as with the national economy, we know we can't solve every problem overnight. The important thing is to create policies that give every tribe the chance to have a strong economy in the long run, to develop the will and the consistency to stick with those policies over time, and to keep working and talking together ...

There has been a great deal of debate this year about the budget of the Indian Health Service ... But I believe the health needs of tribal communities and families and children clearly require special attention. Therefore, I have amended next year's budget to restore more than $120 million in funding for the Indian Health Service.

Finally, as we heard so eloquently today, there is in America, across the lines of race and class and religion, a profound concern for our children. Too many are poor or sick or unsupervised. Too many are likely to use violence or be the victims of violence. Too many are unprepared intellectually for life or work. Yet nothing is so striking in tribal communities as your love of family and extended family and your devotion to your children. Every segment of our society could well take a lesson from you. But in spite of your best efforts, too many of your children also suffer from poor health and inadequate education. And we are trying hard to address those problems ...

As we look back on the American journey, the test ahead is always whether we are moving in the right direction of more tolerance, wider justice, and greater opportunity for all. It is the direction that counts, always the direction. And our choices will set that direction.

Of course, as you well know, our history has not always been a proud one. But our future can be, and that is up to us. Together we can open the greatest era of cooperation, understanding and respect among our people ever. I know that we will. And when we do, the judgment of history will be that the President of the United States and the leaders of the sovereign Indian nations met and kept faith with each other and our common heritage and together lifted our great nations to a new and better place.

[*At this point, the President signed the memorandums.*]

In keeping with a tradition that goes back to the early days of our Republic, I want each of you, in leaving, to receive a miniature replica of the Jefferson Indian Peace Medal. On the front is a picture of our third President, Thomas Jefferson, author of the Declaration of Independence and one of the chief architects of our democracy. When you receive your medal, you will see on the back two hands clasped one with a cuff showing three stripes and three buttons, the other wearing a bracelet engraved with an eagle. The hands join with the inscription, "Peace and Friendship."

As we pray and as we leave, let us hope that this is the beginning of true peace, true friendship, and true progress.

Thank you.

Source: Public Papers of the Presidents of the United States: William Jefferson Clinton, 1994, 1 :800–3, reprinted in Francis Paul Prucha, ed., *Documents of United States Indian Policy* (University of Nebraska Press, 2000 [1975]), pp. 343–5.

Further exploration: Students might be interested in comparing the Indian policies of different presidential administrations by consulting the legislative record.

5. Struggles over the Indian Gaming Regulatory Act

In the 1970s and 1980s, many self-governing tribes hosted high-stakes bingo games. Gambling had long been a part of Native American culture, and as the reservations were not subject to the same state regulations as other towns or the profits to the same taxes, it appeared to be a good opportunity to earn some much needed income. Over time, the industry evolved considerably and became big business. The year 1988 saw the passage of the Indian Gaming Regulatory Act (IGRA). In 2001 a best-selling book by Kim Eisner called The Revenge of the Pequots *made the argument that people who were Indian only by an infinitesimally small blood count, and not by cultural heritage, were making exorbitant profits off innocent people. In fact, however, the Pequots – who had indeed only recently reconstituted themselves as a tribe – were an exceptional case. On many long-standing reservations, the casinos have contributed immensely to economic progress. During the 1990s, discussions of refinements to the law governing Indian gaming became commonplace in Washington, and as recently as 2006 several new amendments were passed. The following is a report produced to accompany the publication of the hearings on the issue. It reveals the complexity of the many issues at stake.*

Calendar No. 466

109th Congress | Report

SENATE

2d Session | 109–261

INDIAN GAMING REGULATORY ACT AMENDMENTS OF 2006
June 6, 2006. Ordered to be printed

Mr. McCain, from the Committee on Indian Affairs, submitted the following
REPORT
[To accompany S. 2078]

The Committee on Indian Affairs, to which was referred the bill, (S. 2078), to amend the Indian Gaming Regulatory Act to clarify the authority of the National Indian Gaming Commission to regulate Class III gaming, to limit the lands eligible for gaming, and for other purposes, having considered the same, reports favorably thereon with an amendment in the nature of a substitute and recommends that the bill (as amended) do pass.

Purpose

The primary purpose of S. 2078, the Indian Gaming Regulatory Act Amendments of 2006, is to clarify and amend provisions of the Indian Gaming Regulatory Act of 1988, Public Law 100–497, 25 U.S.C. Sec. 2501 et seq. ("IGRA"), applicable to the Department of Interior ("DoI"), the National Indian Gaming Commission ("NIGC"), and the Indian tribes. This legislation is necessary to make amendments to the IGRA so that Indian tribes may continue to be the primary beneficiaries of gaming operations conducted on Indian lands, and to reaffirm and further the original goals of the IGRA.

Background

1. Indian gaming pre-IGRA

Indian gaming began in earnest in the late 1970s with several tribes, from New York to Florida conducting "high- stakes" bingo operations. Other tribes quickly followed suit, and by the mid-1980s over 100 tribes were conducting bingo operations, which generated more than $100 million in annual revenues. Some states, particularly Florida and California, attempted to assert jurisdiction over these tribes. The tribes resisted strenuously, citing long-standing Federal law and policy which provided for Federal and tribal jurisdiction over Indian lands, instead of state jurisdiction.

2. Supreme Court Cabazon decision

These legal disputes culminated in a ruling by the Supreme Court in California v. Cabazon Band of Mission Indians, 480 U.S. 202 (1987) ("Cabazon"). In that decision, the Supreme Court, using a balancing test between Federal, state, and tribal interests, found that tribes, in states that otherwise allow gaming, had a right to conduct gaming activities on Indian lands largely unhindered by state regulation. Specifically, the Cabazon Court held that Public Law 83–280 states with laws that regulated, but did not criminally prohibit, all forms of gaming within their borders, could not regulate gaming conducted by Indian tribes on Indian lands in those states. In reaching this decision, the Court also emphasized the Federal government's policy of Indian tribal self-governance, including the policy of encouraging tribal self-sufficiency and economic development.

3. IGRA

The Cabazon decision engendered a great deal of discussion regarding the need for Federal legislation to address Indian gaming and its regulation.

Tribes, satisfied with the Cabazon decision, saw no need for Federal legislation. States sought Federal legislation overruling Cabazon and providing an extension of state jurisdiction over Indian lands for gaming regulation. Some in Congress, including current and past members of this Committee, saw wisdom in creating a comprehensive regulatory framework under Federal law, that would bring some order to the complex relationship between the Federal government, tribes and states as it related to the conduct and regulation of Indian gaming.

The result of those discussions was the IGRA, enacted a year after the Cabazon decision, which established a comprehensive framework for the operation of Indian tribal gaming across the United States. A primary purpose of the IGRA, as stated by Congress, was "to provide a statutory basis for the operation of gaming by Indian tribes as a means of promoting tribal economic development, self-sufficiency, and strong tribal governments."[1] Another purpose was "to provide a statutory basis for the regulation of gaming by an Indian tribe adequate to shield it from organized crime and other corrupting influences, to ensure that the Indian tribe is the primary beneficiary of the gaming operation, and to assure that gaming is conducted fairly and honestly by both the operator and players."[2]

In enacting the IGRA, Congress expressly rejected arguments by states for abrogating tribal sovereignty and imposing state regulation of tribal gaming. Instead, the IGRA established three different categories of gaming and a regulatory system applicable to each. The IGRA also established a Federal regulatory commission, the NIGC, to provide Federal oversight over certain forms of tribal gaming.

The three categories of gaming established by the IGRA, and the regulatory system for each, are:

- Class I, which refers to traditional and ceremonial games conducted by tribes, and for which the IGRA provides exclusive regulation by the tribes;
- Class II, which refers to bingo, games similar to bingo, pulltabs, and some non-banked card games, and for which the IGRA provides primary day-to-day regulation by the tribes and regulatory oversight and enforcement by the NIGC; and
- Class III, which refers to all other types of gaming, and for which the IGRA provides a unique method of shared regulation between tribes and states through mutually agreed upon compacts, and over which the NIGC exercises oversight and enforcement.

The IGRA created the NIGC, a 3-member independent Federal regulatory agency charged with oversight of Indian gaming. Under its mandate, the NIGC is charged with approving management contracts;[3] conducting background investigations;[4] approving tribal gaming ordinances;[5] reviewing and conducting audits of the books and records of Indian gaming operations;[6] and enforcing violations of the IGRA, its own regulations, and approving tribal gaming ordinances.[7]

Pursuant to the compact provisions of the IGRA, many Indian tribes and states developed sophisticated regulatory frameworks to oversee tribal gaming operations. These tribes and states have put in place effective standards for the conduct of Class III games, as well as financial and accounting standards for their operations.

4. *The Seminole decision*

The compacting process, originally envisioned as an opportunity for tribes and states to enter into mutually beneficial agreements addressing legitimate issues of concern to each, became an area of significant discord soon after enactment of the IGRA. Several states, including Florida, asserted legal challenges to the IGRA rather than enter into good faith negotiations for compacts. These challenges culminated in a decision by the U.S. Supreme Court in Seminole Tribe v. Florida, 517 U.S. 44 (1996) ("Seminole"). In that decision, the Court held that provisions in the IGRA which authorized tribes to bring suit in Federal court for "bad faith refusal to negotiate" were unconstitutional infringements on the State of Florida's 11th Amendment immunity to suit. Following the Seminole decision, the Secretary of the Interior, using authority provided by IGRA, promulgated regulations pursuant to which a tribe can request "procedures"[8] for the regulation of Class III gaming in states where such gaming is permissible. Several states have challenged the constitutionality of the Secretary's authority to issue such procedures. To date the Secretary has not issued procedures for any tribe.

5. *The Indian Gaming industry in 2006: A snapshot*

At the time the IGRA was enacted, Indian gaming was a relatively modest industry consisting mainly of what are now known as "Class II" high-stakes bingo operations. At that time, virtually no one contemplated that Indian gaming would become the nearly $20 billion[9] industry that exists today. Indian gaming is providing tribes with much-needed capital for development and employment opportunities where few previously existed.

Though gaming revenues have grown exponentially in the last eighteen years, the IGRA has been amended only once. In 1997, Committee on Indian Affairs Chairman Campbell introduced an amendment that authorized the NIGC to collect increased fees including, for the first time, fees from Class III operations, which would fund the Commission's regulatory efforts in Indian Country.[10] Before the change in the fees structure, the

NIGC was funded almost exclusively with Federal appropriations, and was barely able to keep up with the ever-growing number of tribal gaming operations and its statutorily mandated duties under the IGRA.

Since 1997, the NIGC has made significant strides in its role as the Federal regulatory body charged with oversight in the field of Indian gaming. It has opened five field offices and employed additional staff to oversee tribal gaming operations across the country and fulfill the NIGC's monitoring responsibilities.[11]

Most recently, on May 12, 2006, the President signed Public Law 109–221, which contained the operative provisions of S. 1295, the National Indian Gaming Commission Accountability Act of 2005. S. 1295 was introduced by Senator McCain on June 23, 2005, to amend Section 18 of the IGRA to authorize the NIGC to collect fees from all Class II and Class III operations at a rate not to exceed .08 percent of the gross revenues from each such operation. As a result, for a year in which the Indian gaming industry has gross revenues of $20 billion, the new fee structure provides the NIGC with potential funding of $16 million.

An Overview of the Provisions of S. 2078

On April 27, 2005, Chairman John McCain held an oversight hearing on Indian gaming. At that hearing, Senator McCain stated that the IGRA had not been substantively amended since its enactment in 1988, nearly 17 years before, and expressed his intention to conduct a series of oversight hearings into the IGRA, its implementation and the status of the Indian gaming industry. Subsequently, on May 18, July 27, and September 21, 2005, the Committee held additional oversight hearings on the IGRA, receiving testimony from the DoI, NIGC, local government officials, local community groups, and Indian tribes engaged in gaming. On November 18, 2005, S. 2078 was introduced by Senator McCain. Following introduction of the bill, the Committee held additional oversight hearings on February 1, and February 28, 2006. On March 8, 2006, the Committee held a legislative hearing on S. 2078. The hearings held in 2005 provided the Committee with significant information on much-needed updates and necessary improvements to the IGRA. S. 2078 was drafted based upon that information and information received from other parties. The legislative hearing held on S. 2078 provided additional critical feedback on the bill language. Based on this feedback, on March 29, 2006, the Committee approved a substitute amendment which addressed concerns raised about the bill's language by Committee Members. As approved by the Committee, S. 2078 provides several amendments to the IGRA, including clarifications of the authorities and responsibilities of the NIGC, additional oversight over significant gaming contracts (and parties to those contracts), and several clarifications and amendments to the provisions providing eligibility for gaming under the IGRA on lands acquired after 1988.

Notes

1 Pub. L. 100–497, 102 Stat. 2467, Sec. 3 (1988).
2 See id.
3 See id., Sec. 6(a)(4).
4 See id., Sec. 11(b)(2)(F).
5 See id., Sec. 6(a)(3).
6 See id., Sec. 7(b)(4) and Sec. 11(b)(2)(C).
7 See id., Sec. 14.
8 See infra Note 1, Sec. 11(d)(7)(B)(vii).
9 See National Indian Gaming Commission, Press Release, July 13, 2005.
10 Prior to the 1997 amendment, the NIGC budget was limited to Federal appropriations which could match fees collected from the tribes based on their Class II gaming revenues. The cap on those Class II fees was set at $3,000,000.
11 See e.g. Hearing to Provide Information on the Activities of the National Indian Gaming Commission, Before the Senate Committee on Indian Affairs, S. Hrg. 106–730, 106th Cong., at p. 3 (2000) (Testimony of Montie Deer, Chairman, National Indian Gaming Commission). See also Hearing on Indian Gaming Regulatory Act: Role and Funding of the National Indian Gaming Commission, Before the Senate Committee on Indian Affairs, S. Hrg. 108-67, Pt. 1, 108th Cong., at pp. 3–4 (2003) (Testimony of Philip Hogen, Chairman, National Indian Gaming Commission).

Study: Steven Andrew Light and Kathryn R. L. Rand, *Indian Gaming and Tribal Sovereignty: The Casino Compromise* (University of Kansas Press, 2005).

Further exploration: Students might read Kim Isaac Eisler, *The Revenge of the Pequots* (Simon & Schuster, 2001) in the context of the scholarly study by Light and Rand (cited above) and decide where Eisler, a popular writer, is manipulating the story and where she is being fair.

6. An Elder's Stories for Future Generations

Today many native nations are engaged in attempting to preserve their languages and traditional culture. Courses are being offered to teach young people the tongues they are otherwise in danger of forgetting. Whenever possible, stories are recorded and transcribed so that they will be permanently available to posterity. Paul John, a Yup'ik Eskimo Elder from Nelson Island, Alaska (Qaluyaat) is an example of a man taking an active role in this regard. Born in 1928, John was invited to speak at a local high school for several different days over a two week period in 1977. He told traditional tales in Yup'ik and what he said was recorded. He continued to be active in Yup'ik cultural affairs, and recently an anthropologist has worked to bring his stories into print in both Yup'ik and English. Together, the tales make a 750-page book.

Allamek-gguq ella yuituq

Mat'um nalliini inkut elpeci makut wangkuta, ciuliamta-w' augkut yuullrat niiteng'erpeciu, tua-i-w'elpeceni tuarpiaq piciuvkenani nalluavciu. Taugken makut maa-i aatavet, makut-llu aanama tua-i-w' tangtullruluku. Wiinga-ll' ellmacuar tuarpiaq imumek iqukuinrayagii nauwa show-*rqamta* film-*am iqua alaicecuaqerluni tamaq'erqel', tuacetun tua-i wii ayuqua …*

They say the world is populated by no one else

Even though you hear about what life was like for our ancestors, you don't believe it because you haven't experienced it. But your fathers and mothers saw it. I saw the tail end [of that way of life]. You know how it is when you see the end of a movie and then it's over. Well, it is like that with me. It was like I saw the tail end of our traditional Yup'ik way of life. It is as if I really didn't see [the whole show]. But even though it is like that for me, the things I heard are still in my mind and aren't lost to this day.

Long ago, people did not live like we do now. You know how something is connected to the center and therefore together. That was how our Yup'ik ancestors were. Take me, for instance. I know my relatives in Chefornak, I know my relatives in Bethel, Kipnuk, Tununak, and Newtok.

But it is like you people at the present time have forgotten your relatives because we do not tell you who they are. And it is because our life has become what they call Westernized. We no longer lack anything [in terms of material goods]. We don't inform you, our youngsters, about the relatives.

In those days, before we became Westernized, they told us about our relatives on Nunivak Island or other places, thinking, "If this person starts traveling to other villages and is in need, he is going to feel very desperate if he doesn't know his relatives. But if I tell him who his relatives are by name and where they reside, he will ask for them when he is desperate. 'Where does so- and-so live? Is he here?' And when they say yes, he will say, 'My father or mother has asked me to go to him when I arrive in need of help.'" And he would go to that person knowing who he is without worry if his father or mother had informed him about them. And the person who he goes to see will know he is a relative because he was [also] informed. "I am seeing my relative for the first time." They know they are related because their parents informed them, even though they are seeing each other for the first time. They will help each other, even though they are seeing each other for the first time.

And now, because we are becoming Westernized these days, we no longer inform you [about your family] as if thinking, "If he is at Bethel and needs help, he will ask the BIA [Bureau of Indian Affairs] for help ... Or if he needs help, he will go to the Sleep-off Center..." But here you actually have relatives in Bethel. We no longer tell you about them.

They informed them about their relatives because they were like family, even though they lived far apart. Because they were told about their relatives, if you arrived at a village and didn't have any tobacco, someone would immediately give you some without asking for payment because you are his relative. And he would let you sleep [at his house] without payment if you had no place to sleep because you were told that you are related.

But if we didn't tell [about relatives] and you came along, he wouldn't let you smoke a cigarette or have a chew of tobacco until you paid him twenty-five cents. He wouldn't let you sleep [at his house] at night until you paid him because he doesn't know you. But you were actually related, if only you were told about it ...

Because you weren't told about your relatives, [people] will be reluctant to help you, even though we really shouldn't be reluctant. Because we have become Westernized and no longer lack anything, it is as if we have lost the custom of helping others. You are no longer told about your relatives on Nunivak Island or anywhere in our area. If we always told you about your relatives in other villages ... you would help one another.

Some people say, "This person is no relation and is not from this village." We would not say that if we recalled our past.

Our ancestors used to say, "The world is populated by no one else [but relatives]." They said even if a person saw someone for the first time, it would be better to speak to him openly instead of not talking to him. It would be better not to let him feel uncomfortable and unwelcome. ... They said that the world is populated by no one else [but relatives].

And then they would say, "Even if you see a stranger for the first time, don't just look away. Even if he appears respectable,[4] if you have some food to offer ask him, 'Have you eaten?'" If we fed him if he hadn't eaten, he

[4] Paul John meant, "Even if he does not appear poor or hungry."

would be very grateful in his mind, even though he didn't formally thank you. And he will never forget you when he sees you in his village.

And because he was so very grateful that you fed him when he was hungry, when he sees you in his village he will ask you in return, "I didn't know you were here. You must come and eat." Then you'll go with him. He wouldn't have asked you to eat if you hadn't asked him to eat in your village, if you had looked away after seeing him.

And then one day someone will say to you ... "I realize now who you are, that you are so-and-so's child, and I would like you to eat, I was so very grateful when your mother or father fed me when I went to our village. Okay, come and eat with me."

That is why our ancestors used to say that the world is populated with no one else [but relatives]. They said we are all related. If we are friendly to everyone we see, they will become like our own older or younger brother because of our mutual compassion.

... The adage that existed long ago, that the world is populated with no one else [but relatives], you hear it in the following way: God made all of us human beings. God made Adam and Eve first, and from Adam and Eve, all the people of the world multiplied and dispersed. The people of the world descended from Adam and Eve.

When you think about it, even though they said Yupiit[5] didn't have God in those days, it was as if they knew that all the people descended from Adam and Even when they said that the world is populated by no one else but relatives.

Source and study: Ann Fienup-Riordan, ed., *Stories for Future Generations: The Oratory of Yup'ik Elder Paul John* (University of Washington Press, 2003), pp. 18–25.

7. List of Federally Recognized Tribes Today

Many non-Indian Americans live in a world in which indigenous peoples are largely invisible to them. When Europeans arrive in this country, however, they are struck by the way the landscape is saturated with indigenous names. Americans live in counties, towns, and states with native names. And they cross rivers, play in streams, and climb hills with native names, usually without noticing it. I-95, I-80, and most other east coast interstates were built where earlier main roads once were, and those roads came into being in colonial times following Indian trails. Americans, who often do not think about it, are also surrounded by people of Native American descent. Some of them live in urban areas, some on reservations. Here is a list of the 335 tribes who still exist as political entities in the contiguous United States. There are

[5] Yup'ik people are also called Yupiit.

over 220 more in Alaska, and 30 others which are state-recognized, though not yet federally recognized. Among the latter are the Pamunkey of Virgina, who were ruled by Pocahontas's father, Powhatan, when the first permanent English colony was founded at Jamestown in 1607.

---

1 Absentee-Shawnee Tribe of Indians of Oklahoma
2 Agua Caliente Band of Cahuilla Indians of the Agua Caliente Indian Reservation, California
3 Ak Chin Indian Community of the Maricopa (Ak Chin) Indian Reservation, Arizona
4 Alabama–Coushatta Tribes of Texas
5 Alabama–Quassarte Tribal Town, Oklahoma
6 Alturas Indian Rancheria, California
7 Apache Tribe of Oklahoma
8 Arapahoe Tribe of the Wind River Reservation, Wyoming
9 Aroostook Band of Micmac Indians of Maine
10 Assiniboine and Sioux Tribes of the Fort Peck Indian Reservation, Montana
11 Augustine Band of Cahuilla Mission Indians of the Augustine Reservation, California
12 Bad River Band of the Lake Superior Tribe of Chippewa Indians of the Bad River Reservation, Wisconsin
13 Bay Mills Indian Community, Michigan (previously listed as the Bay Mills Indian Community of the Sault Ste. Marie Band of Chippewa Indians, Bay Mills Reservation, Michigan)
14 Bear River Band of the Rohnerville Rancheria, California
15 Berry Creek Rancheria of Maidu Indians of California
16 Big Lagoon Rancheria, California
17 Big Pine Band of Owens Valley Paiute Shoshone Indians of the Big Pine Reservation, California
18 Big Sandy Rancheria of Mono Indians of California
19 Big Valley Band of Pomo Indians of the Big Valley Rancheria, California
20 Blackfeet Tribe of the Blackfeet Indian Reservation of Montana
21 Blue Lake Rancheria, California
22 Bridgeport Paiute Indian Colony of California
23 Buena Vista Rancheria of Me-Wuk Indians of California
24 Burns Paiute Tribe of the Burns Paiute Indian Colony of Oregon
25 Cabazon Band of Cahuilla Mission Indians of the Cabazon Reservation, California
26 Cachil DeHe Band of Wintun Indians of the Colusa Indian Community of the Colusa Rancheria, California
27 Caddo Indian Tribe of Oklahoma

28 Cahuilla Band of Mission Indians of the Cahuilla Reservation, California
29 Cahto Indian Tribe of the Laytonville Rancheria, California
30 California Valley Miwok Tribe, California (formerly the Sheep Ranch Rancheria of Me-Wuk Indians of California)
31 Campo Band of Diegueno Mission Indians of the Campo Indian Reservation, California
32 Capitan Grande Band of Diegueno Mission Indians of California:

(a) Barona Group of Capitan Grande Band of Mission Indians of the Barona Reservation, California
(b) Viejas (Baron Long) Group of Capitan Grande Band of Mission Indians of the Viejas Reservation, California

33 Catawba Indian Nation (aka Catawba Tribe of South Carolina)
34 Cayuga Nation of New York
35 Cedarville Rancheria, California
36 Chemehuevi Indian Tribe of the Chemehuevi Reservation, California
37 Cher-Ae Heights Indian Community of the Trinidad Rancheria, California
38 Cherokee Nation, Oklahoma
39 Cheyenne–Arapaho Tribes of Oklahoma
40 Cheyenne River Sioux Tribe of the Cheyenne River Reservation, South Dakota
41 Chickasaw Nation, Oklahoma
42 Chicken Ranch Rancheria of Me-Wuk Indians of California
43 Chippewa-Cree Indians of the Rocky Boy's Reservation, Montana
44 Chitimacha Tribe of Louisiana
45 Choctaw Nation of Oklahoma
46 Citizen Potawatomi Nation, Oklahoma
47 Cloverdale Rancheria of Pomo Indians of California
48 Cocopah Tribe of Arizona
49 Coeur D'Alene Tribe of the Coeur D'Alene Reservation, Idaho
50 Cold Springs Rancheria of Mono Indians of California
51 Colorado River Indian Tribes of the Colorado River Indian Reservation, Arizona and California
52 Comanche Nation, Oklahoma (formerly the Comanche Indian Tribe)
53 Confederated Salish and Kootenai Tribes of the Flathead Reservation, Montana
54 Confederated Tribes of the Chehalis Reservation, Washington
55 Confederated Tribes of the Colville Reservation, Washington
56 Confederated Tribes of the Coos, Lower Umpqua and Siuslaw Indians of Oregon
57 Confederated Tribes of the Goshute Reservation, Nevada and Utah
58 Confederated Tribes of the Grand Ronde Community of Oregon

59 Confederated Tribes of the Siletz Reservation, Oregon
60 Confederated Tribes of the Umatilla Reservation, Oregon
61 Confederated Tribes of the Warm Springs Reservation of Oregon
62 Confederated Tribes and Bands of the Yakama Indian Nation of the Yakama Reservation, Washington
63 Coquille Tribe of Oregon
64 Cortina Indian Rancheria of Wintun Indians of California
65 Coushatta Tribe of Louisiana
66 Cow Creek Band of Umpqua Indians of Oregon
67 Cowlitz Indian Tribe, Washington
68 Coyote Valley Band of Pomo Indians of California
69 Crow Tribe of Montana
70 Crow Creek Sioux Tribe of the Crow Creek Reservation, South Dakota
71 Cuyapaipe Community of Diegueno Mission Indians of the Cuyapaipe Reservation, California
72 Death Valley Timbi-Sha Shoshone Band of California
73 Delaware Nation, Oklahoma (formerly Delaware Tribe of Western Oklahoma)
74 Delaware Tribe of Indians, Oklahoma
75 Dry Creek Rancheria of Pomo Indians of California
76 Duckwater Shoshone Tribe of the Duckwater Reservation, Nevada
77 Eastern Band of Cherokee Indians of North Carolina
78 Eastern Shawnee Tribe of Oklahoma
79 Elem Indian Colony of Pomo Indians of the Sulphur Bank Rancheria, California
80 Elk Valley Rancheria, California
81 Ely Shoshone Tribe of Nevada
82 Enterprise Rancheria of Maidu Indians of California
83 Flandreau Santee Sioux Tribe of South Dakota
84 Forest County Potawatomi Community, Wisconsin (previously listed as the Forest County Potawatomi Community of Wisconsin Potawatomi Indians, Wisconsin)
85 Fort Belknap Indian Community of the Fort Belknap Reservation of Montana
86 Fort Bidwell Indian Community of the Fort Bidwell Reservation of California
87 Fort Independence Indian Community of Paiute Indians of the Fort Independence Reservation, California
88 Fort McDermitt Paiute and Shoshone Tribes of the Fort McDermitt Indian Reservation, Nevada and Oregon
89 Fort McDowell Yavapai Nation, Arizona (formerly the Fort McDowell Mohave-Apache Community of the Fort McDowell Indian Reservation)

90 Fort Mojave Indian Tribe of Arizona, California and Nevada
91 Fort Sill Apache Tribe of Oklahoma
92 Gila River Indian Community of the Gila River Indian Reservation, Arizona
93 Grand Traverse Band of Ottawa and Chippewa Indians, Michigan (previously listed as the Grand Traverse Band of Ottawa and Chippewa Indians of Michigan)
94 Graton Rancheria, California
95 Greenville Rancheria of Maidu Indians of California
96 Grindstone Indian Rancheria of Wintun-Wailaki Indians of California
97 Guidiville Rancheria of California
98 Hannahville Indian Community, Michigan (previously listed as the Hannahville Indian Community of Wisconsin Potawatomie Indians of Michigan)
99 Havasupai Tribe of the Havasupai Reservation, Arizona
100 Ho-Chunk Nation of Wisconsin (formerly known as the Wisconsin Winnebago Tribe)
101 Hoh Indian Tribe of the Hoh Indian Reservation, Washington
102 Hoopa Valley Tribe, California
103 Hopi Tribe of Arizona
104 Hopland Band of Pomo Indians of the Hopland Rancheria, California
105 Houlton Band of Maliseet Indians of Maine
106 Hualapai Indian Tribe of the Hualapai Indian Reservation, Arizona
107 Huron Potawatomi, Inc., Michigan
108 Inaja Band of Diegueno Mission Indians of the Inaja and Cosmit Reservation, California
109 Ione Band of Miwok Indians of California
110 Iowa Tribe of Kansas and Nebraska
111 Iowa Tribe of Oklahoma
112 Jackson Rancheria of Me-Wuk Indians of California
113 Jamestown S'Klallam Tribe of Washington
114 Jamul Indian Village of California
115 Jena Band of Choctaw Indians, Louisiana
116 Jicarilla Apache Nation, New Mexico (formerly the Jicarilla Apache Tribe of the Jicarilla Apache Indian Reservation)
117 Kaibab Band of Paiute Indians of the Kaibab Indian Reservation, Arizona
118 Kalispel Indian Community of the Kalispel Reservation, Washington
119 Karuk Tribe of California
120 Kashia Band of Pomo Indians of the Stewarts Point Rancheria, California
121 Kaw Nation, Oklahoma

122 Keweenaw Bay Indian Community, Michigan (previously listed as the Keweenaw Bay Indian Community of L'Anse and Ontonagon Bands of Chippewa Indians of the L'Anse Reservation, Michigan)
123 Kialegee Tribal Town, Oklahoma
124 Kickapoo Tribe of Indians of the Kickapoo Reservation in Kansas
125 Kickapoo Tribe of Oklahoma
126 Kickapoo Traditional Tribe of Texas
127 Kiowa Indian Tribe of Oklahoma
128 Klamath Indian Tribe of Oregon
129 Kootenai Tribe of Idaho
130 La Jolla Band of Luiseno Mission Indians of the La Jolla Reservation, California
131 La Posta Band of Diegueno Mission Indians of the La Posta Indian Reservation, California
132 Lac Courte Oreilles Band of Lake Superior Chippewa Indians of Wisconsin (previously listed as the Lac Courte Oreilles Band of Lake Superior Chippewa Indians of the Lac Courte Oreilles Reservation of Wisconsin)
133 Lac du Flambeau Band of Lake Superior Chippewa Indians of the Lac du Flambeau Reservation of Wisconsin
134 Lac Vieux Desert Band of Lake Superior Chippewa Indians of Michigan
135 Las Vegas Tribe of Paiute Indians of the Las Vegas Indian Colony, Nevada
136 Little River Band of Ottawa Indians of Michigan
137 Little Traverse Bay Bands of Odawa Indians, Michigan (previously listed as the Little Traverse Bay Bands of Odawa Indians of Michigan)
138 Lower Lake Rancheria, California
139 Los Coyotes Band of Cahuilla Mission Indians of the Los Coyotes Reservation, California
140 Lovelock Paiute Tribe of the Lovelock Indian Colony, Nevada
141 Lower Brule Sioux Tribe of the Lower Brule Reservation, South Dakota
142 Lower Elwha Tribal Community of the Lower Elwha Reservation, Washington
143 Lower Sioux Indian Community in the State of Minnesota (previously listed as the Lower Sioux Indian Community of Minnesota Mdewakanton Sioux Indians of the Lower Sioux Reservation in Minnesota)
144 Lummi Tribe of the Lummi Reservation, Washington
145 Lytton Rancheria of California
146 Makah Indian Tribe of the Makah Indian Reservation, Washington
147 Manchester Band of Pomo Indians of the Manchester-Point Arena Rancheria, California

148 Manzanita Band of Diegueno Mission Indians of the Manzanita Reservation, California
149 Mashantucket Pequot Tribe of Connecticut
150 Match-e-be-nash-she-wish Band of Pottawatomi Indians of Michigan
151 Mechoopda Indian Tribe of Chico Rancheria, California
152 Menominee Indian Tribe of Wisconsin
153 Mesa Grande Band of Diegueno Mission Indians of the Mesa Grande Reservation, California
154 Mescalero Apache Tribe of the Mescalero Reservation, New Mexico
155 Miami Tribe of Oklahoma
156 Miccosukee Tribe of Indians of Florida
157 Middletown Rancheria of Pomo Indians of California
158 Minnesota Chippewa Tribe, Minnesota:

(a) Bois Forte Band (Nett Lake)
(b) Fond du Lac Band
(c) Grand Portage Band
(d) Leech Lake Band
(e) Mille Lacs Band
(f) White Earth Band

159 Mississippi Band of Choctaw Indians, Mississippi
160 Moapa Band of Paiute Indians of the Moapa River Indian Reservation, Nevada
161 Modoc Tribe of Oklahoma
162 Mohegan Indian Tribe of Connecticut
163 Mooretown Rancheria of Maidu Indians of California
164 Morongo Band of Cahuilla Mission Indians of the Morongo Reservation, California
165 Muckleshoot Indian Tribe of the Muckleshoot Reservation, Washington
166 Muscogee (Creek) Nation, Oklahoma
167 Narragansett Indian Tribe of Rhode Island
168 Navajo Nation, Arizona, New Mexico, and Utah
169 Nez Perce Tribe of Idaho
170 Nisqually Indian Tribe of the Nisqually Reservation, Washington
171 Nooksack Indian Tribe of Washington
172 Northern Cheyenne Tribe of the Northern Cheyenne Indian Reservation, Montana
173 North Fork Rancheria of Mono Indians of California
174 Northwestern Band of Shoshoni Nation of Utah (Washakie)
175 Oglala Sioux Tribe of the Pine Ridge Reservation, South Dakota
176 Omaha Tribe of Nebraska
177 Oneida Nation of New York

178 Oneida Tribe of Indians of Wisconsin (previously listed as the Oneida Tribe of Wisconsin)
179 Onondaga Nation of New York
180 Osage Tribe, Oklahoma
181 Ottawa Tribe of Oklahoma
182 Otoe-Missouria Tribe of Indians, Oklahoma
183 Paiute Indian Tribe of Utah:

(a) Cedar City Band of Paiutes
(b) Kanosh Band of Paiutes
(c) Koosharem Band of Paiutes
(d) Indian Peaks Band of Paiutes
(e) Shivwits Band of Paiutes

184 Paiute–Shoshone Indians of the Bishop Community of the Bishop Colony, California
185 Paiute–Shoshone Tribe of the Fallon Reservation and Colony, Nevada
186 Paiute–Shoshone Indians of the Lone Pine Community of the Lone Pine Reservation, California
187 Pala Band of Luiseno Mission Indians of the Pala Reservation, California
188 Pascua Yaqui Tribe of Arizona
189 Paskenta Band of Nomlaki Indians of California
190 Passamaquoddy Tribe of Maine
191 Pauma Band of Luiseno Mission Indians of the Pauma and Yuima Reservation, California
192 Pawnee Nation of Oklahoma
193 Pechanga Band of Luiseno Mission Indians of the Pechanga Reservation, California
194 Penobscot Tribe of Maine
195 Peoria Tribe of Indians of Oklahoma
196 Picayune Rancheria of Chukchansi Indians of California
197 Pinoleville Rancheria of Pomo Indians of California
198 Pit River Tribe, California:

(a) Big Bend
(b) Lookout
(c) Montgomery
(d) Creek and Roaring Creek Rancherias
(e) XL Ranch

199 Poarch Band of Creek Indians of Alabama
200 Pokagon Band of Potawatomi Indians, Michigan and Indiana (previously listed as the Pokagon Band of Potawatomi Indians of Michigan)

201 Ponca Tribe of Indians of Oklahoma
202 Ponca Tribe of Nebraska
203 Port Gamble Indian Community of the Port Gamble Reservation, Washington
204 Potter Valley Rancheria of Pomo Indians of California
205 Prairie Band of Potawatomi Nation, Kansas (formerly the Prairie Band of Potawatomi Indians)
206 Prairie Island Indian Community in the State of Minnesota (previously listed as the Prairie Island Indian Community of Minnesota Mdewakanton Sioux Indians of the Prairie Island Reservation, Minnesota)
207 Pueblo of Acoma, New Mexico
208 Pueblo of Cochiti, New Mexico
209 Pueblo of Jemez, New Mexico
210 Pueblo of Isleta, New Mexico
211 Pueblo of Laguna, New Mexico
212 Pueblo of Nambe, New Mexico
213 Pueblo of Picuris, New Mexico
214 Pueblo of Pojoaque, New Mexico
215 Pueblo of San Felipe, New Mexico
216 Pueblo of San Juan, New Mexico
217 Pueblo of San Ildefonso, New Mexico
218 Pueblo of Sandia, New Mexico
219 Pueblo of Santa Ana, New Mexico
220 Pueblo of Santa Clara, New Mexico
221 Pueblo of Santo Domingo, New Mexico
222 Pueblo of Taos, New Mexico
223 Pueblo of Tesuque, New Mexico
224 Pueblo of Zia, New Mexico
225 Puyallup Tribe of the Puyallup Reservation, Washington
226 Pyramid Lake Paiute Tribe of the Pyramid Lake Reservation, Nevada
227 Quapaw Tribe of Indians, Oklahoma
228 Quartz Valley Indian Community of the Quartz Valley Reservation of California
229 Quechan Tribe of the Fort Yuma Indian Reservation, California and Arizona
230 Quileute Tribe of the Quileute Reservation, Washington
231 Quinault Tribe of the Quinault Reservation, Washington
232 Ramona Band or Village of Cahuilla Mission Indians of California
233 Red Cliff Band of Lake Superior Chippewa Indians of Wisconsin
234 Red Lake Band of Chippewa Indians, Minnesota (previously listed as the Red Lake Band of Chippewa Indians of the Red Lake Reservation, Minnesota)

235 Redding Rancheria, California
236 Redwood Valley Rancheria of Pomo Indians of California
237 Reno-Sparks Indian Colony, Nevada
238 Resighini Rancheria, California (formerly the Coast Indian Community of Yurok Indians of the Resighini Rancheria)
239 Rincon Band of Luiseno Mission Indians of the Rincon Reservation, California
240 Robinson Rancheria of Pomo Indians of California
241 Rosebud Sioux Tribe of the Rosebud Indian Reservation, South Dakota
242 Round Valley Indian Tribes of the Round Valley Reservation, California (formerly known as the Covelo Indian Community)
243 Rumsey Indian Rancheria of Wintun Indians of California
244 Sac and Fox Tribe of the Mississippi in Iowa
245 Sac and Fox Nation of Missouri in Kansas and Nebraska
246 Sac and Fox Nation, Oklahoma
247 Saginaw Chippewa Indian Tribe of Michigan (previously listed as the Saginaw Chippewa Indian Tribe of Michigan, Isabella Reservation)
248 St. Croix Chippewa Indians of Wisconsin (previously listed as the St. Croix Chippewa Indians of Wisconsin, St. Croix Reservation)
249 St. Regis Band of Mohawk Indians of New York
250 Salt River Pima–Maricopa Indian Community of the Salt River Reservation, Arizona
251 Samish Indian Tribe, Washington
252 San Carlos Apache Tribe of the San Carlos Reservation, Arizona
253 San Juan Southern Paiute Tribe of Arizona
254 San Manual Band of Serrano Mission Indians of the San Manual Reservation, California
255 San Pasqual Band of Diegueno Mission Indians of California
256 Santa Rosa Indian Community of the Santa Rosa Rancheria, California
257 Santa Rosa Band of Cahuilla Mission Indians of the Santa Rosa Reservation, California
258 Santa Ynez Band of Chumash Mission Indians of the Santa Ynez Reservation, California
259 Santa Ysabel Band of Diegueno Mission Indians of the Santa Ysabel Reservation, California
260 Santee Sioux Tribe of the Santee Reservation of Nebraska
261 Sauk-Suiattle Indian Tribe of Washington
262 Sault Ste. Marie Tribe of Chippewa Indians of Michigan
263 Scotts Valley Band of Pomo Indians of California
264 Seminole Nation of Oklahoma
265 Seminole Tribe of Florida:

(a) Dania Reservations
(b) Big Cypress Reservations
(c) Brighton Reservations
(d) Hollywood Reservations
(e) Tampa Reservations

266 Seneca Nation of New York
267 Seneca–Cayuga Tribe of Oklahoma
268 Shakopee Mdewakanton Sioux Community of Minnesota (previously listed as the Shakopee Mdewakanton Sioux Community of Minnesota (Prior Lake))
269 Shawnee Tribe, Oklahoma
270 Sherwood Valley Rancheria of Pomo Indians of California
271 Shingle Springs Band of Miwok Indians, Shingle Springs Rancheria (Verona Tract), California
272 Shoalwater Bay Tribe of the Shoalwater Bay Indian Reservation, Washington
273 Shoshone Tribe of the Wind River Reservation, Wyoming
274 Shoshone–Bannock Tribes of the Fort Hall Reservation of Idaho
275 Shoshone–Paiute Tribes of the Duck Valley Reservation, Nevada
276 Sisseton–Wahpeton Sioux Tribe of the Lake Traverse Reservation, South Dakota
277 Skokomish Indian Tribe of the Skokomish Reservation, Washington
278 Skull Valley Band of Goshute Indians of Utah
279 Smith River Rancheria, California
280 Snoqualmie Tribe, Washington
281 Soboba Band of Luiseno Indians, California (formerly the Soboba Band of Luiseno Mission Indians of the Soboba Reservation)
282 Sokaogon Chippewa Community, Wisconsin (previously listed as the Sokaogon Chippewa Community of the Mole Lake Band of Chippewa Indians, Wisconsin)
283 Southern Ute Indian Tribe of the Southern Ute Reservation, Colorado
284 Spirit Lake Tribe, North Dakota
285 Spokane Tribe of the Spokane Reservation, Washington
286 Squaxin Island Tribe of the Squaxin Island Reservation, Washington
287 Standing Rock Sioux Tribe of North and South Dakota
288 Stockbridge Munsee Community, Wisconsin (previously listed as the Stockbridge-Munsee Community of Mohican Indians of Wisconsin)
289 Stillaguamish Tribe of Washington
290 Summit Lake Paiute Tribe of Nevada
291 Suquamish Indian Tribe of the Port Madison Reservation, Washington
292 Susanville Indian Rancheria, California

293 Swinomish Indians of the Swinomish Reservation, Washington
294 Sycuan Band of Diegueno Mission Indians of California
295 Table Bluff Reservation – Wiyot Tribe, California
296 Table Mountain Rancheria of California
297 Te-Moak Tribes of Western Shoshone Indians of Nevada:

(a) Battle Mountain Band
(b) Elko Band
(c) South Fork Band
(d) Wells Band

298 Thlopthlocco Tribal Town, Oklahoma
299 Three Affiliated Tribes of the Fort Berthold Reservation, North Dakota
300 Tohono O'odham Nation of Arizona
301 Tonawanda Band of Seneca Indians of New York
302 Tonkawa Tribe of Indians of Oklahoma
303 Tonto Apache Tribe of Arizona
304 Torres-Martinez Band of Cahuilla Mission Indians of California
305 Tule River Indian Tribe of the Tule River Reservation, California
306 Tulalip Tribes of the Tulalip Reservation, Washington
307 Tunica-Biloxi Indian Tribe of Louisiana
308 Tuolumne Band of Me-Wuk Indians of the Tuolumne Rancheria of California
309 Turtle Mountain Band of Chippewa Indians of North Dakota
310 Tuscarora Nation of New York
311 Twenty-Nine Palms Band of Mission Indians of California (previously listed as the Twenty-Nine Palms Band of Luiseno Mission Indians of California)
312 United Auburn Indian Community of the Auburn Rancheria of California
313 United Keetoowah Band of Cherokee Indians in Oklahoma (previously listed as the United Keetoowah Band of Cherokee Indians of Oklahoma)
314 Upper Lake Band of Pomo Indians of Upper Lake Rancheria of California
315 Upper Sioux Community, Minnesota (previously listed as the Upper Sioux Indian Community of the Upper Sioux Reservation, Minnesota)
316 Upper Skagit Indian Tribe of Washington
317 Ute Indian Tribe of the Uintah and Ouray Reservation, Utah
318 Ute Mountain Tribe of the Ute Mountain Reservation, Colorado, New Mexico, and Utah
319 Utu Utu Gwaitu Paiute Tribe of the Benton Paiute Reservation, California

320 Walker River Paiute Tribe of the Walker River Reservation, Nevada
321 Wampanoag Tribe of Gay Head (Aquinnah) of Massachusetts
322 Washoe Tribe of Nevada and California:

- (a) Carson Colony
- (b) Dresslerville Colony
- (c) Woodfords Community
- (d) Stewart Community
- (e) Washoe Ranches

323 White Mountain Apache Tribe of the Fort Apache Reservation, Arizona
324 Wichita and Affiliated Tribes, Oklahoma:

- (a) Wichita
- (b) Keechi
- (c) Waco
- (d) Tawakonie

325 Winnebago Tribe of Nebraska
326 Winnemucca Indian Colony of Nevada
327 Wyandotte Tribe of Oklahoma
328 Yankton Sioux Tribe of South Dakota
329 Yavapai–Apache Nation of the Camp Verde Indian Reservation, Arizona
330 Yavapai-Prescott Tribe of the Yavapai Reservation, Arizona
331 Yerington Paiute Tribe of the Yerington Colony and Campbell Ranch, Nevada
332 Yomba Shoshone Tribe of the Yomba Reservation, Nevada
333 Ysleta Del Sur Pueblo of Texas
334 Yurok Tribe of the Yurok Reservation, California
335 Zuni Tribe of the Zuni Reservation, New Mexico

Source: Federal Register, July 12, 2002, vol. 67, no. 134, pp. 46327–33.

Study: Charles Wilkinson, *Blood Struggle: The Rise of Modern Indian Nations* (Norton, 2005).

Questions for consideration

Note: The other questions in this book are addressed to students of any race. This set of questions, however, is especially addressed to non-native college students.

1 If you were Native American, what do you think you would find most hurtful about popular attitudes toward Indians?
2 If you were native, which recent political, cultural, or economic issue do you think would be most important to you?
3 Which American Indian reservation is nearest to your home?
4 When did the land your house occupies pass out of native hands?

Selected Bibliography

Rolena Adorno and Patrick Charles Pautz, eds., *The Narrative of Cabeza de Vaca* (University of Nebraska Press, 2003).

Peter Aleshire, *The Fox and the Whirlwind: General George Crook and Geronimo: A Paired Biography* (John Wiley, 2000).

Sherman Alexie, *The Lone Ranger and Tonto Fistfight in Heaven* (Atlantic Monthly Press, 1993).

James Axtell, *The Invasion Within: The Contest of Cultures in Colonial North America* (Oxford University Press, 1986).

Philip Barbour, ed., *The Complete Works of John Smith* (Institute of Early American History and Culture, 1986).

Julianna Barr, *Peace Came in the Form of a Woman: Indians and Spaniards in the Texas Borderlands* (University of North Carolina Press, 2007).

Carol Blackburn, *Harvest of Souls: The Jesuit Missions and Colonialism in North America, 1632–1650* (McGill-Queen's University Press, 2000).

David Blanchard, "High Steel! The Kahnawake Mohawk and the High Construction Trade," *Journal of Ethnic Studies* 11 (Summer 1983): 32–60.

Tamara Bray, ed., *The Future of the Past: Archaeologists, Native Americans, and Repatriation* (Garland, 2001).

James Brooks, *Captives and Cousins: Slavery, Kinship, and Community in the Southwest Borderlands* (University of North Carolina Press, 2002).

Dee Brown, *Bury My Heart at Wounded Knee* (Holt, Rinehart & Winston, 1970).

Colin Calloway, *The American Revolution in Indian Country* (Cambridge University Press, 1995).

Colin Calloway, *The Shawnees and the War for America* (Viking, 2007).

Colin Calloway, *The Western Abenaki of Vermont, 1600–1800: War, Migration and the Survival of an Indian People* (University of Oklahoma Press, 1990).

Colin Calloway, ed., *The World Turned Upside Down: Indian Voices from Early America* (Bedford/St. Martin's, 1994).

Gae Whitney Canfield, *Sarah Winnemucca of the Northern Paiutes* (University of Oklahoma Press, 1983).

George P. Castile, *To Show Heart: Native American Self-Determination and Federal Indian Policy, 1960–1975* (University of Arizona Press, 1998).

Alfred Cave, *Prophets of the Great Spirit: Native American Revitalization Movements in Eastern North America* (University of Nebraska Press, 2006).

Joyce Chaplin, *Subject Matter: Technology, the Body, and Science on the Anglo-American Frontier, 1500–1676* (Harvard University Press, 2001).

Inga Clendinnen, *Aztecs: An Interpretation* (Cambridge University Press, 1991).

Amanda Cobb, *Listening to Our Grandmothers' Stories: The Bloomfield Academy for Chickasaw Females, 1852–1949* (University of Nebraska Press, 2000).

Michael D. Coe, *Breaking the Maya Code* (Thames & Hudson, 1992).

Michael D. Coe and Mark Van Stone, *Reading the Maya Glyphs* (Thames & Hudson, 2001).

William S. E. Coleman, ed., *The Voices of Wounded Knee* (University of Nebraska Press, 2000).

William Cronon, *Changes in the Land: Indians, Colonists, and the Ecology of New England* (Hill & Wang, 1983).

Philip J. Deloria, *Playing Indian* (Yale University Press, 1998).

Philip J. Deloria and Neal Salisbury, eds., *A Companion to American Indian History* (Blackwell, 2002).

Vine Deloria, Jr., *Custer Died for Your Sins: An Indian Manifesto* (Macmillan, 1969).

Raymond J. DeMallie, ed., *The Sixth Grandfather: Black Elk's Teachings Given to John C. Neihardt* (University of Nebraska Press, 1984).

John Demos, *The Unredeemed Captive: A Family Story from Early America* (Alfred Knopf, 1994).

L. James Dempsey, *Blackfoot War Art: Pictographs of the Reservation Period, 1880–2000* (University of Oklahoma Press, 2007).

Kathryn Zabelle Derounian-Stodola, ed., *Women's Indian Captivity Narratives* (Penguin, 1998).

Mary Crow Dog with Richard Erdoes, *Lakota Woman* (Harper Collins, 1990).

James Drake, *King Philip's War: Civil War in New England, 1675–1676* (University of Massachusetts Press, 1999).

Oliver Dunn and James Kelley, Jr., eds., *The Diario of Christopher Columbus's First Voyage to America, 1492–1493* (University of Oklahoma Press, 1989).

R. David Edmunds, *Tecumseh and the Quest for Indian Leadership* (Pearson Longman, 2007).

Kim Isaac Eisler, *The Revenge of the Pequots* (Simon & Schuster, 2001).

Ann Fienup-Riordan, ed., *Stories for Future Generations: The Oratory of Yup'ik Elder Paul John* (University of Washington Press, 2003).

Kathleen Fine-Dare, *Grave Injustice: The American Indian Repatriation Movement and NAGPRA* (University of Nebraska Press, 2002).

Donald Fixico, *Termination and Relocation: Federal Indian Policy, 1945–1960* (University of New Mexico Press, 1986).

Theresa Strouth Gaul, *To Marry an Indian: The Marriage of Harriett Gold and Elias Boudinot in Letters, 1823–1839* (University of North Carolina Press, 2005).

Frederic Gleach, *Powhatan's World and Colonial Virginia: A Conflict of Cultures* (University of Nebraska Press, 1997).

Kay Graber, *Sister to the Sioux: The Memoirs of Elaine Goodale Eastman, 1885–1891* (University of Nebraska Press, 1985).

Greg Grandin, *The Blood of Guatemala: A History of Race and Nation* (Duke University Press, 2000).

Greg Grandin, *The Last Colonial Massacre: Latin America in the Cold War* (University of Chicago Press, 2004).

Rayna Green, "The Pocahontas Perplex: The Image of Indian Women in American Culture," *Massachusetts Review* 16/4 (1975).

Stephen Greenblatt, *Marvelous Possessions: The Wonder of the New World* (University of Chicago Press, 1991).

Stephen Greenblatt, *New World Encounters* (University of California Press, 1993).

Allan Greer, ed., *The Jesuit Relations: Natives and Missionaries in Seventeenth-Century North America* (Bedford/St. Martin's, 2000).

Allan Greer, *Mohawk Saint: Catherine Tekakwitha and the Jesuits* (Oxford University Press, 2005).

George Gurney and Therese Thau Heyman, eds., *George Catlin and His Indian Gallery* (Smithsonian American Art Museum, 2002).

Ramón Gutiérrez, *When Jesus Came, the Corn Mothers Went Away: Marriage, Sexuality, and Power in New Mexico, 1500–1846* (Stanford University Press, 1991).

Charles Wilson Hackett, ed., *Revolt of the Pueblo Indians of New Mexico and Otermín's Attempted Reconquest, 1680–1682* (University of New Mexico Press, 1942).

Laurence M. Hauptman, *The Iroquois Struggle for Survival: World War II to Red Power* (Syracuse University Press, 1976).

David S. Heidler and Jeanne T. Heidler, *Indian Removal* (Norton, 2007).

Inés Hernandez-Avila, ed., *Reading Native American Women: Critical/Creative Representations* (Altamira, 2005).

J. N. B. Hewitt, "Iroquoian Cosmology," *Twenty-First Annual Report of the Bureau of American Ethnology, 1899–1900* (US Government Printing Office, 1903), pp. 255–95.

Ruth Bradley Holmes and Betty Sharp Smith, *Beginning Cherokee*, 2nd edn. (University of Oklahoma Press, 1977).

David Howard, *Conquistador in Chains: Cabeza de Vaca and the Indians of the Americas* (University of Alabama Press, 1997).

Frederick E. Hoxie, *A Final Promise: The Campaign to Assimilate the Indians, 1880–1920* (University of Nebraska Press, 1984).

Frederick E. Hoxie, ed., *Talking Back to Civilization: Indian Voices from the Progressive Era* (Bedford/St. Martin's, 2001).

Frederick E. Hoxie and Jay Nelson, eds., *Lewis and Clark and the Indian Country: The Native American Perspective* (University of Illinois Press, 2007).

Peter Iverson, ed., *"For Our Navajo People": Diné Letters Speeches and Petitions, 1900–1960* (University of New Mexico Press, 2002).

Troy R. Johnson, *The Occupation of Alcatraz Island: Indian Self-Determination and the Rise of Indian Activism* (University of Illinois Press, 1996).

Alvin M. Josephy, ed., *Lewis and Clark through Indian Eyes* (Knopf, 2006).

Alvin M. Josephy, Jr., Joane Nagel, and Troy Johnson, eds., *Red Power: The American Indians' Fight for Freedom*, 2nd edn. (University of Nebraska Press, 1999 [1971]).

Benjamin Keen, *The Aztec Image in Western Thought* (Rutgers University Press, 1971).

Isabel Thompson Kelsay, *Joseph Brant, 1743–1807: Man of Two Worlds* (Syracuse University Press, 1984).

Karen Ordahl Kupperman, *Indians and English: Facing Off in Early America* (Cornell University Press, 2000).

Jill Lepore, *A is for American: Letters and Other Characters in the Newly United States* (Knopf, 2002).

Jill Lepore, *The Name of War: King Philip's War and the Origins of American Identity* (New York: Vintage Books, 1998).

Steven Andrew Light and Kathryn R. L. Rand, *Indian Gaming and Tribal Sovereignty: The Casino Compromise* (University of Kansas Press, 2005).

Daniel F. Littlefield, ed., *Native American Writing in the Southeast, 1875–1935* (University Press of Mississippi, 1995).

James Lockhart, *The Nahuas after the Conquest: A Social and Cultural History of the Indians of Central Mexico, Sixteenth through Eighteenth Centuries* (Stanford University Press, 1992).

James Lockhart, *Nahuatl as Written* (Stanford University Press, 2001).

James Lockhart, ed., *We People Here: Nahuatl Accounts of the Conquest of Mexico* (University of California Press, 1993).

K. Tsianina Lowawaima, *They Called It Prairie Light: The Story of Chilocco Indian School* (University of Nebraska Press, 1994).

Garrick Mallery, "Picture-Writing of the American Indians," *Tenth Annual Report of the Bureau of American Ethnology, 1888–89* (US Government Printing Office, 1893), pp. 266–87.

Peter C. Mancall, ed., *Envisioning America: English Plans for the Colonization of North America, 1580–1640* (Bedford/St. Martin's, 1995).

Barbara Alice Mann, *George Washington's War on Native America* (Praeger, 2005).

Barbara Alice Mann, *Native Americans, Archaeologists, and the Mounds* (Peter Lang, 2003).

Barbara Alice Mann, ed., *Native American Speakers of the Eastern Woodlands: Selected Speeches and Critical Analyses* (Greenwood, 2001).

Bunny McBride, *Molly Spotted Elk: A Penobscot in Paris* (University of Oklahoma Press, 1995).

Sally McClain, *Navajo Weapon* (Rio Nuevo, 1994).

Russel Means with Marvin J. Wolf, *Where White Men Fear to Tread: The Autobiography of Russell Means* (St. Martin's, 1995).

James H. Merrell, *The Indians' New World: Catawbas and their Neighbors from European Contact Through the Era of Removal* (University of North Carolina Press, 1989).

Jane Merritt, *At the Crossroads: Indians and Empires on a Mid-Atlantic Frontier, 1700–1763* (University of North Carolina Press, 2003).

Joseph Mitchell, "The Mohawks in High Steel," foreword to Edmund Wilson, *Apologies to the Iroquois* (Farrar, Straus & Cudahy, 1959), pp. 27–36.

Gary E. Moulton and Thomas W. Dunlay, eds., *The Journals of the Lewis and Clark Expedition*, vol. 6 (University of Nebraska Press, 1990).

John Neihardt, ed., *Black Elk Speaks: Being the Life Story of a Holy Man of the Oglala Sioux* (University of Nebraska Press, 2000 [1932]).

Jill E. Neitzel, ed., *Pueblo Bonito: Center of the Chacoan World* (Smithsonian, 2003).

Roger Nichols, ed., *Black Hawk's Autobiography* (Iowa State University Press, 1999).

Barry O'Connell, ed., *A Son of the Forest and Other Writings by William Apess, a Pequot* (Universit of Massachusetts Press, 1997).

Jeffrey Ostler, *The Plains Sioux and U.S. Colonialism from Lewis and Clark to Wounded Knee* (Cambridge University Press, 2004).

Timothy R. Pauketat, *Ancient Cahokia and the Mississippians* (Cambridge University Press, 2004).

Leonard Peltier, *Prison Writings: My Life is My Sundance* (St. Martin's, 1999).

Theda Perdue, ed., *Cherokee Editor: The Writings of Elias Boudinot* (University of Tennessee Press, 1983).

Theda Perdue, *Cherokee Women: Gender and Culture Change, 1700–1835 (University of Nebraska Press, 1998).*

Theda Perdue and Michael D. Green, eds., *The Cherokee Removal: A Brief History with Documents* (Bedford/St. Martin's, 2005).

Kenneth R. Philip, *Indian Self-Rule: First-Hand Accounts of Indian–White Relations from Roosevelt to Reagan* (Chicago: Howe Bros., 1986).

Ann Marie Plane, *Colonial Intimacies: Indian Marriage in Early New England* (Cornell University Press, 2000).

Miguel León Portilla, *The Broken Spears: The Aztec Account of the Conquest of Mexico* (Beacon Press, 1962).

Francis Paul Prucha, ed., *Documents of United States Indian Policy* (University of Nebraska Press, 2000 [1975]).

Francis Paul Prucha, *The Great Father: The United States Government and the American Indian* (University of Nebraska Press, 1984).

Andrés Reséndez, *A Land So Strange: The Epic Journey of Cabeza de Vaca: The Extraordinary Tale of a Shipwrecked Spaniard who Walked across America in the Sixteenth Century* (Basic Books, 2007).

Matthew Restall, Lisa Sousa, and Kevin Terraciano, eds., *Mesoamerican Voices: Native-Language Writings from Colonial Mexico, Oaxaca, Yucatan, and Guatemala* (Cambridge University Press, 2005).

Daniel Richter, *Facing East from Indian Country: A Native History of Early America* (Harvard University Press, 2001).

Daniel K. Richter, *The Ordeal of the Long-House: The Peoples of the Iroquois League in the Era of European Colonization* (Institute of Early American History and Culture, 1992).

Sherry Robinson, *Apache Voices: Their Stories of Survival as Told to Eve Ball* (University of New Mexico Press, 2000).

James Ronda, *Lewis and Clark among the Indians* (University of Nebraska Press, 1984).
Helen Rountree, *Pocahontas, Powhatan, Opechancanough: Three Indian Lives Changed by Jamestown* (University of Virginia Press, 2005).
Helen Rountree, *Pocahontas's People: The Powhatan Indians of Virginia through Four Centuries* (University of Oklahoma Press, 1990).
Helen Rountree, *The Powhatan Indians of Virginia: Their Traditional Culture* (University of Oklahoma Press, 1989).
Neal Salisbury, ed., *The Sovereignty and Goodness of God by Mary Rowlandson with Related Documents* (Bedford/St. Martin's, 1997).
Linda Schele and David Freidel, *A Forest of Kings: The Untold Story of the Ancient Maya* (William Morrow, 1990).
Paul Schneider, *Brutal Journey: The Epic Story of the First Crossing of North America* (Henry Holt, 2006).
Eric Schultz, *King Philip's War: The History and Legacy of America's Forgotten Conflict* (Norton, 1999).
Amy Schutt, *Peoples of the River Valley: The Odyssey of the Delaware Indians* (University of Pennsylvania Press, 2007).
Peter Silver, *Our Savage Neighbors: How Indian War Transformed Early America* (Norton, 2007).
David Silverman, *Faith and Boundaries: Colonists, Christianity, and Community Among the Wampanoag Indians of Martha's Vinyard* (Cambridge University Press, 2005).
David Curtis Skaggs and Larry L. Nelson, eds., *The Sixty Years' War for the Great Lakes, 1754–1814* (Michigan State University Press, 2001).
Thomas P. Slaughter, *Exploring Lewis and Clark: Reflections on Men and Wilderness* (Knopf, 2003).
Susan Sleeper-Smith, *Indian Women and French Men: Rethinking Cultural Encounter in the Western Great Lakes* (University of Massachusetts Press, 2001).
Paul Chaat Smith and Robert Allen Warrior, *Like a Hurricane: The Indian Movement from Alcatraz to Wounded Knee* (New Press, 1996).
Gregory Smoak, *Ghost Dances and Identity: Prophetic Religion and American Indian Ethnogenesis in the Nineteenth Century* (University of California Press, 2006).
John R. Stein, Dabney Ford, and Richard Friedman, "Reconstructing Pueblo Bonito," in Jill E. Neitzel, ed., *Pueblo Bonito: Center of the Chacoan World* (Smithsonian Books, 2003), pp. 44–54.
David Stuart, "Ten Phonetic Syllables," *Research Reports on Ancient Maya Writing* 14 (1987).
David E. Stuart, *Anasazi America* (University of New Mexico Press, 2000).
Geoffrey Symcox and Blair Sullivan, eds., *Christopher Columbus and the Enterprise of the Indies: A Brief History with Documents* (Palgrave Macmillan, 2005).
David Hurst Thomas, *Skull Wars: Kennewick Man, Archaeology, and the Battle for Native American Identity* (Basic Books, 2000).
Camilla Townsend, *Malintzin's Choices: An Indian Woman in the Conquest of Mexico* (University of New Mexico Press, 2006).

Camilla Townsend, *Pocahontas and the Powhatan Dilemma* (Hill & Wang, 2004).
Alan Trachtenberg, *Shades of Hiawatha: Staging Indians, Making Americans, 1880–1930* (Hill & Wang, 2004).
Kerry A. Trask, *Black Hawk: The Battle for the Heart of America* (Henry Holt, 2006).
Bruce Trigger, *Natives and Newcomers: Canada's "Heroic Age" Reconsidered* (McGill-Queen's University Press, 1985).
Christopher Vecsey, *Imagine Ourselves Richly: Mythic Narratives of North American Indians* (Harper, 1991).
Christopher Vecsey, *The Paths of Kateri's Kin* (University of Notre Dame Press, 1997).
Paul Wallace, *Thirty Thousand Miles with John Heckewelder* (University of Pittsburgh Press, 1958).
David J. Weber, *What Caused the Pueblo Revolt of 1680?* (Bedford/St. Martin's, 1999).
Nicolás Wey-Gómez, *The Tropics of Empire: Why Columbus Sailed South to the Indies* (Duke University Press, 2006).
Richard White, *The Middle Ground: Indians, Empires and Republics in the Great Lakes region, 1650–1815* (Cambridge University Press, 1991).
Charles Wilkinson, *Blood Struggle: The Rise of Modern Indian Nations* (Norton, 2005).
Glenn Williams, *The Year of the Hangman: George Washington's Campaign against the Iroquois* (Westholme, 2005).
Edmund Wilson, *Apologies to the Iroquois* (Farrar, Straus & Cudahy, 1959).
Raymond Wilson, *Ohiyesa: Charles Eastman, Santee Sioux* (University of Illinois Press, 1983).
Peter H. Wood, Gregory A. Waselkov, and M. Thomas Hatley, eds., *Powhatan's Mantle: Indians in the Colonial Southeast* (University of Nebraska Press, 1989).
Margarita Zamora, *Reading Columbus* (University of California Press, 1993).
Sally Zanjani, *Sarah Winnemucca* (University of Nebraska Press, 2001).

Index

Abenakis, 66, 68–72
Africans, enslaved, 41, 65, 119
agriculture, 4, 47–8, 104
  see also corn
Akwesasne Notes, 201–5
Alaska, 91–4, 216–19
Alcatraz proclamation, 186–7
alcohol, 35, 57, 113, 169, 192–4
Aleuts, 92–4
Alexie, Sherman, 207
American Indian (as term), 7, 39, 191
American Indian Movement (AIM), 192–4, 195
American Indian Religious Freedom Act, 207
American Indian Trust Management Reform Act, 207
American Revolution, 81, 84–5
Amherst, Sir Jeffery, 76–81
ancestors, 9–11, 13, 14, 22–3, 29–30, 69, 113, 122–3, 217–19
  see also under fathers
Anishinabe, 94, 205
annals, historic *see* Tlatelolco
Apache, 146–52
  images of, 165–6, 169
Apess, William, 118–20
archaeology, 9–11, 14–16, 72–3, 199–201
architecture, 14
Arizona, 12, 148
Arts & Crafts Act of 1935, 171–4
Atkins, J.D.C., 154–7
authors, indigenous *see* books
Aztecs, 12, 27–32

babies, 12, 144
  see also childbirth, children
Bannock War, 135–6
baptism *see* conversion
Barrett, S.M., 147–9
Baum, L. Frank, 6
beads, shell, 199–200
beadwork, 171, 174
beavers, 69
Becenti, Alice, 161–4
Bedonkoho Apache, 151
Beverly, Robert, 198–9
Bible, 60
  see also Christianity
Black Elk, 138–42
Black Hawk, 112–18
Black Hills, 138
Blackfeet Lakota, 126–35
Blackfoot Indians, 176
boarding schools *see under* education
bones *see* Native American Graves Protection and Repatriation Act
books:
  as dictated to others, 112–17, 146–52, 216–19

as written by indigenous authors, 118, 122, 135, 157, 189, 192, 205–7
Bouquet, Colonel Henry, 76–81
Brant, Joseph, 21
Brave Bird, Mary *see* Crow Dog, Mary
Brief and True Report of the Newfound Land of Virginia, 17, 43
Brooklyn, 177
Brulé Lakota Sioux, 126–35, 193
buffalo, 126–35, 143, 193
Buffalo Bill's Wild West Show, 139, 164
Bureau of Indian Affairs, 154, 167–8, 184–6
  see also Commissioner of Indian Affairs
Burned Thighs *see* Brulé Lakota Sioux

Cabazon decision, 212–13
Cabeza de Vaca, Alvar Núñez, 41–2
Cahokia, 14, 17
calendar: Mesoamerican, 9, 27–8; in winter counts, 125
California: activism in, 186–8; boarding schools in, 135, 161
Canada, 6, 21, 50–4, 118
canoes, 20, 40, 59–60, 93
captivity, 52–4, 57–60, 64–7, 85
  in southwest, 166
Carlisle Indian School, 166
casinos *see* Indian Gaming Regulatory Act
Cathérine Tegahkouita, Saint *see* Kateri
Catlin, George, 117
Caughnawaga *see* Kahnawake
ceremony, 12–13, 14, 28, 61–2, 208
Chaco Canyon, 14–16
Cherokee, 21, 74–5, 99–101
  images of, 190
  and removal, 102–11
Cherokee Phoenix, 99–101
Chesapeake Bay, 31, 44
Chicago, 168, 184
Chickasaws, 72–6, 81–4
childbirth, 13, 22, 24–5, 122–3, 192
  see also women
children:
  as captives, 65–7
  growing up on the plains, 122–4, 138–41
  in massacres, 144–6, 201–2
  in schools, 157–65
  see also childbirth
Chiricahua Apache, 146
Choctaw, 74–5
Christianity, 29–30, 32, 144–6, 156, 180
  see also conversion, Dominicans, Franciscans, Jesuits, Moravians
Christmas, 144
circles, images of, 72–6
Civil War, 136
Clark, William, 89–91
Clatsops, 89–91
Clinton, Bill, 207–11
code talkers *see* Navajo
Collier, John, 171
Columbus, Christopher, 39–41
  in native imagination, 160, 169
Commissioner of Indian Affairs, 142, 154–7, 171, 185
Connecticut, 118
Continental Congress, 82, 84
conversion, 31, 52–4, 70
  by captive Protestants to Catholicism, 65–7
  as a goal of colonizers, 40, 43–4, 156
  leading to inner conflict, 146, 180
  rejected by Indians, 29–30, 31, 56, 61–2
Cooper, James Fenimore, 137
corn:
  as central factor in treaty negotiations, 112–16
  as object of worship, 30
  origins and spread, 4–5, 14, 17
Cortés, Hernando, 27–8, 146
Crazy Horse, 140, 194
Creeks, 74–5
Crow Dog, Leonard, 192
Crow Dog, Mary, 192–4
Crows, 126–34

Custer, George Armstrong, 6, 136–8, 141–2, 193
Custer Died for Your Sins, 189

Dakota Sioux, 8, 122–4
dance *see* music
Dartmouth, 122, 164, 205
Dawes Act, 154
de Bry, Theodor, 17–20
Dear John Wayne, 205–6
deception, 36, 48, 55–6, 95
Declaration of Indian Purpose, 184–6
Deer, Ada, 181–2
Deklugie, Asa, 148, 150
Delawares, 78, 94, 97
Deloria, Vine, 189–91
Diabo, Orvis, 177–80
Diné *see* Navajo
disease, 31, 50–4, 125–9
  at boarding schools, 161–3
  see also smallpox
doctors, indigenous:
  ancient healers, 12–13
  graduates of medical school, 122, 166
dolls, 173
Dominicans, 31–3
don Luis *see* Velasco, don Luis de
Duane, James, 84
Dutch, 33–6

Eastman, Charles, 122–4, 142, 144–7
Eastman, Elaine *see* Goodale, Elaine
Eastman, John, 55–7
economic development, 207–16
education, indigenous, 122–4, 125
  in boarding schools, 122, 135, 155–7, 157–61, 161–4, 193
  in Termination era, 181–2
English, 43–8, 55–60, 64–72, 76–81
Erdrich, Louise, 205–6
Eskimo, 216–19
Ethnic Newswatch, 205
exoticism, 7, 157–8, 164–6, 190–1, 205–6
Experiences of Five Christian Indians, 118–20
extermination *see* genocide

famine *see* hunger
fathers, 21, 22, 23, 135, 136, 139–40, 148, 157, 165–6, 179–80, 205, 218
  colonial protectors, 69, 70, 82, 83, 96–7, 113, 115, 143, 186
  as symbol of ancestors, 3, 69, 107, 110, 113, 157, 187
Federal Bureau of Investigation (FBI), 195
First Nations, 7
fishing, 20, 89–90
Florentine Codex, 12–13
Florida, 41, 75, 81
  and gaming law, 212–14
  used for imprisonment of indigenous, 146, 201–5
food:
  in celebration or welcome, 24, 45, 90–1, 162–3, 218–19
  specific dishes described, 143, 179
  see also hunger
Fort Pitt, 77–8
Franciscans, 29, 61–2
Frelinghuysen, Theodore, 102, 108–11
French, 50–4, 64–75, 96, 128–9
French and Indian War *see* Seven Years War

Gandeaktena (early Christian convert), 52–4
genocide, 6, 47–8, 137–8, 144–6, 201–5
Georgia, 82, 102–11
Geronimo, 146–52
ghost dance, 142–4
Gist, George *see* Sequoyah
gods, 12–13, 21, 30, 34, 70, 113
Goodale, Elaine, 142–4
Great Depression, 171
Great Spirit, 21, 34, 70, 113
Guatemala, 9, 201–5

Handsome Lake, 179 n2
Harriot, Thomas, 17, 43–4
Harrison, William Henry, 94–6
Haudenosaunee *see* Iroquois
heart, imagery of, 12, 30, 71, 82–3, 186
Heckewelder, John, 33–7
Hewitt, John, 21, 25
Hiawatha, 166
history, indigenous memory of:
  found in archaeological remains, 9, 14–17
  passed on through stories, 27, 123, 125–35
  in relation to dominant histories, 1–2
horses:
  as feature of life, 136, 139
  images of, 74, 126–34
Hudson River, 36
Huitzilopochtli (Aztec god of war), 28
humor:
  and children, 123
  in irony, 30, 90
  as method of coping with the past, 194, 206
  in practical jokes, 141, 159–60
  in sarcasm, 186, 189–91
  in story-telling tradition, 33–6, 177–80
  in trickster myth, 24–5
hunger, 8, 12–13, 30, 59, 112–16, 126–34
hunting:
  causing competition for land, 47, 68–9
  mythic image of, 21–5
  as way of life, 90, 112, 123, 126–35, 193
Huron, 50–2, 66, 97

Immigration and Naturalization Service (INS), 203–4
Indian (as term) *see* American Indian
Indian Bureau *see* Bureau of Indian Affairs
Indian Gaming Regulatory Act, 209, 211–16
"Indian question", 137
Indian Removal Act, 102
  see also removal
Indian Reorganization Act of 1934, 171
indigenous history *see* history, indigenous
indigenous languages *see* language, indigenous
infants *see* babies
intermarriage, 119–20, 144, 193
interpreters *see* translators
Iroquois, Five Nations of the, 2, 65–6, 68, 72, 86, 118, 177–80
  see also Mohawk, Oneida, Seneca
Iwo Jima, 176

Jackson, Andrew, 102, 105–8
Jamestown, 44–8, 198
Jefferson, Thomas, 89, 105, 210
Jemison, Mary, 60
Jesuits, 50–4
Jesus Christ, native images of, 99, 120
Jews, 120
John, Paul (Yup'ik elder), 216–19

Kahnawake, 52, 177
Kanjobal Maya, 202–5
Kateri, 52, 54
Kennedy, John F., 184
Ke-o-kuck (rival of Black Hawk), 113–15
kidnapping, 31
King George's War, 64–6, 71
King Philip *see* Metacom
King Philip's War, 55–60

La Flesche, Francis, 3, 7, 157–61
Lakota Sioux, 125–34, 138–45, 189–96
language, indigenous:
  attempts to preserve, 12, 21, 216
  attempts to wipe out, 154–7
  efforts of colonizers to learn, 33, 43, 50, 142
  samples: Cherokee, 100–1; Clatsop, 90; Mohawk, 22; Nahuatl, 12–13; Navajo, 175–6; Yup'ik, 217
  vital to understanding of indigenous, 3, 5 n2, 9–10, 21, 36

laughter *see* humor
Lewis, Meriwether, 89
Lincoln, Abraham, 164
Little Big Horn, battle of the, 138–42
Lone Dog, 125–34
Lone Ranger and Tonto Fistfight in Heaven, 207
Longhouse Religion, 179–80
Louisiana Purchase, 89
Love Medicine, 205

Maine, 68
maize *see* corn
Malinche, 54
Mallery, Garrick, 125
Mandans, 89
Manhattan, 33–6, 186
manito, 34–5
maps, indigenous, 73–6
marriage, 9, 21, 23, 24, 53 n1, 66, 177
  see also women, intermarriage
Massachusetts, 57–8
massacres, 28, 201–5
  see also Wounded Knee
Massassoit, 55, 56
Maya, 9–11, 201–5
McCain, John, 211, 215
McKiernan, Kevin, 195–6
Means, Russell, 194
medal of peace, Jeffersonian, 91, 210
medicine men, 127, 131–3, 138–42
  see also doctors, priests, prophets
Menominees, 181–2
Metacom, 55–7, 60, 120
Mexica *see* Aztecs
Mexico, 4–5, 9–13, 27–30, 31
  in the Plains Indian wars, 146–9
military:
  and Indian removal, 114–17
  indigenous in, 175–6
  officers of remembering Indian wars, 136–7, 152
  see also Seventh Cavalry
Minneconjou Lakota Sioux, 126–34, 144–6
Minnesota, 8, 122
Mississippi River, 72–3, 112
Mitchell, Joseph, 177–80
Mohawk (Iroquois), 64–5, 201
Montezuma, Carlos, 166–70
Montezuma (Aztec emperor), 28
Moravians, 33
mothers, 12, 163–4, 141
  see also childbirth, children
music, 28, 123, 141–4, 161, 180
myth, 21–5

Nahuatl *see* language, indigenous
Naiche (Apache leader), 146, 152
Native American (as term), 7
Native American Graves Protection and Repatriation Act (NAGPRA), 198–201
Native American Housing Assistance and Self-Determination Act, 207
native press, 99–101, 166–70, 201–5
Navajo, 161–4, 175–6
Neihardt, John, 139–42
Nelson, Molly Dellis, 180–1
New Mexico, 12, 14, 61–2, 161–4, 171
New Yorker, 177
Newhouse, Seth, 21
Nicholson, Francis, 72, 75
North Dakota, 205
Northwest Coast, 89–91, 93
Norton, John, 21–22

objectification *see* exoticism
Oglala Lakota Sioux, 126, 139–42, 192–4
Ohio Valley, 33
Ohiyesa *see* Eastman, Charles
Oklahoma, 102, 147
Omaha Indians, 157–61
Oneida (Iroquois), 87, 174
orality, 1, 12, 123
Ottawas, 76, 94
otter, 92–3

Paiutes, 135–6
Pamunkeys, 44, 171, 174, 220

pan-Indian movements, 94–9, 184–8, 201–5
Paquiquineo *see* Velasco, don Luis de
Paris, 50, 181
Peltier, Leonard, 195–6
Pennsylvania, 76–81
Penobscots, 180–1
Pequots, 118, 211
pictographic writing, 1, 5, 9–11, 27, 125–35, 176
  artificial, 171, 174
Piedras Negras, 201
Pilgrims, 190
Pine Ridge Reservation, 144–6, 192–3, 195–6
Pocahontas, 44–6, 220
polytheism, 29–30
  see also myth
Pontiac, 76
  as name of car, 205
Powhatan (paramount chief of Virginia Indians), 44–6, 220
prayer, 12–13
  see also ceremony
press *see* native press
priests, 29–30
  see also prophets, medicine men
prison, Indians in, 122, 146, 193–4, 195–6
prophets, 94–6, 114–16
  see also priests, medicine men
Prophetstown, 94
protein, 4
Pueblo Bonito, 14–16
Pueblo Revolt of 1680, 61–2

Quarterly Journal, 166–70
Quebec Bridge Disaster, 180

red man (as term), 98, 137–8, 192
religion, 12, 40, 67, 132, 170, 178, 179 n2, 187, 208: freedom of, 208
  see also ceremony, Christianity, conversion, gods, myth, prayer, prophets
religious orders *see* Dominicans, Franciscans, Jesuits, Moravians
removal, Indian, 102–12, 112–17
reservation:
  art on, 173–4, 176
  life on, 142, 146, 167–8, 178–9, 192–4
Rhode Island, 55
Roanoke, 17, 43–4
Roosevelt, Theodore, 147–8
Ross, John, 102–5
Rowlandson, Mary, 57–60
Russians, 91–4, 155

Ša, Zitkala, 170
Sacagawea, 54
  see also Clark, William
Sahagún, Bernardino de, 12
Saint Lawrence River, 50, 76
Sans Arc Lakota Sioux, 126–35
Santee Dakota Sioux, 124, 139, 141
Sauk, 112–18
scalping, 140–1
Secotan, 17–19
Seneca (Iroquois), 60
Sequoyah, 99–100
Seven Years War, 68, 76
Seventh Cavalry, 136, 144–46
Shawnees, 78, 94, 97
Sherman Institute, 161–4
Shoshoni *see* Snake Indians
Sioux, 122–35, 138–45, 166, 169–70, 189–90, 192–6
Sitcha, 93–4
Sitting Bull, 166, 194
slavery:
  of Africans *see* Africans, enslaved
  among Indians, 53–4
smallpox, 76–81, 126
  see also disease
Smith, John, 44–6
Snake Indians, 91, 130
Son of the Forest, 120
sorcery, 51, 62
South Carolina, 72, 75
South Dakota, 122, 125, 138, 142, 167

Spanish, 27–33, 39, 41–2, 61–62, 83
Spiro Mounds, 72–3
Spotted Elk, Molly *see* Nelson, Molly Dellis
Spotted Tail (Lakota chief), 193–4
Stacher, Samuel, 161–4
Standing Bear, Luther, 124, 161
steelwork, 177–80
sterilization, 193
Stevens, Phineas, 68–72
Stoddard, William, 164–6

technology, 4, 43–4
Tecumseh, 94–9, 138
Tegahkouita, Cathérine *see* Kateri
Tenskwatawa (Tecumseh's brother), 94–5
Termination, 181–2
Texas, 41
Tippecanoe River, 94
Tlaloc (Aztec god of rain), 12–13, 30
Tlatelolco, annals of, 27–9
tourism, 171–4
trade, 35–6, 40, 46, 57, 69, 72–6, 99
  trading posts, 127–4
Trail of Tears, 102
translation:
  difficulties of, 2–3, 29, 95–6, 158
  process of, 148–9
translators:
  in courtroom setting, 62
  as federal employees, 112–13, 125
  former captives as, 68
  young Indians as, 32
treaties, 36, 55, 138
  goals clarified, 81–8
  negotiations recorded, 68–72
  rejected as void, 95–9, 111–13
  see also deception
Tribal Self-Government Act, 207
tribes
  federally recognized, 219–31
  state-recognized, 220
trickery *see* deception
turtle, imagery of, 21–5
Two Kettles Lakota Sioux, 126–35

Uncpapa Lakota Sioux, 126–35, 139–40
United States Congress, 102–11
United States Constitution, 81, 155, 207
United States Supreme Court, 102, 214
uprisings:
  of 1622, 46
  of Dakota, 8, 122
  of Pontiac, 76
  of Pueblo, 61
  of Sitcha, 93–4
urban life, 177–81

Velasco, don Luis de, 31–2
Virginia, 43–8, 198–201

Wampanoags, 55
wampum belts, 68–9
  see also beads
War of 1812, 112, 118
warfare:
  and art, 176
  as part of lifestyle, 123, 126–35
  tactics in, 41–2, 46, 53, 57–60, 76–81, 135–6
  threatened at treaty negotiations, 68–72, 83–4
warriors *see* warfare
Washington, George, 33, 83–4, 103, 160
wasičun, 142, 194
Waterhouse, Edward, 46–8
Wayne, John, 205–6
Wheelock, Eleazar, 164
White, John, 17–18, 20
White House, 207
wild west shows, 169–70, 179
  see also Buffalo Bill's Wild West Show
Wilson, Richard, 195
Winnemucca, Lee, 135–6
Winnemucca, Sarah, 135–6
winter counts, 125–35, 194
Wisconsin, 181–2
women:
  as captives, 52–4, 55–6, 65–7
  as corn farmers, 112–13
  as daughters representing fathers, 99, 116, 152

as mothers, 12, 141, 163–4
in religious imagery, 13, 21–4
as royal consorts, 9–10, 45
as victims of violence, 145, 192–3, 202
as writers and activists, 135, 170
Wonderful Wizard of Oz, 6
World War Two, 175–6, 180–1
Wounded Knee Creek:
1890 massacre at, 6, 144–6, 170
1973 occupation of, 192–4, 195–6

Yankton/Yanktonai Sioux, 126–35, 139, 170
Yavapai, 166–9
Yellow Robe, Chauncey, 166, 169–70
Yupiit, 216–19